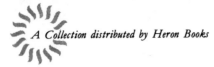

WOMEN
WHO
MADE
HISTORY

Silver coin of Cleopatra

THE LIFE
AND TIMES
OF
CLEOPATRA

BY
CARLO MARIA FRANZERO

Preface by the author

Distributed by
HERON BOOKS

13 014 04

CONTENTS

LIST OF ILLUSTRATIONS

EDITOR'S FOREWORD

Everybody has heard of Cleopatra, the dazzling Queen of Egypt, the lover of Caesar and Mark Antony, who died by her own hand rather than fall captive to the Romans. Shakespeare wrote of her:

> *Age cannot wither her, nor custom stale*
> *Her infinite variety; other women cloy*
> *The appetites they feed, but she makes hungry*
> *Where most she satisfies...*

Indeed over the centuries the story of Cleopatra has inspired a host of poems, paintings, plays and films. All of them, almost without exception, celebrate Cleopatra as the great lover, the starcrossed Queen; but was she perhaps something more than this? Could she also have been—in the title of our series—a Woman Who Made History?

Signor Franzero states unequivocally, in his preface written expressly for this new edition of his book, that Cleopatra was a " woman of immense political ambition." She was undoubtedly in love with Caesar, and may well have cherished Mark Antony as well; nevertheless there can be little question but that she used both men to further her overriding ambition. And this ambition was to unite her ancient kingdom, wealthiest in the known world, on an equal basis with Rome, the most powerful nation of her time.

The stakes were high; and it was therefore not wholly by chance that she chose Caesar, the greatest man of her age, to further her ambitions—and when Caesar fell, Mark Antony, who in turn came close to achieving her goal. With either man she might have become co-ruler of the entire civilized world.

Cleopatra, it is clear, had the strength and talent to match her towering ambitions. Although as Pharaoh she ruled

Egypt with all the immemorial rites of that ancient kingdom, she was by extraction Macedonian and thus heir to the incomparable learning of Greece. She spoke over half a dozen languages with ease and in conversation was more than able to hold her own with the learned Greek philosophers with whom she adorned her court. Although perhaps not matchlessly beautiful in face and figure, her proverbial wit and charm amply made up for any deficiencies, while her untold wealth enabled her to live a life of ostentatious splendour.

A glance at the Historical Appendix at the back of this book will bring out even more clearly the importance of Cleopatra in history. Her drama was played out at a fateful time in the history of the Ancient World, when most of the rich Hellenic kingdoms of the eastern Mediterranean had submitted to conquering Rome—with the notable exception of Egypt, still nominally independent. If Cleopatra could ally Egypt with Rome, thus preserving her throne, the balance between East and West would in a measure be restored—and she would become Queen of the world. If she failed, Rome's domination of the civilized world of the time would be complete. Here was the breathtaking extent of Cleopatra's ambition.

She failed, and in the subsequent upheavals the Mediterranean became a Roman lake, the Republic gave way to the Empire, and the 3,000-year-old Egyptian kingdom, as well as Cleopatra's own proud Ptolemaic dynasty, disappeared from history. Cleopatra's fate was intimately connected with all these climactic events; she was indeed a Woman Who Made History.

Courtlandt Canby
Editor of the Series

PREFACE

It was Somerset Maugham who said that "an author is probably the last person who can write fitly of his own work." Yet, in writing a preface for this new edition of *Cleopatra*, I feel that the fortune of this book—which culminated with the great Epic Film that was made from it—was due to my having followed my Latin instinct in the interpretation of the famous Queen of Egypt.

I felt impatient with the stilted and disparaging picture that dramatists and poets had made of Cleopatra to suit popular tradition. I felt convinced that Cleopatra was not only a woman of great beauty and charm, but also of immense political ambition; a Queen who thought politically and at the same time loved passionately—a woman who was vital, vivid, scheming and imperious: an enchantress moved both by passion and greatness.

The writer, in his historical and artistic re-creation of Cleopatra, has very little to go by. Nothing remains of Alexandria, the marvellous city that was the *summa* of the culture and refinement of Cleopatra's time, and not one unarguably authentic image of the wondrous Queen has escaped the ruthless hand of time. All that remains is the legend of Cleopatra's life and loves, echoing along the Halls of History; and the writer can but endeavour to recreate as best he may the character and personality of this Queen, who was loved by Caesar and having hoped to join the fortunes of her ancient kingdom with those of Rome, was to endure the shock of seeing disinherited the son she had given Caesar, who was Caesar's only son.

That shock, my Latin instinct told me, was the determining point of Cleopatra's career and drama. Throughout her remaining years she was hounded by the memory of Caesar and of her own love for Caesar; and it was this memory and the shattering disappointment that was involved in it that urged her and almost goaded her to take vengeance upon Rome, until she was reduced to defending herself from Rome's relentless expansion, and Nemesis overtook her in the person of Caesar's legal heir and successor, the young Octavian—not yet acclaimed " Augustus." All the rest, all the events that followed Cleopatra's return from Rome after Caesar's assassination, were but the links of the chain which closed with the asp's bite.

Even the glamorous liaison and marriage with Mark Antony was but an episode, albeit the most important one, in her schemes for the survival of the Kingdom of Egypt and of herself and of Caesar's son. Indeed, at the very end, she thinks only of Caesarion's safety, and dies trusting that Caesar's son shall escape and survive.

It is even doubtful whether Cleopatra really loved Mark Antony—the brave, the gallant, the Herculean Mark Antony, whose pride was at the height of its ascension when he could come before Cleopatra as the knight before his lady to demand, as the reward of victory, a kiss for himself, and for the bravest of his horsemen a golden suit of armour. How soon, how soon Cleopatra must have seen through the bombast of Mark Antony, who could not conquer Persia with all the treasure of Egypt she had put at his disposal, and who abandoned the decision at Actium to chase after her in a mad fit of passion!

At an early stage Cleopatra must have realised that Mark Antony lacked a sense of responsibility as a prince—this reproach weighs only too heavily upon him—and in a similar way that he preserved so little of the patriotic spirit for Rome during his life in Egypt that he did not even want to leave his ashes to his Fatherland. Cleopatra sensed in Mark Antony's indolent nature a lack of creative spirit, for he followed the impulses of the moment without reflecting what might be their ultimate consequences. Yet, Mark Antony was Cleopatra's last throw against Rome, and she exercised a dominion

10

over him that led to his destruction and her own—the tragedy, the pity of it!

This was the drama of Cleopatra, as it appeared to my Latin mind. And considering that Rome's domain was already encircling the whole Mediterranean basin, Cleopatra's effort to delay the inevitable take-over of Egypt by Rome was both imaginative and pathetic. For Cleopatra was an extraordinary person. At her death she was but thirty-eight years of age. Her power over men rested not so much on actual beauty as on her fascinating manners and her extreme readiness of wit. She fully believed in her divine descent. Even in her follies there was magnificence. We may estimate the real power of her mental qualities by observing the impression her character made upon the Roman poets of the time: no meditated praise could have borne such testimony to her greatness as the lofty strain in which Horace celebrates her fall and congratulates the Roman world on its escape from the ruin with which she threatened it.

One day, in Rome, I stood gazing at the three slender white columns, still joined by their trabeation, that rise like beautiful flowers on the very edge of the ruins of the Forum. Many have thought these columns to be all that remains of the Temple of Venus Genetrix which Julius Caesar had erected to impress upon the Romans his divine descent. In that Temple Caesar had placed the statue of Cleopatra, deified as Venus'—Cleopatra who had born Caesar his only son; Cleopatra who in those fateful months before the Ides of March held court for Caesar in the Villa Transtiberina; Cleopatra who urged Caesar to crown himself King and rule the world with her as his Queen. The sight of those three beautiful columns seemed to give me the key to the mystery of Cleopatra: brilliant of mind and strong of will as a great Queen should be, yet possessing that touch of frailty that is part of the enchantment of femininity that stirs the emotions and imaginations of great men.

Carlo Maria Franzero
Cobham, Surrey, 1968

BOOK ONE

CLEOPATRA AND HER WORLD

I

WHEN Cleopatra was born in the year 68 B.C., the Trojan War for Helen of Troy had taken place more than eleven hundred years before; Athens and Greece had become a Roman Province; Julius Caesar—who was to change Cleopatra's life and destiny—was 34 years of age; and the Kings and Queens of Egypt had ruled over the Nile for more than two thousand years.

Olympus, her personal Doctor, kept a journal: it gives us the best information of the personal appearance of Cleopatra at the time she became Queen of Egypt.

At eighteen, Cleopatra had a definite Macedonian head, not Grecian, but rather the head and profile of the very beautiful women of Smyrna. Her skin was naturally golden, the skin of those rare women into whom the sun has put its glow. Her hair was neither fair nor dark; a natural burnt-amber. Her eyes could, with her changeable moods, be grey pools or turn, in moments of passion, to that bluish mauve that is the blue of violets. But, in her commanding moments, her eyes, of a limpid splendour, had a strange, penetrating quality.

She was not very tall; a girlish stature, lithe and supple, the form that is at all ages so attractive and alluring.

The features of her face were delicate, but well marked, her nose small and aristocratically aquiline with delightful nostrils, that made her look both coquettish and imperious. Her mouth was small, but not too small, large enough to have character and to promise sensuality, whilst the turn of her chin had a delightful roundness, perfect in shape.

Her beauty was not incomparable;[1] there were other women of greater beauty, but Cleopatra possessed a most wonderful appeal and had an intense magnetism. She was splendid to look at, and capable of conquering the most hardened heart.[2]

The bust in the British Museum—one of the few reliable figurations of Cleopatra—gives quite definitely the image of a woman who was petite, with soft hair, a good mouth and general beauty that is, perhaps, intensified by the vacant eyes that in the ancient stone portraits seem to hold such mystery and fascination. And above those eyes, her eyebrows are pleasantly arched and full.[3]

Cleopatra had an irresistible charm; her very presence, her seductive and cultured speech, the strangeness that radiated from all her manners and attitudes, exercised an attraction that made, at times, a man almost wild. There was a sweetness in her voice,[4] and the enchantment of her speech was such that she gained to her views all listeners.[5] Her grace was equally irresistible. Her manner could be girlish and naïve, or, in a fanciful mood, be ambitious and capricious. Or she could be turbulent and stormy, or throw herself into rough play; but she always retained a natural dignity and could be disdainful and proud.[6] She could be scheming—like the eternal

---

[1] Plutarch.
[2] Dio Cassius.
[3] Some historians rely for Cleopatra's likeness on the general accuracy of the Egyptian coins portraits, for " a long tradition of splendid and life-like portrayals always characterized the Alexandrian coinage ". (E. T. Newell, *Royal Greek Portraits Coins*).
[4] Plutarch.
[5] Dio Cassius.
[6] Pliny and Cicero.

woman. But by nature she was impulsive and full of spontaneity. She enjoyed life with the high spirits of a young woman, and took with candour all the pleasures that came her way.

Intellectually, she was most gifted. Her repartee was prompt and witty; and at eighteen she already spoke many languages. Seldom had she need of interpreters; alone of all the Ptolemys she could speak Egyptian, and could converse fluently in Greek, Latin, Ethiopian, Hebrew, Arabic, Syrian, Persian and even in the strange tongue of the Troglodytes.

Since an early age she had evinced a strong interest in politics, and believed passionately in the independence of ancient Egypt and the greatness of her dynasty. She was ambitious and watched with care that the due honours were paid to the throne.[1] Even at that young age, Cleopatra carried a burning ambition to become Empress of the World.

Was she, as a young girl, taken to the Temple at Thebes and deflowered, in the old custom, on the altar of Amon-Rê? Did she, in the corrupt atmosphere of the Palace and of her city, allow herself a few amorous adventures? And most important of all—was she a sensual woman, as Josephus called her, " a slave to her senses "? The answer is perhaps simple and eternal: there is no beautiful and intelligent and gifted woman who is not also a woman of the senses. A woman who does not carry the flame of passion and love in her heart is not a great woman, neither upon a throne nor in ordinary life. It was also a time of much licence and the intrigues of love were the order of the day; but when, in the history of all times and countries, was not love the moving power of events?

[1] Dio Cassius.

17

But above every other trait, Cleopatra was a cultured woman. She had the artistic temperament of her Greek forebears. Throughout her life she patronized and promoted science and art. In her honour, in after years, the mathematician Photinus published his work entitled, as a due homage, *The Canons of Cleopatra,* and the works of the physician Dioscorides were composed at her prompting and have since been read by scholars throughout the ages. Cleopatra was familiar with the astronomer Sosigenes and it was due to her influence that Caesar adopted Sosigenes' plan for the reform of the Calendar.

She believed in the Gods and in their power; she believed indeed with equal faith in the divinity of Royalty; she had a firm belief in her own divine descent.

And, at that early age of eighteen, she was already desperately fighting for her throne.

II

CLEOPATRA—seventh Queen of that name and the last of the Ptolemys—was the fourth daughter of a second marriage of Ptolemy XIII: in fact, an aura of illegitimacy hangs around her childhood, for history has not recorded the name of her mother.

She grew up in the Palace, amidst the murders of her Royal relatives for a quicker succession to the throne, and the unending intrigues to secure from the Roman Senate the assent and protection that meant staving off the invasion of Egypt by the Legions of Rome.

The Dynasty of the Ptolemys was fast approaching its end. It was founded by Ptolemy, a Macedonian General who had been the personal bodyguard to Alexander. At the Conqueror's death, Egypt with Libya and several sections of Arabia and Syria had fallen to the lot of

1. An idealized Greek head of Cleopatra.

2, 3, 5. Cleopatra's story in coins: below, *first line* (left to right): Cleopatra on a silver tetradrachm of 49 B.C., and on an 80-drachma bronze coin. *Second line*: Silver coin of Octavian. *Third line*: Ptolemy I Soter, first king of Ptolemaic Egypt, and Ptolemy III, Energetes. *Fourth line*: Tetradrachma showing Antony and Cleopatra together.

4, 5. *First line*, below: Gold coin showing Sextus Pompey, Pompey the Great and Gnaeus Pompey the Younger. *Second line*: A coin of Julius Caesar. *Third line*: Marcus Junius Brutus, leader of the conspiracy against Caesar, with the assassins' daggers on the reverse. *Fourth line*: Mark Antony (left) and Lepidus, leaders of the Caesarian party immediately after the assassination.

6. Presumed portrait head of Cleopatra.

Ptolemy, who became automatically the depositary of the mortal remains of Alexander, who had decreed that his body should be buried at Alexandria. From his own father's name Lagus, Ptolemy called his dynasty Lagidae, and took the Royal name of Ptolemy I Soter, or The Saviour.

The King was Greek and so was the capital. The new Kings never wore the Egyptian dress except on official occasions and none of them bothered to learn the Egyptian language.[1] Circumstances induced the Egyptians to accept these foreigners as the successors of their ancient Kings and they gave to the Ptolemys the titles that had belonged to the Pharaohs: they called the Ptolemys " Image of Amon ", " Son of the Sun " and " the Chosen of Ptah ". In the temples were erected their statues with the insignia of the ancient Pharaohs—the double crown of Upper and Lower Egypt, the horns and feathers of Amon, their brows encircled by the Royal snake. In this dress the Ptolemys paid adoration before the Cow Hathor, and bent low before the Crocodile Sebak whilst they burnt incense to the Cat Bast, the Gods of the Egyptian people that were two thousand and more years old. The Ptolemys were depicted in the arms of Isis, saluted by Osiris and receiving the kiss of Nut, Mother of the Skies.

Alexandria was connected with Egypt and the fabulous Nile only by her trade and the government offices. Rarely did the Ptolemys visit Egypt proper and then only for brief visits to an important or holy city.

The Ptolemys never felt Egyptian although they encouraged and fostered the national life. They were cruel sovereigns with a contempt for human life.

---

[1] Plutarch.

19

Terrible crimes marked their history and they murdered one another without compunction. And having murdered fathers and mothers and brothers and friends, they took delightful and noble surnames: Soter the Saviour, Philadelphus the Friend of Brothers, Energetes the Beneficent, Philopator His Father's Friend (whom he had murdered), Epiphanes the Illustrious, Philometor His Mother's Friend. Only Cleopatra's father, who was a great bibber, had the wit to call himself Neos Dionysos, but his subjects had nicknamed him Auletes the Flute Player, for he used to solace himself by playing the flute, and the nickname passed to history.

No less violent and murderous were the women of the family but they did not give themselves solemn surnames.

The Ptolemys were remarkable also for other traits. Only the first three Ptolemys had shown talents and high qualities; the others excelled in debauchery and degeneration. Their life in the Palace at Alexandria was a continuous orgy. Some of them indulged in gorging themselves at the table till their excesses were revolting. When Scipio the African visited Egypt, he found the grandfather of our Cleopatra so chocked with food that he was unable to walk; he was indeed nicknamed Physkon, the Bloated. As the King insisted in walking with the Roman General from the quay to the Palace, Scipio remarked that his visit to Alexandria had at least the benefit of enabling the people of that city to see their King walking. Bloated with food and wine, Ptolemy XI moved about the rooms on two crutches; but when he was completely drunk he recovered the use of his legs and then he enjoyed parading about the Palace followed by his Court and companions.

As for Cleopatra's father, Ptolemy Auletes, he regarded sobriety with such aversion that he threatened to put to death the philosopher Demetrius for refusing to get drunk at a banquet: to save his life, Demetrius had to appear in public the following day completely inebriated. When Ptolemy Auletes was sober the plaintive notes of his flute filled the rooms of the Palace and the shady gardens; otherwise his life was an orgy, punctuated by plots to save his throne. And it was under Ptolemy XIII that relations between Egypt and Rome reached the critical phase that was to change the course of history.

The early years of Cleopatra were filled with the muffled sounds of family murders and the echoes of her father's journeys to Rome to " buy " the safety of his throne.

Having obtained the control of the Hellenic world, Rome had been busy in securing the control of the Eastern Mediterranean, and towards the middle of the last century B.C. was turning covetous and impatient eyes upon Egypt: Alexandria's trade and the immense wealth of Egypt were a tempting prize. Rome's ambitions were fostered also by another factor, the family dissensions of the Ptolemys. It appeared easy to sweep away this effete dynasty of Macedonian upstarts who had planted themselves in Egypt. The very complexities of their line of succession made them as puppets in the hands of Rome. On the death of Ptolemy XII, one of his children proclaimed himself Pharaoh of Egypt and was accepted by the people of Alexandria. He was a bastard with an unknown mother. Yet to refuse to recognise him would have meant declaring the line extinct and this was tantamount to inviting a Roman occupation. A second brother took the crown of Cyprus, also calling himself Ptolemy.

But no sooner had Cleopatra's father taken possession of the throne and become Ptolemy XIII than he discovered that his predecessor had voluntarily put an end to the dynasty by leaving in his will Egypt to the Roman Republic. Such a strange bequest had other precedents in history: the kingdoms of Pergame, Cyrenaica and Bithinia had been left to Rome by testament. Perhaps Ptolemy XII had done it to secure for himself the moral support of Rome at the time of his accession. Be that as it may, the Roman Senate claimed the validity of the will; Ptolemy XIII's party contested it; and albeit there were no doubts as to the authenticity of the will, its validity was another matter: quite probably the will was made before the accession of its signatory to the throne, thus giving away what was not yet his to give; and indeed, the will could be valid only in the case of there being no rightful heir, while the people of Egypt had accepted Ptolemy XIII as such. Rome, however, was not ready for a campaign overseas and was therefore content to seize as Roman heritage all that could be seized of the dead King's estate, and took no steps to dethrone Ptolemy XIII or his brother the King of Cyprus. The reason was that an important party in Rome was averse to an Oriental adventure; and, on the other hand, the Senate was very reluctant to put into the hands of any one man the power represented by the immense resources of Egypt, for Egypt was considered as important, in rank and resources, as Rome herself; and Alexandria held the key to the wealth of the south and opened the road to Arabia and India. The income of the Palace at Alexandria was reputed to be no less than the total income of Rome; and Alexandria had succeeded Athens as the centre of culture, and had indeed surpassed it.

Alexandria was considered by the Romans to be the second city of the world.

Ptolemy XIII, better known as Auletes, was more than frightened by the will of his father, and spent his life in assuaging the Roman greed.

In the year 63 Pompey annexed Syria in the name of Rome, and Auletes sent him propitiatory presents of money and military supplies. He also invited the victorious General to visit Egypt, but Pompey accepted the presents and declined the invitation.

At last, in the year 59, Ptolemy Auletes decided to go to Rome in person, hoping to obtain, through Pompey's support, the Senate's recognition of his right to the throne of Egypt. It was a pitiful affair. In Rome, Auletes showered magnificent presents upon the more influential Senators; and when his cash resources were exhausted he borrowed a large sum from the great financier Rabirius Postumus, who induced several friends to invest in an " Auletes loan ". In fact, a sort of syndicate was formed for the purpose of backing the Egyptian King; should Auletes' claims succeed, the King would reimburse the syndicate with generous interest.

But Auletes' visit had come at a critical moment. The third war against King Mithridates and the wars against the pirates had depleted the treasury, and Rome was in urgent need of money. In the Senate and in the clubs the politicians discussed openly the immediate advantage of annexing Egypt. Crassus, Rullus and Julius Caesar were for an immediate occupation. When everything seemed lost Auletes made a personal present of 6,000 talents of gold to Caesar and the situation was saved. The bargain was sealed with the " Julian Law for Egypt ", that Caesar made the Senate pass: the Julian

Law called Ptolemy XIII " ally and friend of the Roman people."

No sooner had Auletes obtained the support of Rome than the Egyptian people revolted under the burden of the taxes imposed by him for the repayment he had to make to the Roman syndicate. The administration was also irritated by the refusal of Ptolemy Auletes to defend Cyprus against Rome, who annexed it promptly the following year.([1]) Auletes was chased from Egypt. Stopping at Cyprus, he heard that Cato was still on the island. Thinking of the " kindness " he had shown in Rome to the worthy Senator, Auletes sent him a Royal invitation to visit him. Cato, who had that day an attack of liver, replied that if Auletes wanted to see him, he was in his quarters. When Ptolemy Auletes entered the room, Cato did not even rise from his chair: with a flick of his hand he motioned him to be seated and gave him a severe reprimand for his idea of returning to Rome to plead his case. " All Egypt turned into gold "—he said—" would no longer satisfy the greed of the Roman politicians ". But Auletes took sail for Rome.

In the interval, a daughter of Ptolemy Auletes, Berenice, seized the throne and reigned as Berenice IV. She, and her sister, who died soon after, were the only children of the first marriage of Ptolemy Auletes.

A refugee in Rome, Auletes presented himself before the Senate as a King deprived of the throne that Rome had recognised as his right. Again he bribed and bought out the men of influence; again he borrowed right and left although the syndicate, this time, was not so sanguine about the soundness of the investment. Caesar could not be bought for he was in Gaul, busy conquering that

[1] 58 B.C.

province. Pompey declined Auletes' money, but gave him hospitality in his villa near Albano, on the charming shores of Lake Nemi. Hostile to the idea of seeing Auletes back, the people of Alexandria sent an embassy to Rome: Auletes hired some assassins and had the embassy murdered near Pozzuoli; the survivors he bought with money.

Everything might have turned out favourably for Auletes had not one of his opponents discovered in the Sibyls Books an oracle which said that if the King of Egypt came to ask for assistance, Rome should give him the help of her friendship but not of her arms. Out of his patience and wits, poor Auletes shook the dust of Rome off his sandals and retired to Ephesus in Asia Minor.

Three years later the statesmen of Rome were still discussing the case of Ptolemy XIII; but so strong was the Senate's apprehension of entrusting to a single commander the task of subjecting Egypt, with or without a local King, that no decision was ever reached. It was suggested that the Governor of Cilicia, Lentulus Spinther, should be sent to Egypt with an army, but leaving Auletes in Ptolemais: ([1]) in this way the Sibyls's oracle would have been bypassed. But Auletes smelt danger and opposed the plan. At last, Auletes made for the return of his kingdom the colossal offer to Rome of 10,000 talents. The Governor of Syria, Aulus Gabinius, pressed by his personal debts, promised to obtain the consent of the Senate to an invasion of Egypt, in spite of the Sibyls. At the end, Gabinius declared war on Archaelaus, who had married Berenice IV, on the pretext that Archaelaus gave encouragement to the pirates of the North African coast;

---

[1] Now St. John of Acre.

and soon a Roman army was crossing the desert from Gaza towards Pelusium. It is worth noting that the cavalry was commanded by a young officer of twenty-seven by the name of Mark Antony. Pelusium was taken; the legions marched on Alexandria, the capital was occupied, Queen Berenice was killed and Ptolemy Auletes was replaced on the throne.

From that moment, a strong contingent of Roman troops, infantry and cavalry, remained in the city " to keep order ". The young officer Mark Antony stayed there some months. In the course of his visits to the Palace he was introduced to Princess Cleopatra who was then fourteen years old, and he thought she looked " an exquisite flower ".

The last remaining years of Ptolemy XIII were spent in staving off his Roman creditors. He ended by appointing the chief creditor Rabirius Postumus his own Finance Minister, so that all taxes and revenues passed through his creditor's hands.

In the year 54 the Alexandrians tried to be rid of the Roman bailiffs sitting in their house, and chased away Rabirius. Immediately Rome turned her attention to Alexandria: Egypt must be annexed without delay. If Crassus had not died in the catastrophe of the Parthian War, the march on Egypt would not have been delayed.

But in the year 51 Ptolemy XIII Auletes died, replete with food and worries. In his will, one copy of which had been deposited with the Aerarium in Rome, Auletes had stated that his eldest daughter, Cleopatra, should succeed him together with his eldest son, enjoining the two children to reign conjointly and imploring the Roman Senate to see that his will be respected: he named the Roman people as guardians to the new King and Queen.

This succession of the eldest daughter to reign jointly with a brother but ten years old presupposed, in the tradition of Egypt, their marriage, and the Ptolemys had conformed to the ancient Egyptian usage of marriages between brothers and sisters which had been the Pharaohs' custom from the time that Osiris had married his sister Isis. Dynastically, the custom, thousands of years old, was due to the right of the female line to succeed to the throne, and was also bound with the religious attributes of the Royal lineage. Often such marriages were merely symbolical.

Cleopatra was eighteen years of age.

III

EGYPT was no longer the land of the Pharaohs, although the Sphinx, the Pyramids and the mysterious Gods with the animal heads—the Cat, the Crocodile, and the Jackal —still ruled over the life of the Egyptian people. The mighty Nile still flowed from the great table-land and the cataracts of Nubia, distributing its fertilising inundations through the canals and locks built more than one thousand years before, " the Nile which supplies all men with nourishment and food ".

Alexandria was great and splendid, it was the most beautiful city of the ancient world. No other city could compare with it for splendour, culture and wealth. And it was the most modern of the western cities, governing in an ancient way a kingdom and a race that were a world unto themselves. Alexandria was also a world apart from Egypt; as much a world apart from the valley of the Nile as Carthage was from Africa. It was built on a tongue of land of the Nile's delta where for centuries and centuries the Pharaohs had never ventured.

The city was bordered on one side by the Mediterranean, on the other by Lake Mareotis, and in this respect Alexandria was even more separated from Africa than was Carthage by her semicircle of hills.

Alexander the Great, after his conquest of Egypt, had intended to build Alexandria strictly as a Greek colony that would receive all the Greek trade bound for Egypt, and carry all the products of the Nile bound both for the East and the West. Alexander had, therefore, chosen the position behind the delta with the purpose of creating a city that would be the head of Egypt and yet remain apart from it. Egypt, indeed, was to the Alexandrians almost an unknown land. There was not one Alexandrian out of ten thousand who had ever found himself face to face with the Sphinx. This is very important in understanding the spirit of the city and of its people and civilization.

Alexandria was a world apart from the cliffs of the desert, from the immense river, from the ancient temples, the tombs, the continuous creaking of the water-wheels of the irrigation canals that sounded like cries in the night. Even the sky, the weather, the climate of Alexandria belonged to another world. The people of Alexandria did not know the desert shimmering under the blazing sun, the white tracks of the camels across the dunes, the great cataracts of the Nile over the rocks of black granite in the Nubian land, the vastness of the river's seasonal floods. The climate of Alexandria was cool and temperate; even in the summer months the sea-breeze fanned pleasantly the gardens. And in the lovely gardens, the flowers were those of the Greek hills.

In front of Alexandria was the great harbour which was enclosed by two tongues of land extended by two

mighty breakwaters, which reached to the island of
Pharos running low and parallel to the city. The first
sight for the arriving traveller was the " Pharos " the
famous lighthouse, erected upon the eastern point of the
isle and dominating the main entrance to the port. The
great lighthouse had been built two hundred years before,
under Ptolemy Philadelphus, by Sostratus of Cnidos, and
it was one of the seven marvels of the world, entirely built
of white marble, five hundred and forty feet high. It
was a series of towers, erected one above the other, like
the biblical tower of Babel; the lower towers were quad-
rangular and the higher ones rounded. A raised path led
to the entrance at the base, and along a spiral road the
fuel was brought to the top to feed the great lamp whose
light, by means of a large mirror (which was supposed to
be still in existence in Mahomet's time), was intensified to
such brilliance that the sailors could see it thirty-five miles
at sea. That lighthouse was dedicated " to the Saviour
Gods, for the help of those who travel across the seas " ;
and the Romans had taken it as a model for their light-
houses at Ostia, Rhodes and Messina.

The Heptastadion, a quay one mile in length, divided
the port in two vast basins and it joined the Pharos with
the city. A passage at each end of the quay connected
the two basins, the western which was the Port of Eunostos
or Safe Return, and the eastern one or Great Port which
was situated between the Pharos and the Diabathra or
breakwater which was continuing the promontory of
Lochias. Under the sun the Port shone like a green
mirror, through which one could perceive the undulations
of the sandy bed covered with sea-weeds of wonderful
colours.

And before the traveller rose the marvellous skyline of

Alexandria with the Royal Palace in front view. The Royal Palace was, in fact, a series of magnificent royal buildings, each one vying with the others, for each Ptolemy had built himself a new palace; and they were all surrounded by beautiful gardens.

The little island of Antirhodes was the Royal Port, with its pavilion for the Royal travellers. The private quay descended to the azure waters in long low steps of marble, so that the largest galleons could moor. On a hill not far from the harbour was the theatre of Dionysos, the divine ancestor of the Ptolemys. In this unending water-front the splendid buildings followed in magnificent succession: most conspicuous was the Museum or University with its long arcades, the lecture halls and, at the northern end above the sea line, the famous Library which, when Cleopatra was born, contained seven hundred thousand manuscript books, many unobtainable elsewhere: in that library was the Septimus, the first translation of the Ancient Testament made, under Ptolemy Philadelphus, by seventy-seven learned Egyptian Jews, who had called it the Biblion, or the Book of Books.

The actual founder of the Museum and the Library had been Ptolemy I, who made of Alexandria a shrine of the spiritual life of Greece. At first the collection of books was intended for private use of the King, and was housed in a wing of the Royal Palace; but soon it was made accessible to scholars and students, and transferred to the Library: the Museum was a treasury of science and culture and its library gave birth to the Alexandrian school, to which posterity owes many Greek literary works. The teaching given at that University, the methods employed, the accuracy of the scientific instruments, even the quality of the papyrus supplied to the students for their notes, all were famous throughout the world.

In the Museum there was one large hall where visitors could sit; another where they could converse and hold learned discussions; and there was a large dining-hall. Students and teachers were considered as servants of the Queen, and were given every opportunity of devoting themselves to their studies. Many of the teachers had been famous: chief among them the Peripatetic Demetrius Phalereus who had been the first to suggest the idea of founding a Library and Museum, and had been artistic adviser to the first Ptolemys. There had been the grammarian Philetas of Cos, author of many amatory poems and tutor of Ptolemy II, and the philosopher Hegesias who preached the doctrine of pessimism with such convincing eloquence that his teaching produced an epidemic of suicides. And the father of geometry, Euclid; Herophilos, physician and anatomist, the first to dissect a corpse, and who promoted an anatomical institute; Zenodoros of Ephesus, who devoted his life to an edition of Homer; Theocritus of Syracuse, the greatest pastoral poet of ancient times; Callimachus whose elegies and epigrams were famous. And Eratosthenes studied mathematical geography and cosmogony, and was the first to compute the size of the earth and draw a map of the world with lines of latitude and longitude; and at the Alexandrian school, two hundred years before Cleopatra, an attempt was made to reform the Calendar.

Between the Museum and Lochias rose the theatre, from the tiers of which the crowds could see the ships sailing beyond the island of Antirhodes. Behind the theatre rose the Paneum or Temple of Pan, that Strabo described as being in the shape of a huge pine-cone, artificially rocky, that one climbed along a spiral path, and from the top one could see the whole city lying below.

On the left stood the Gymnasium, with a portico five hundred feet long, and around it were the Law Courts, surrounded by gardens and groves. Further west was the Forum, and, upon the quay, the Temple of Neptune. In the centre of a walled space, called Soma, rose the tombs of the Ptolemaic Kings, the new Dynasty, set around the venerated mausoleum which contained the body of Alexander the Great inside a sarcophagus of crystal; the original coffin of the Great Conqueror had been of gold, and within that golden coffin the first Ptolemy had brought the body of Alexander to the city of his name, but this old coffin had been stolen.

This part of the city was called the Bruchion or Royal City. Its noble buildings of white stone, mirrored in the clear waters of the Port, the statues and monuments, the gardens, the marble steps reaching to the sea, the wide streets, the vast squares, all composed a splendour that had no equal. The majesty of the city appeared even greater when the traveller went beyond the front view. Traversing the Forum one entered the Canopus Road, three miles long, deriving its name from the pilot of Menelaus, and going from the Gate of the Necropolis at the western end beyond the Port of Safe Return, as far east as the Gate of Canopus, further east than Lochias. This magnificent avenue was flanked all the way by colonnades, through which one could see the Museum, the Soma, the Royal Palace within its gardens, and on the south side, the Gymnasium with its splendid portico, and the Paneum raising its peak towards the sky.

Further east one reached the Jewish district, with the synagogue and national buildings; and passing under the

Gate of Canopus, cut into the city walls, one reached the Hippodrome which twenty thousand spectators could barely fill. There the soil was sandy, the rocks white, the grass scarce.

Between the Road of Canopus and the open land, the Grove of Nemesis formed a resting place along the seashore; and nearby was the Temple of Aphrodite-Astartés, where the girls dedicated to the Goddess were instructed in the art of love.

Some three miles from the city was the summer resort of Nicopolis; and at the other end of Canopus, which was also called **Meson Pedion**, was the district of Rhakotis, where the low-class Egyptians lived, just behind the quay used by the cargo-boats: and Rhakotis was the name of the little Egyptian village which had stood on the site before Alexander built the new city. It was the busiest district, with its vast docks and warehouses served by an inner port, from which a canal, passing under the Canopus, joined the Lake at the back of the city.

Behind Rhakotis, upon a hill, was the stupendous Temple of Serapis. No other building in the world, except perhaps the Temple of Jupiter Capitolinus in Rome, surpassed the Serapeion in splendour; to reach it one had to mount a hundred steps. Rising high upon the hill, the massive temple towered above the humming life of the city. At the back of the temple, outside the city walls, was the Stadium; and further west a vast Necropolis of beautiful mausoleums and gardens.

Parallel with the southern walls was Lake Mareotis, with a port and locks around a narrow branch that went deep inside the city: a road as large as the Canopus, which was cutting it at right-angles, joined the port on the Lake with the Great Port on the Mediterranean: the

33

southern gate was dedicated to the Sun, the northern to the Moon. The warehouses on the Lake were richer than those on the sea, as at Lake Mareotis ended their journey the barges arriving from all parts of Egypt over the Nile and the canals. The shores of Lake Mareotis were most fertile; it was on the shores of the lake that grew the papyrus which supplied all the world with writing paper. And the villas scattered along the lake had beautiful gardens.

Alexandria's gardens had enchanted Strabo no less than the sumptuous buildings: the wealth of flowers and shrubberies gave a soft fragrance to the air; for nearly three centuries the Ptolemys had spent enormous sums for the embellishment of Alexandria. The population was cosmopolitan: Greeks, Egyptians, Latins, Phoenicians, Persians, Lybians, Armenians and people from Crete and Cyprus. The Greek element was still predominant, and a number of aristocratic families claimed to be the descendants of the soldiers and administrators brought by Alexander the Great. Nearly everybody spoke both Egyptian and Greek, and the official documents were set in both languages; many Greeks added to their name an Egyptian one, and many Egyptians adopted a second Greek name. Inter-marriages—except on the part of Jews—had brought about a mixed race; indeed, there goes back to those times what is now called a " Levantine ". Respectable or plausible merchants, sailors and pirates, political refugees from Rome and elsewhere, criminals and debtors, all were granted permission to enter and settle in Alexandria on condition of serving in the Army: and the Army, in constant quarrel with the Macedonian troops of the Palace, was a fantastic force made up with mercenaries from Germany and Gaul and all the scoundrels who could find no better trade.

The aristocracy was a mixture of cosmopolitan officers of the Army, of Greek and Egyptian State Officials, of rich merchants and bankers of western or Syrian and Jewish extraction. The students and teachers at the Museum were under the direct patronage of the Court and formed a class apart.

The populace, mostly Greeks and Egyptians of mixed blood, were a turbulent and excitable crowd, always quarrelling with the Jews. Greeks and Egyptians were often undistinguishable, and had come to terms even about spiritual matters, and all adored Serapis, while Greek Art was accepted by all as the last word of artistic expression. Alexandria was, in fact, the Paris of the ancient world, where the Greek and Oriental artists sought their fortune and success. Alexandria was also a city of pleasure. For the feast of the sacred bull Apis, the carnival lasted a long time.

But one and all the Alexandrians were totally devoid of patriotism and were utterly disinterested in public affairs. The word " people " had certainly no political meaning for them. The Greek wit had given nicknames even to the Ptolemy Kings. On the other hand, the Greco-Egyptians were a vain lot, most pretentious in their appearance; and the luxury of the merchants' houses and villas surpassed anything known in Rome. Their love of good food and their cooks were a by-word.

It was a vast population; some three hundred thousand which, together with slaves and soldiers and foreigners, made a total of no less than a million.

A great business city, gorgeously beautiful and fabulously wealthy. It was also a most immoral city. A huge meeting-place of all peoples and races, teeming with trade and commerce, overflowing with prosperity, full of contrasts and passions, it was the melting-pot of all the vices of mankind. Hordes of prostitutes of every grade found an easy market in a city where the most popular Goddess was Aphrodite. Since the time of Ptolemy II the prestige of the hetaerae was great, and the stark sensuality of Greece was combined with the more feverish eroticism of the East. The Greeks had considered sensuality the most stimulating side of life; in Alexandria it had degenerated into open vice. Aphrodite had a temple with a garden full of women dedicated to the art of love; the poets addressed odes to Priapus. And the degeneracy was helped by the ancient custom of the Egyptian of marriages between brothers and sisters, which allowed concubines for the men. Lake Mareotis was, at night, full of pleasure-boats on which people danced and gave themselves to all manner of licentiousness.

And the only God that really was worshipped by the Alexandrians was Mammon. To grow rich was the only thing that mattered.

Beyond Alexandria was the real Egypt: the thirty thousand towns which formed the kingdom of Cleopatra: Bubastes, where the Goddess of Love reigned; Memphis, sleeping at the feet of the Pyramids; Thebes, the Holy City; Hermonthis, called the glory of the Two Heavens, and the legendary land where each cluster of grapes needed two men to carry it to the wine presses.

The real Egypt, which had remained unchanged for two thousand five hundred years with its Gods, the mummies, the hieroglyphic writing, the administration that was still the same as under the Pharaohs, the people being Serfs of the State, and all they produced belonged to the

36

Queen and the whole machinery of the State was set in motion by the will of the Queen alone; the taxes were paid to fill the Queen's treasure, wars were undertaken for the Queen's renown, great buildings were erected in the Queen's honour, all the property of the country was the Queen's by right, and the people were only allowed to share it for they belonged one and all to the Queen and the Queen could dispose of their lives at will.

The Queen still wore, although only on ceremonial occasions, the insignia of the Pharaoh Kings; her names and titles were the same as the names and titles of Rameses II one thousand years before.

This was the stage upon which the drama of Cleopatra's life was acted.

IV

THE marriage of Cleopatra with her younger brother Ptolemy was never celebrated. Cleopatra put it aside.

The young Ptolemy fell under the influence of three men: his Greek tutor Theodotus, the Egyptian Commander of the Palace troops, Achillas, and the chief eunuch Pothinus, a trio that soon took Royal powers into their hands.

Cleopatra suffered an eclipse. She was a young girl, and her councillors were less resolute than the three unscrupulous advisers of her brother.

In the meantime events in Rome were fast approaching a crisis. In the rivalry between Julius Caesar and Pompey the Great a civil war might explode at any moment.

And Cleopatra and her brother, or her brother's advisers, took opposite views.

Two years after Auletes' death, Marcus Calpurnius Bibulus, Proconsul of Syria, sent his two sons to Alexandria with orders to transfer the Roman troops which had been left in the city by Gabinius in the year 55 to keep order, to the army in readiness for a new campaign against the Parthians. The troops, mostly German and Gaul cavalry, called themselves " Milites Gabiniani ", had married Alexandrian women and were finding Alexandria a most agreeable residence. At the order to strike camp there was a mutiny, and Bibulus' sons were murdered by the drunken soldiery.

Cleopatra ordered the arrest of the murderers and sent them in chains to Bibulus. The grieved Proconsul, however, sent the murderers back to the Queen with the message that the Roman Senate alone could decide the punishment.

The following year, 49, Pompey sent his son to the Egyptian Court in order to obtain a fleet and troops in readiness for the inevitable civil war. The Gabinian men, thinking a war against Caesar more tempting, did not revolt. Fifty ships and a regiment of cavalry left Alexandria and joined the forces of Bibulus, now Admiral to Pompey in the Adriatic. Pompey appeared, at the moment, master of the Roman world, and Cleopatra remembered the support he had given to her father.

But the following year, in Alexandria, the crisis was reached between brother and sister. Supported by the tutor, the eunuch and the General, Ptolemy proclaimed himself sole King of Egypt. Afraid for her life, Cleopatra fled, not to Rome, but to Syria, and there she promptly collected together an army of mercenaries and at their head crossed the desert and marched upon Alexandria to reconquer her throne.

At the very moment the curtain was rising over the Royal drama, the unexpected result of the civil war between Julius Caesar and Pompey changed the whole destiny of Cleopatra.

Julius Caesar had crossed the Rubicon and in sixty days had become master of Italy; Pompey had crossed the Adriatic into Thessaly, swiftly followed by Caesar who told his pilot: " Fear nothing; thou carriest Caesar and his fortune! "

The great clash took place at Pharsalia. But the vast army of Pompey—more than 45,000 men of infantry and 14,000 of cavalry against Caesar's 22,000—was utterly defeated, because, as Plutarch says, some of the principal Romans and Greeks, when the dreadful moment of action approached, could not help considering to what sorry plight the avarice and ambition of two men had brought the Roman empire: the same arms on both sides, the same standards, the strength and manhood of one and the same city turned upon itself!

After the battle, in Pompey's camp all the tents were found crowned with myrtle, the beds strewn with flowers, the tables covered with cups and bowls of wine, in preparation for the victory. Pompey fled to Mitylene, to take up his wife Cornelia and his son; with them he went to Cyprus, and from there, in a Seleucian galley, set sail for Egypt to seek refuge.

On the 28th of September at Pelusium, where they faced each other in arms, Cleopatra and Ptolemy were informed that the ship carrying the fleeing Pompey the Great was in sight, and was sending a messenger to beg the King of Egypt's protection.

Ptolemy was very young, and his Prime Minister Pothinus called a council. The fate of Pompey the Great was decided by Theodotus from Chios, by Pothinus the eunuch and the Egyptian soldier Achillas. The soldier was for sending to Pompey an order to depart; the eunuch for giving him an honourable reception and avoid the danger of Pompey making an alliance with their enemy Cleopatra: perhaps the unsuccess at Pharsalia could still be redressed.

But the rhetorician Theodotus insisted that they were both wrong: " If you receive him, you will have Caesar for your enemy and Pompey for your master. If you send him off, Pompey may one day revenge the affront and Caesar resent your not having delivered him in his hands. The best solution is to send for Pompey and put him to death. By this means you will do Caesar a service and have nothing to fear from Pompey ". And Theodotus added: " Dead men do not bite."[1]

It was a pitiful thing that the fate of the Great Pompey was left in the hands of those three scoundrels, while Pompey thought it beneath him to be indebted to Caesar for his safety. The execution of the black deed was committed to Achillas. The Egyptian took with him Septimius, who had formerly been one of Pompey's officers, a centurion named Salvius, and with three or four assistants went up to Pompey's ship in a small boat. When Pompey's friends and officers perceived that there was nothing magnificent in their reception, but a few men in a fishing boat, they urged Pompey to get back to the open sea while he was out of reach of missive weapons.

But the boat approached and Septimius addressed Pompey as Imperator. Then Achillas saluted him in Greek and invited him to come into the boat, because the water was very shallow towards the shore. At the same time Achillas saw several of the King Ptolemy's ships getting ready and the shore covered with troops, so that

---
[1] Plutarch.

if Pompey changed his mind it would have been too late. Pompey embraced Cornelia, and ordered two centurions, one of his freedmen named Philip and a servant called Scenes to get into the boat before him. When Achillas took his hand in support and he was on the point of jumping into the boat, Pompey turned to his wife and son and repeated the line of Sophocles: *" Seek'st thou a tyrant's door? Then farewell freedom! "*[1]

While the boat was being rowed towards the shore, noticing that not a man was speaking to him, he looked at Septimius and said: " I think I remember you as one of my fellow soldiers ", which Septimius answered merely with a nod. Silence again took place, and Pompey took out a paper, in which he had written the speech in Greek that he intended to make to Ptolemy, and busied himself reading it.

From the ship Cornelia and her friends were watching the event with anxiety. She saw a number of the King's officers coming down to the shore in all appearance to receive her husband. But as Pompey was taking hold of Philip's hand to jump out of the boat, Septimius came from behind and stabbed him with his broad sword: Salvius and Achillas did the same. From the ship they saw the wounded Pompey take his toga with both hands and cover his face; then without uttering a word, he fell dead. He was fifty-nine years of age and it was the day after his birthday. Cornelia gave a shriek that was heard as far as the shore, and quickly the Seleucian galley weighed anchor and departed helped by a gale.

The murderers cut off Pompey's head; then they threw the body out of the boat naked and left it exposed in sight of all. Only later the freedman Philip washed the body

---

[1] Plutarch.

41

with sea-water and wrapped it in his own garment, having nothing else at hand. Then he saw on the shore the fateful fishing boat, and made a pile for the poor naked and headless body. While he was thus collecting the wood for a pyre an old Roman, who had been a campaigner under Pompey, came up to Philip: " Who are you that are preparing the funeral of Pompey the Great? " Philip answered: " I am his freedman." And the old soldier said: " But you shall not have this honour entirely to yourself." In this humble manner was the funeral of Pompey conducted.

Next day Lucius Lentulus, who knew nothing of what had happened because he was travelling from Cyprus, arrived, and saw the funeral pile, and Philip standing by it. He called out: " Who has finished his days upon this shore? " and after a pause he sighed: " Ah, Pompey the Great! Perhaps you are the unlucky man." Soon after, Lentulus went ashore and was instantly slain by Achillas' men.

Four days afterwards Caesar, in pursuit of Pompey, landed at Alexandria. Theodotus presented him at once with the head of his great rival: Caesar turned from it in horror. They presented him with Pompey's ring, which had upon the signet a lion holding a sword. Caesar took the ring, and looked at it with tears in his eyes.

Then Caesar sent messengers to Ptolemy and Cleopatra ordering them to retire to their own camps: he had come to set order in Egypt.

BOOK TWO

CLEOPATRA AND JULIUS CAESAR

I

CLEOPATRA was in her tent at Pelusium. It was the easternmost port on the Mediterranean coast; the citadel upon the delta on the route that was joining Egypt with Syria. From the fortress of Pelusium the Queen of Egypt could gaze into Asia. But now, surrounded by her own armies and the adverse soldiery of her brother, her eyes were turned upon Alexandria.

The capital of her kingdom: and it was now occupied by Caesar, the invincible victor! And Caesar had sent for her. Impatient she was to go; and yet she delayed.

News of the events in Alexandria had reached her day by day without official messengers or spies. News in the East had a way of travelling fast. She had heard that Caesar had ordered the head of Pompey to be buried on the sea-shore, in the little grove of Nemesis—what a symbol!—and that a monument was to be built. She learnt that Caesar had sent the ashes of Pompey to the widow Cornelia, by a special ship in mourning, and Caesar had taken up residence at the Palace at Bruchion and showed no hurry to leave Egypt. He had disembarked from his galley, set his foot upon the imposing steps of black marble that descended broad and deep into the sea and from there he had looked round. Two legions had disembarked after him and a small escort of 800 German cavalry.

She had heard that the people had not been completely submissive, and the Egyptian Ministers had shown an

45

inclination to ambiguities. So Caesar had thought it better to make a second entry into Alexandria, more solemn and more formal, more like a conqueror who intends not to leave the people in two minds. Caesar had made the legions march through the city, and he had led the march, preceded, like the Consular Processions in Rome, by the Lictors carrying the Fasces topped by the hatchet. The Lictors and the Fasces. The Consul was taking possession in name of Rome.

The people of Alexandria—so gay, so carefree!—had furrowed their brows at the sight of the Consular Procession. The dark shadow of Rome, after so long, was now darkening the Canopus! People had murmured against this affront to the majesty of Egypt and to the King and Queen. For several days news had reached Pelusium of riots and disturbances. Caesar had sent for reinforcements from the near East.

Ah, to be in Alexandria now! But Cleopatra knew that she would be twice lost: an enemy of Caesar, and at the mercy of her brother and his eunuch counsellor.

Cleopatra sat in her tent on the hill above the sea and calmly she weighed the chances of her plan, studying, as a woman does, her changing images in her mirrors.

And she felt deep within herself that her way to success was to side with Caesar.

She thought of him only as a man. There was no Roman invader, no great Dictator, no unconquerable General, no triumphant victor of the Egyptian dynasty; there was only a man—Caesar. What was he, this great man Caesar?

And Cleopatra thought of the strange things she had heard from her father, when she was a girl, about this man Caesar. In recent times, after her father's death,

46

her own agents had sent reports that were even more impressive and intriguing.

The portraits she had seen of him were only stamped upon coins. The image she had formed of him was one of her own imagining out of all the strange and great tales she had heard of him. She thought of him, a man well over fifty, trying to hide his baldness by bringing up the hair from the back of his head. But the neck seemed proud of holding Caesar's head. He had an extraordinary face, small and sharp, with dark brown eyes, and a little aquiline nose, (and her finger touched her own aristocratic little nose), and a thin mouth, that could be hard and yet so seductive. And he had the greatest and the worst reputation any man could have. Never mind his wars and victories—great Generals must be victorious! Disregard his unscrupulous politics—political affairs are never scrupulous. But his affairs with women! People said that he was a great connoisseur of women; and yet he was already half-way through his fifties, a dangerous age for any man. Was he a marvellous lover? They said no woman was safe from him. And people said he always lived like an aristocrat and yet the Roman rabble loved him and his soldiers adored him. And people said that his talk was plain and his voice was deep and throaty. And people said—ah! They also said of him, that his only sorrow, his deepest, his most grievous sorrow was not to have had a child of his own, a child to inherit his name and his power and his fortunes!

Thus did Cleopatra ponder in her tent—Cleopatra, perhaps no longer Queen of Egypt. She decides that she will obey the order, and present herself to Caesar.

In Alexandria Caesar grows impatient. This Egypt,

he thinks, is baffling. He has been to the tomb of Alexander the Great—his hero!—the body of the dead Alexander in the coffin of crystal, perfectly preserved, under the painted bandages, the mighty form of the Great Conqueror, buried in his own city, greater and more famous than all the heroes of the *Iliad!* Caesar has been told that the original golden sarcophagus had long been stolen; but the crystal coffin under the bronze lid was a sight to inspire him. To have seen, to have touched the dead form of Alexander the Great!

Caesar has visited Alexandria, the great Port, the locks, the docks, the stupendous schools and Library. All in such marvellous order; everything so well organized, so practical, so advanced! A city worthy of a great Empire; worthy of Rome—and of Caesar. If only this young boy of a King were not so shy and effeminate! And this eunuch Pothinus, so elusive, so irritating! And ·so treacherous. Caesar knows that despite his humility in his presence, all he had said and done in public was intolerably insolent. The corn he had supplied to the Roman soldiers was old and musty, yet this scum of a eunuch was bold enough to say: "They ought to be satisfied, since they don't pay for it."(1) He had placed only wooden and earthen vessels on the young King's table, saying that Caesar had taken all the gold and silver plate for his father's old debt: for the late Auletes had owed Caesar seventeen million five hundred thousand drachmas since the days of the syndicate in Rome that had backed his claims to the throne. Now, in Alexandria, Caesar had remitted to his children seven millions and a half and had demanded only ten millions in settlement; but Pothinus, instead of paying the money, had advised

---

[1] Plutarch.

7. The Pharos, or lighthouse, of Alexandria, one of the seven wonders of the world, built by Ptolemy II Philadelphus about 280 B.C. From a sixteenth century engraving.

8. Navigation on the Nile in Roman times, reminiscent of Cleopatra's voyage along the Nile with Julius Caesar. From a Roman mosaic.

him to go and finish the great affairs he had upon his hands, after which he should have his money with thanks. The impudence of it! Caesar had answered back that " he had no need of Egyptian counsellors ", and had commanded Cleopatra to appear before him. What was she like this girl who had not followed her brother in submission?

Apollodorus, the faithful Sicilian servant, rowed the boat around the delta, under the walls of the Palace, and landed near the steps. He unloaded a rolled carpet, tied with a string at the ends; one of those bundles in which any working-class Egyptian carried his belongings and the strip of matting that served him as a bed. Apollodorus was a big strong fellow, and having stepped out of the boat he threw the big bundle easily over his shoulder and passed the Palace gates. He stopped at a door and told the Roman sentry that he was bringing a beautiful carpet to the mighty Caesar, a gift from the King Ptolemy. The mighty Caesar appeared at the door, a question in his eyes. Two quiet eyes answered with an honest look; Apollodorus was nodded into the room.

The tall Sicilian slave unrolled the carpet before Caesar —and out of it rose Cleopatra as in a fairy tale.([1]) The little Queen bounced up with all the quickness and lightness of a young girl; shook her hair free and then boldly looked Caesar in the face. And Caesar, the Great, the Mighty, the Unconquerable and also the ladies-man, laughed.

Now she was speaking, a beautiful Latin, a little too fast with her Greek accent; she was telling him that she felt she had no other way of reaching Caesar safely;

[1] Plutarch.

but Caesar did not hear half she was saying, he was looking at her. This slip of a girl, a wit, with a voice that was like music, and such a lovely mouth, such a daring bosom under her silks, dishevelled and charming, fearful and audacious, an Aphrodite rising out from inside a carpet!

So Caesar stood looking at her, with his thin finely chiselled mouth that could be so authoritative and so captivating, his clean-shaven face that smelled of well-groomed skin, laughter in his eyes—and they each noticed that the other had white, glistening teeth.

II

THAT meeting in the night—the famous meeting of Caesar and Cleopatra which historians and poets have told in a thousand ways, and yet may be better left to the imagination—that first meeting born of surprise and spent in pleasant talk in the quietude of the autumn night in the gorgeous Palace, for Cleopatra had two decisive results: she gained the throne of Egypt and she fell in love with Caesar.

The Caesar that Cleopatra had met was a conqueror with the halo of his resounding victory at Pharsalia, and he was now the absolute Master of the Roman world. And he was all that Cleopatra had heard or imagined of him, and more, infinitely more.

Cleopatra discovered that Caesar was a man that might be compared only to Alexander—the founder of her kingdom and dynasty.

At fifty-four—he had indeed celebrated his fifty-fourth birthday a few days before—Caesar was the sublimation of all the virtues and vices that composed his rare nature.

He was the unscrupulous man he had always been, in his public and private life; a man without any particular religion, except an absolute faith in his own destiny, which is the real faith of any great man; but he had no trace of hypocrisy or pretension to virtue, and did not care to mask his errors. In matters of money he retained the sublime indifference and lack of principles that in the early years of his career had made him contract enormous debts, till he owed his creditors such vast sums that could only be paid with the spoils of victories—or not paid at all.

His magnanimity was as great as his cruelty: in Alexandria he had wept when they had shown him the head of his enemy Pompey; and yet at Uxellodunum, during the Gallic Wars, he had ordered thousands of prisoners to be mutilated by cutting off their right hands so that they could no longer hold a sword or spear. During the campaign in Gaul he had killed one million men and another million he had sent to be used as slaves; and to the young Tribune Metullus, who had the impertinence to ask whether Caesar had any right to appropriate the public funds for his wars, he had replied that he would put him to death if he persisted in such nonsense: " And take note, young man, that it is more unpleasant for me to say it than to do it."

Yet, in spite of all the laxity of his life and his many amours, he still was what he had always been: a man and a soldier of unsurpassable vigour; who shared all the fatigues and privations of a campaign; who was frugal to the point of eating with indifference a dish of asparagus upon which had been poured a sauce accidentally made with a balm. For many years he had not touched wine— an abstinence enforced by the state of his health. And he

51

could still sit a horse as he had done many times in view of his troops, galloping with his hands behind his back.

The years had already lined his face; and the indulgence in pleasures no less than the fits of epilepsy of which he suffered, had ravaged it. But it was a head and a face full of grace. For Caesar looked, at fifty-four, an aristocrat; a man of fine breeding, with a rare hidden power, one of those men of destiny who are born at very long intervals, perhaps to remind us that we humans are descended from the Gods; men born to command and to outlive death into eternity.

His body was spare and lithe; his face was as sharp and keen with flat cheekbones, the brown eyes deep and piercing; the mouth thin and well designed, perhaps hard and cynical but the lips could quickly form into a smile, and the pale colour of his skin, all these revealed an inflexible power mixed with sensuality. By his appearance he showed the care he gave to his person. His hair, alas, was sparce, but combed to hide his baldness. His white toga was bordered with a large band of purple with a gold fringe. There was a touch of preciosity in his elegance; and although he wore nothing but his signet ring, it was known that he was partial to jewels for had he not himself given vent to the rumour that he had invaded Britain because he hoped to find there beautiful pearls for his mistresses? Every great man has some affectations, which are, in such men, the spontaneous expression of their complex nature.

Such was Caesar at the time of that meeting, the new Master of Rome, who could look at the young and exquisite Cleopatra with the appraising and mocking eyes of an old rake, and yet talk so urbanely, with the charm of a man of the world, in a cultured, agreeable voice, perhaps a little high, but with such a joyful hint of persiflage.

For Caesar was already a little tired of the " orientalism " of the Palace and its eunuchs full of deceit, and the unexpected little Queen was such an enchanting change! Should he try to conquer this seductive girl who had chosen to present herself in that rather absurd manner?

But Cleopatra had already fallen in love with Caesar, in love as a girl of eighteen can fall in love with a man of fifty-four who happens to be Caesar. And it was her first love.

III

THE following day Caesar called to his presence both Cleopatra and her brother Ptolemy, and read to them the will of their father Auletes, of which he was executor on behalf of the Roman people, and enjoined them to obey the testament's terms, according to which they must reign jointly and peacefully.

But Ptolemy felt that Caesar's decision to discard him from the throne was already taken, and tearing from his head the diadem he flew into a rage, hastening from the room and calling for his friends. A tumult followed outside the Palace, and Caesar had to show himself at a window and harangue the crowd inviting them to assemble on the following day in the Gymnasium.

Cleopatra listened to his voice, and wondered at his unconcerned tone. Caesar turned from the window, and with a smile hovering on his lips gave orders that her apartments were to be guarded.

What was in Caesar's mind? Was the great Caesar touched by the admiration in the young woman's eyes?

Did he read in that admiration the devotion that was to come? That night Cleopatra invited Caesar to dine as her guest. Her guest? He was the conqueror, he was arbiter of her future. Yet, Caesar accepted with the grace of a courtier.

All day Cleopatra had wandered through the Palace; the Palace from which six months before she had been forced to flee. She touched the silken curtains, the alabaster benches, the doors of scented woods. It was such a marvel to be back again, to be once more the Queen.

She adorned herself for the dinner; Caesar presented his officers " to the Queen of Egypt ". He conversed with her lightly and gallantly; then he informed her that on the morrow he would read to the people Auletes' will, and reinstate both children, and so that no opposing parties could be formed again in the Palace, he would restore Cyprus to Egypt. And then he expressed his admiration of her beautiful Sidonian silks.

He did not say that he intended to be the real master of Egypt, and consider Alexandria a Roman conquest— Alexandria the greatest commercial port of the Mediter- ranean, the gateway to the unknown lands of the East. The West he had already conquered; Pharsalia had placed Greece and Asia Minor at his feet; Cleopatra would offer to him as an unparallelled appanage the splendid Alexandria.

The people of Alexandria had so long been afraid of a Roman landing that they were taken aback when they heard Caesar announce the re-instatement of their King and Queen and the return of Cyprus to their sovereignty in the persons of Cleopatra's younger brother and sister, Prince Ptolemy and Princess Arsinoë.

Caesar went further. He informed the Alexandrians that he was forfeiting the largest part of the debts contracted in Rome by King Auletes, and was satisfied to fix at the very moderate sum of ten million drachmas the total claim on behalf of the Roman creditors. He informed the people that he was imposing on Alexandria no war contribution as might be his right in view of the open support that Egypt had given to his enemy Pompey.

But trouble was growing within the Palace on behalf of the almost discarded King Ptolemy.

For the wealthy city Alexandria, it was nothing to pay ten million drachmas. Yet, the cunning eunuch and Prime Minister Pothinus gave order to melt the Palace gold plate and the temple vases to turn them into money for Caesar. On the Royal table he gave orders to put wooden vessels so that everyone might see to what poverty the grasping avarice of Caesar had reduced Egypt. The Roman troops were still supplied with corn of inferior quality. Here and there hostilities and affrays broke out.

Caesar struck a first blow to the plotters. Being informed that Pothinus and Ptolemy were in secrecy arming their ships, which were at anchor in the west part of the Great Harbour, Caesar sent his men to set fire to the Egyptian Fleet: eighty vessels of the coastal squadron and the fifty war galleys which had been previously placed at the disposal of Pompey. The rest of the fleet was landlocked in the basin of the Port of Safe Return. The conflagration had terrific results: many of the fine buildings along the quay were destroyed and the famous Library suffered irreparable damage. But it was a strong lesson; and Caesar gained control of the Great Harbour and occupied the isle of Pharos with the lighthouse. He also fortified the vulnerable points of his land defences.

One day his barber, a young man who had his nose everywhere, informed Caesar of a plot to murder him. The eunuch Pothinus was arrested during a banquet for the reconciliation of Ptolemy and Cleopatra, and was beheaded without delay.

The first act of hostility that caused Caesar to feel alarmed was the pollution of the water reservoirs. New wells of excellent water were luckily found; but the poisoning of the reservoirs had made Caesar give thought to the abandoning of Alexandria.

Soon after, news reached him that the XXXVII Legion, which had sailed from Asia Minor with arms and provisions, was at anchor outside the Egyptian waters. In high spirits, Caesar sailed with all his fleet to meet the convoy, leaving his troops at their strongholds around the city. The ships saluted and joined forces and Caesar returned to the Royal anchorage under the walls of the Palace. Sure now of his strength, he tried to seize also the Port of Safe Return. But a dangerous reverse was imminent. While commanding in person the attack at the southern point of the Heptastadium, the Egyptians of Achillas made a sortie from the south, in their eagerness a number of Roman soldiers jumped on the boat that was carrying their commander and instead of giving him assistance they caused the ship to capsize.

The crowd watching the battle from the promontory of Lochias saw Caesar jump in the water, holding aloft in his left hand a roll of important papers, and swim vigorously, holding between his teeth his scarlet mantle that trailed behind him on the water. Now and then his bald head disappeared under water, to avoid the missiles of the Egyptian archers, who were already shouting in victory. Caesar landed unarmed on the Palace steps. His scarlet mantle was fished out by an Egyptian and held up, amid jeers, on a boathook. It was a lost battle.

But the revenge came quickly. An army was coming to Caesar's help, from across the desert, under the combined command of Mithridates of Pergamus,([1]) of the Jewish King Antipater, father of Herod, and of the Arab chief Iamblichus. Now Caesar could "put things in order" in Egypt. The Royal army was endeavouring to deliver the little King Ptolemy from Alexandria and reconquer the city. Caesar ordered Ptolemy to go—to rejoin his army. It was the simplest, and the cleanest, way to be rid of the troublesome brother of Cleopatra. The little King understood the intention of his Roman enemy, and when the order came, he wept and begged to be allowed to remain in the Palace. But he was pushed out; he was forced to go and fight against Caesar.

The Syrian army had already taken Pelusium and was marching along the east side of the delta, crossing the Nile near Memphis. Ptolemy was obliged to give battle to the forces of Mithridates and his allies. He had retrenched at the foot of a hill, on the flank of the Nile. After a battle lasting two days, he was defeated. Ptolemy, trying to escape, jumped into a boat, but the boat overturned. His body was later identified by the heavy breastplate of gold that he had worn. He was fifteen. His death saved Caesar from the embarrassment of taking him prisoner to Rome and putting him to death after his Triumph. On the 19th of March, Caesar re-entered Alexandria triumphally. The gates of the capital were now opened to him. As a sign of total submission the people of Alexandria dressed themselves in mourning. They brought before Caesar the images of their Gods.

---

[1] Natural son of the Great Mithridates.

On his charger Caesar traversed the city and went to the Palace. Cleopatra received him as a hero and her liberator. She was the undisputed Queen of Egypt.

Caesar considered this war for Egypt too trivial for his pen, and entrusted the recording of his *De Bello Alexandrino* to a friend.

IV

CLEOPATRA found that now Caesar was in the mood for taking a holiday. He was in no hurry to leave Egypt and return to Rome. Indeed, he lived at the Palace the most joyful existence. Had not the Roman Senate informed him on the 25th of October that Rome had appointed him Dictator for the whole year 47?

During the winter Cleopatra and Caesar came to know each other better. For Cleopatra this romance had the tender and pathetic magic of a new experience. Caesar, with his imperiousness in public affairs, the fascination of his manners in their meetings, appeared to her as an ideal lover. And for Caesar, it was something he had not experienced before. He was now experiencing the sentimental hunger which comes to men who have lived a life of excesses. He thought of Cornelia, the lovely Cornelia he had loved when he was seventeen; he thought of Pompeia, the statuesque Pompeia grand-daughter of Sulla, who had betrayed him with Clodius and he had divorced her " because Caesar's wife must be above suspicion ", and he thought of Servilia, the voluptuous, insatiable Servilia; and the noble Calpurnia to whom he had now been married ten years; and he thought of all the great Roman beauties and the foreign princesses and the women in all the lands he had conquered; but Cleopatra seemed

58

to unite all the charms and all the arts of love. Caesar was fifty-five and Cleopatra was twenty-one.

No, Caesar was in no hurry to depart. He was sitting in this Palace, and was finding it congenial, for it was more than a royal house. The Bruchion, as it was called, had been founded by Alexander, and each Ptolemy had added to it. It stood upon an elevation, where the hills swept down to the sea; and it was a small city in itself, a magnificent compound of buildings of great splendour, in which the massiveness of Egyptian architecture was blended with the more refined taste of Greek art. The part actually used by Cleopatra had been specially arranged by Ptolemy Auletes, the flute player, who had delighted in adorning it with the most perfect works of art. The rooms were furnished with chairs of ivory and ebony, tables of exquisite design, coffers encrusted with gold, finely carved candelabra. In tripods of bronze and silver burned the incense of Arabia; colourful carpets enhanced the floors of red porphyry and black marble; and here and there stood statues and groups by Praxiteles, Myron and Phidias. The terraces were connected by great marble steps to the luxuriant gardens; in the ponds and fountains the water was clear as crystal; the roses from Persia exhaled a pleasant fragrance; the palms moved like fans in the gentle breeze. And above was the beautiful Egyptian sky.

Now that the winter had passed, ships were arriving from Rome with despatches for Caesar. Rome, said the messengers, was anxiously awaiting Caesar's return. The seats of the Pompeians in the Senate were unoccupied; hundreds of Senators and Knights were still in hiding, fearing the Dictator's vengeance. The situation in Italy was insecure, for no one could tell how the Dictator would use his power. There was Mark Antony, representing the Master; but who could say whether his decrees really interpreted the Dictator's will?

And Caesar listened to the messengers and scanned the dispatches and gave no reply as to his return. He heard how Antony and Dolabella had fought in the Forum because one had stolen the other's wife, a shocking spectacle, and they were his two most trusted friends and representatives. He heard how the people put up statues to him all over Italy; but he also heard how thousands of his own soldiers were marauding or enlisting in the army of the sons of Pompey, because they were despairing of ever receiving the pay that was due to them or the land which should have been their due after the victory. Rome was without her leader; and it seemed as though Caesar had deserted Rome. But Caesar, the ageing son of Venus, was in love. He had now spent nearly six months in the Palace, and he had found a happiness he had not known before. He spent his days interesting himself in the ancient ways of Egyptian life controlled by Alexandria, that was almost a foreign city; and at night he discovered new pleasures in the arms of Cleopatra.

At the end of the winter Cleopatra told Caesar that in the summer she would bear him a son. And she stood before him, bashful and proud.

Caesar's brown eyes widened with pleasure and he smiled. Almost with embarrassment he asked her how she knew it would be a boy. Cleopatra, carried away with her own ecstasy, was certain it would be.

V

Now the condition of the Queen could no longer be concealed. Cleopatra must show to her people that their Queen is not merely the mistress of the Roman Dictator. After the death of her young brother Ptolemy, she was officially a widow. Cleopatra put around the rumour that Caesar was the incarnation of the Great God of Egypt, and that the child she was soon to have would be the fruit of her Divine union.

Caesar consented to let himself be recognised by the Egyptians as the incarnation of the God Amon. Had he not found it simple and useful, ungodly as he was, to affirm in Rome that he was descended from Venus, for the Julian family descended from Julius, son of Aeneas, issued from the union of Anchises and Venus? So Alexander the Great had pretended before the people of Egypt to be son of Amon, and allowed himself to be represented with the horns of the ram on the sides of his head. And Alexander was Caesar's own personal hero.

Cleopatra used all her influence to induce Caesar to believe in their divinity. She firmly believed in her own divine descent. From her childhood she had seen herself honoured as a daughter of Isis and proclaimed immortal in the Temples. Her very power as Queen she held on behalf of the Gods. She never doubted that she was the representative of the Sun-God. Did not every Egyptian —although the Alexandrians smiled cynically—prostrate themselves in her presence, their face against the hearth, as one does in the sight of God, and call her a Goddess, as their forefathers had called Gods the Pharaoh Kings? Yes, she believed in her divine, superhuman, immortal person. The Gods of Egypt had guided her life and her destiny; the Gods had sent Caesar to Egypt for her to love and to bear him a son and to rule with him over the world.

The people of Egypt accepted the announcement of the marital rite by the High Priests. On the walls of the Temple of Hermonthis at Thebes a bas-relief was set, representing the nuptials of Cleopatra with the God Amon, depicted as a human, the head with the ram's horns being a stylization of Caesar's lean features. Later, the events of Cleopatra's reign were dated from this superhuman occurrence; there still exists an epitaph bearing the date " twentieth year from the union of Cleopatra with Amon-Caesar ".

Thus Cleopatra has made of Caesar a King of Egypt. Now she feels sure of her kingdom and of her destiny.

Politically, no other union could be more acceptable to the Egyptians than the marriage of their Queen with the Dictator of Rome. But a much greater vista opens in her mind. With her womanly insight, Cleopatra has guessed that soon Caesar will want to reign, not only to rule, over the Roman Empire he has conquered. And she can bring to him an unparallelled dowry, the kingdom of Egypt, with its untold wealth, its ancient prestige, and the open route to the Indies. All this she can share with Caesar, she will be the Empress of the Roman-Egyptian world, and pass it on, one day, to her own son, Caesar's son. What a dream to unfold! Maternity somewhat quieted her fiery nature. Exalted by these ambitions, she has already forgotten her father's pleadings with the Roman usurers for the safety of the throne; she brushes disdainfully aside the recent memories of her own fight for survival, Pothinus the perfidious eunuch, her little brother drowned with his breastplate of gold. She is the Daughter of the Sun, Sister of the Moon, Wife of Caesar descendant of Venus; and in her womb already moves the child that shall reign after her!

How much and how far did the same thoughts pass in Caesar's mind?

A man of Caesar's nature could not live six months in the intimacy of Cleopatra without savouring to the full the inebriating air of royalty. Between the Dictatorship wrenched from an unstable mob and the serene sublimity of absolute Royal power held in the name of the Gods, the difference was as tempting as his greatest victories.

On the other hand, by falling in with Cleopatra's wishes, he was compromising nothing. For a long time Rome had looked at Alexandria and Egypt as the most desirable prey. Outside the Roman Republic Egypt was the richest and the most powerful country in the world. The importance of Alexandria, of her trade, of her culture, was the biggest prize he could now offer to Rome. What could the Roman people refuse him after this? His policy was clearly dictated by the circumstances. His " marriage " with Cleopatra could be easily explained and discounted in Rome: the ancient Laws forbade bigamy; but was not the Dictator above the law? Calpurnia could be divorced on account of her sterility. And now there was this child on the way—would it be a son? A son, the heir that no other woman had given him, for was Brutus really his son?

Those obscure hopes and ambitions made Caesar delay his departure. He was now impatient to learn whether the child would really be a son. He felt loth to depart before events would give him this answer.

And in the hope of a son, he thought of the possibility of ruling over an Empire and at the same time founding a House of Royal lineage. And Caesar was already convinced that the Roman Republic had lasted too long, and it had produced only factions and civil wars. Rome needed a King.

VI

CLEOPATRA ordered the thalamegos to be prepared, and with Caesar embarked upon a journey on the Nile, to show Caesar her kingdom.

The thalamegos, the Royal barge, was a floating palace. There were spacious apartments, and the main lounge was panelled in cedar and cypress wood, painted in gay colours and gold. The furniture was in Greek style, but the banqueting room was decorated in Egyptian tradition. Caesar's apartment had a frieze with scenes from the *Iliad,* and on the deck were little sanctuaries dedicated to Venus and Dionysos. The ships had rest-decks for morning hours and for the evening there was a small garden.

Caesar ordered a considerable number of his troops to embark on a fleet of four hundred river-boats: his intention was to travel as far as the deep interior of the Sudan. Had he plans of military nature? Did he fear the attitude of the populations up country?

From Alexandria the expedition moved into the nearest branch of the Nile, and set a southernly course, in the direction of Memphis. Propelled by the steady rowing of fifty Nubians with ebony oars, the beautiful thalamegos glided at first between leagues of emerald foliage. After the first few days the vegetation grew scanty, the shores were now barren, the horizon a vast stretch of sand, which melted away under the blazing sun; here and there the aloes shot in the quivering air their blade-like branches.

The ancient city of Memphis appeared. The thalamegos dropped anchor opposite the Pyramids. The long line of Pyramids, stretching for miles along the western ridge of the hills; the unique tombs of the Pharaohs, rising from the plateau, each surrounded by the smaller tombs of courtiers.

Cleopatra and Caesar disembarked and went to gaze at the Great Sphinx. Caesar compared the delicate grace of his Queen with the tremendous proportions of the Sphinx. Lying on her bed of sand, with the sun setting behind the Libyan hills, the monster seemed about to rise from a vast ocean of gold. What question did Caesar put to the Sphinx?

They visited Thebes, the sacred city, where the central of the three great temples measured fifteen hundred feet in width, and about the same in length; the ancient capital of the earlier Empire, that was nine miles long.

At Caesar's suggestion, Cleopatra ordered the obelisk of the Pharaohs to be moved from the Temple at Thebes and be transported to Alexandria where it was re-erected near the Forum, with an inscription added at the foot recalling the event.([1])

They passed Elephantine, and on the thirtieth day of their voyage they stopped at Philae, a pearl in its double setting of blue sky and blue water, both so pure, so transparent; the island city that was reserved to the Priests of Isis.

At last they reached Assouan and the first cataract of the Nile.

But the task of making the boats jump the rapids appeared super-human. The Roman troops were awed by the huge falls of the cataracts upon the rocks of basalt as

---

[1] It is the obelisk which now stands on the Thames Embankment in London, and is popularly called " Cleopatra's Needle ".

black as the walls of Avernus. The Officers reported an attempt to mutiny. The fearless Legionaries of Caesar, who feared no enemy, had taken fright at the Great Nile.

The thalamegos turned on its return journey. But Caesar was studying with great interest the country and the life of the Egyptian people. Cleopatra was always ready to supply the right information. Her knowledge of the life, of the administration, of the people's customs, was to Caesar as surprising as the land he was traversing.

In its entire length, Egypt was framed in rocky walls, which sometimes reached a height of eight hundred feet; hills that instead of rising to peaks, formed the edge of a large table-land with larger plateaux here and there. The table-land was entirely without water, covered with the sand of the desert. The life and prosperity of the country depended on the periodical floods of the Nile, which spread upon the land coolness, dampness and fertility, reviving the whole country from the dryness of the summer heat. Because of this the ancient people had fixed their New Year's Day on the 15th of September, the date at which the Nile's floods were at their highest, the time when the fate of the country was in the balance; if the water rose insufficiently by one-tenth part, the canals carrying the water to the higher level would not fill, and the result was famine. If the flood rose slightly too high, sad devastation ensued; embankments and dykes would be thrown down, and freshly cultivated fields would be covered by the inundation. From the earliest times, the rise of the Nile was closely watched and controlled by government officials, who regulated the taxes by the result of the floods. There existed nilometers, wells in which the height of the water was marked by a water gauge; the nilometers were under the protection of the State; the height of the inundation was notified from province to province.([1])

At the time of Cleopatra, the height of a good flood at Memphis was said to be sixteen ells, and in the beautiful statue of the Nile in the Vatican Museum the boy who represents the sixteenth ell looks down with great content from the cornucopia up which he has clambered. This genie of the sixteenth ell is also to be seen on an Alexandrian coin presenting his cornucopia to Father Nile.

The people of Egypt, Cleopatra explained to Caesar, did not possess the light-heartedness of the Greeks, although the sky of Egypt smiled more brightly than that of Hellas. The life of the Egyptian labourer was a hard one: and yet he was content to know that all the fruits of his toil would be accepted by the Queen on behalf of the Gods.

The making of the canals, the dykes and shrines had been done in old time; a colossal work which had taxed the ingenuity of the people, and accustomed the people to systematic work. As the upkeep of this system of irrigation could be carried out only by a supervisory body, it was impossible for the Egyptians to be a free people of peasants like the people of Rome. The hard logic of facts, Cleopatra told Caesar, proved that an autocratic government was necessary in order to control the flood of the Nile and the prosperity of the country. And she smiled with gravity and sweetness, while Caesar beheld the mighty River, the amazing irrigation works, and he, who had built so many bridges in the course of his campaigns, noted the clever use of the Archimedes' screw.

---

[1] An ancient nilometer still exists on the island of Elephantine, in the extreme South of Egypt.

At night, in the exquisite rooms of the thalamegos, he told Cleopatra episodes of his life; unfolded the story of what had been accomplished and the dreams that were in his heart. When he spoke of his ambitions a metallic hardness came into his voice—and Cleopatra asked, had he ever consulted an oracle? No, Caesar did not believe in oracles; he believed only in his destiny. But he looked at her with tenderness when her hand went, in the way a carrying woman does, to her belly; and he would then ask in his mind: " Is it to be a son? "

They returned to Alexandria at the end of June. On the first week of July Cleopatra gave birth to her child: it was a boy.

The people of Egypt proclaimed the child, Son of the God Amon, appearing on Earth in the person of Caesar. But Cleopatra named her son Caesarion, the Greek diminutif of Caesar. An inscription in two languages described the child of Caesar and Cleopatra: " Ptolemy, equally called Caesar—*Ptolemys zed nef Kysares.*"[1]

Soon after the birth of his son Caesar departed for Rome. He was returning to Rome—he told Cleopatra —to create that Monarchy that they would share over the World.

VII

Rome was in joyful mood. The civil war was ended; Caesar, the Dictator, was preparing his Triumph, in fact, four triumphs: it was going to be a marvellous show. And now, in time for Caesar's Triumphs, Cleopatra Queen of Egypt was arriving: the fabulous mistress of Caesar, bringing with her Caesar's son.

[1] The inscription is preserved in the Egyptian Museum of Turin, in Italy.

In all truth, the visit had necessitated a good deal of private and official juggling. When Cleopatra had first suggested her visit, Caesar had demurred. Suitable excuses were not lacking; his letters to her were as affectionate as ever; she should not take much notice of the rumours about his attachment to Queen Eunoc, wife of the King of Mauretania, it was but a passing fancy. (The ageing lover dwelt upon it with a touch of cynical pride underlining the episode . . .) But there were still wars to be ended, situations in Rome to be sorted out. Cleopatra suggested that the official reason of her visit would be to obtain for Egypt the title of *Socius Republicae*—ally of the Roman Republic. The suggestion seemed but a trifling excuse: it was totally unnecessary for the Queen to journey to Rome in person to settle a point that the Ambassadors could easily settle. Eventually however, the Senate extended an official invitation.

More important than anything else was the curiosity of the populace: the romance of Caesar with Queen Cleopatra was known in every detail. By the Gods, she must have cast a magical spell indeed, this Egyptian Queen, to come as an honoured guest instead of joining the gang of the vanquished Kings who would walk in chains behind Caesar's chariot!

It was a glorious June day when Cleopatra arrived in Rome. Huge crowds lined the route with mixed feelings. All kinds of strange stories were about: the Queen of Egypt was a courtesan, a kind of Oriental siren, glittering with pearls and gold; a sorceress whose evil influence drove all men to perdition. Above all, she was an alien, a woman from the East, a thing that the people of Rome despised more than anything on earth.

The Royal procession opened with black slaves wearing

69

big gold ear-rings. Then came the Court Eunuchs clothed in long robes, like women. Eunuchs?—the people tittered; eunuchs, what for? To keep the Queen's husbands in the Royal harem? Then came the Queen's Ministers, with heavy wigs and extraordinary beards; and then the Egyptian soldiers, almost naked, their heads adorned with things looking like antennae, that made them look like huge insects. The astronomers drew laughters of derision; the sight of the standards on which the sacred symbols were painted called for a jeer: the jackal's head, the vulture, the bull! The Roman populace laughed at a religion that had animals for emblems.

The Royal litter appeared in the midst of flashing spears and shields. All eyes were fixed on Cleopatra. Yes, she was beautiful; indeed, her beauty took the crowd's breath away. Rome had never seen anything like it.

Cleopatra's resplendent face, her curious head-dress from which a snake of gold peered forth. Bit by bit it was noted that her complexion was golden; her eyes were so painted with antimony that they seemed to reach her temples; and her lips had a vividness that no other woman in Rome could equal, and their shapely arch gave such a sensuous touch to her superb appearance that every man in the crowd felt his heart melting away. Her tunic was of a transparent tissue that made her perfect breasts appear bare.

But however beautiful this Queen of Egypt might be, she could not silence the people of Rome more than by holding upon her knees her child. And this child bore an astonishing likeness to Caesar.

With all the pomp of the Roman Republic, the

9. Cleopatra as imagined by a French miniaturist. From a manuscript dated 1505.

10. A feast worthy of Cleopatra: "A Scene in the Life of the Pharaohs" as envisaged in a fifteenth century German manuscript.

Dictator, surrounded by the Senators and the Tribunes, welcomed the Queen of Egypt in the Forum. Then the Oriental procession resumed its march to the villa that Caesar had placed at the disposal of the Queen of Egypt.

The villa was situated in the Horti Transtiberini, a private estate of Caesar's, on the right bank of the Tiber, approximately where there are now the vast gardens of the Villa Pamphili; and it comprised a charming house surrounded by pleasant gardens; Caesar and his legitimate wife Calpurnia resided in the town residence of the Dictator.

That night Caesar came, privately, to the villa.

Perhaps his passion for Cleopatra had now cooled and in that year and a half of separation Caesar had considerably aged: his appearance was haggard, his nose more arched, his mouth more than ever a thin line, his hair still more carefully brought from the back over the top to hide his baldness. Only his brown eyes were still full of youthful sparks, flashing with power and humour. A terrible malady was consuming his emaciated body; the epileptic attacks occurred now only too often. But his enthusiasm, and his courage and his ambition irradiated around him like an aura.

He came to the villa to greet his Queen, his mistress. The memories of those nine months in Egypt—nine months to the day, what a cynical recollection!—were very sweet. Cleopatra's youth and beauty, Cleopatra's love and passion, Cleopatra's exquisite, unique company.

Caesar entered the garden alone, and walked up the well-kept path flanked by marble seats and little groves. Cleopatra was waiting for him; dressed in a simple robe, exhaling her unforgettable perfume; her smile as girlish as on the night when he had seen her spring out like a toy from the unrolled carpet. Caesar pressed her to him, with the tenderness of an old lover. And then he bent, their arms still interlaced, to look at the child. Yes, it was his very image. And he told her so.

His son. His own son. The son that no other woman had given him.

It was quite worth defying Rome.

VIII

CLEOPATRA watched the Triumph of Caesar seated next to his wife, Calpurnia, in the official stand. The Triumph lasted four days. Caesar had never celebrated a Triumph in Rome. Now all his victories and all his conquests, upon the barbarians whom he had made vassals and subjects of Rome, and upon his rivals in the civil war, were to be celebrated together, in a series of Triumphal processions lasting four consecutive days.

But in the very first day a horrible omen occurred. When the Victor's chariot with the board breast high was approaching the official stand, carrying Caesar crowned with golden laurel saluting the people with his right hand uplifted, his face taut and proud, his eyes seeking not Calpurnia's but Cleopatra's eyes, a cracking sound was heard above the joyous shouts of the crowd; Caesar was seen to be staggering forward; then he lightly leapt to the ground. What had happened? The crowd surged round the Dictator, promptly pushed back by the troops; somebody shouted that the axle of the Triumphal chariot had broken. In no time a second chariot was brought up, and Caesar remounted; the procession went on.

But Cleopatra shuddered. To her mind it looked like a terrible omen.

72

The first day the Triumph celebrated the conquests of Gaul. That night Caesar ascended the Capitol in the light of a thousand torches fixed to the back of forty elephants, and he paid homage to Jupiter, Protector of Rome. Vercingetorix, the Gauls' leader, who had been kept prisoner in Rome for six years, was executed on the Tarpeian Rock, according to custom.

The second day was given to the Egyptian Triumph. The official interpretation was that it was intended to do honour to the Queen Cleopatra as an Ally of Rome. For the populace it meant the defeat of the Pompeian Party. Cleopatra's eyes rested upon the images of the already slain enemies, Achillas and Pothinus. Her sister Arsinoë walked behind Caesar's chariot, in chains.

A colossal statue of the Old Nile and a reproduction of the Pharos, seventh marvel of the world, enchanted the people as much as the strange specimens of Egyptian fauna, among which was a delightful giraffe proudly looking down from her high neck. When the triumph was over, Princess Arsinoë was spared as a particular homage to the Royal House of Cleopatra. But the sight of her disloyal sister dragged in fetters behind the Roman conqueror, was for Cleopatra a thing that she was never to forget: infinitely better, she thought, immensely more dignified to choose death as her Uncle had done in Cyprus, rather than be dragged behind the Victor's chariot!

For the moment, however, the unhappy thought was soon cancelled. She was seated on the official stand and Caesar's eyes from his chariot were seeking hers.

The third day was given to the conquest of Pontus in Asia Minor. The procession was headed by an immense standard, bearing the proud and immortal message that

73

Caesar had sent from his camp to the Roman Senate:
" *Veni, Vidi, Vici.*"

And on the fourth day were celebrated the victories in
North Africa. In all truth, this last procession offended
the national sentiments. The African campaign had been
conducted by Caesar solely against the last survivors of
the Pompeian Party: to drag behind his chariot the old
King Juba of Numidia did not hide Caesar's real purpose
of celebrating his final victory upon all his rivals. And
the pictures showing caricatures of Cato (who had lived
and died in Utica imagining himself in Plato's Republic)
offended both the aristocracy and the populace.

Yet, the four days of Triumph had given the people a
marvellous show; and Cleopatra enjoyed the glorification
of her lover, and laughed with the crowd at the rough
jests shouted by the veterans about their beloved General,
even if now and then she winced at the impudent wit-
ticisms intended for her ears.

Three months later, in September, Cleopatra received
from Caesar a gesture that could not be surpassed. It
was the greatest homage that the Queen might receive at
the hands of her all-powerful lover.

Cleopatra had been delighted when, soon after her
arrival in Rome, Caesar had asked her to sit for a big
statue by the famous Roman sculptor, Archesilaus. The
statue was progressing rather slowly; but Cleopatra was
quite happy with the sketches for the head.

Suddenly Caesar took a great interest in the statue. He
sent for the sculptor: " How long will it take to finish
the job? " Archesilaus pondered for a minute, then began
to explain the time it was bound to take to complete the
great task of working the marble and the ivory and over-

laying it with gold: "Ten years, at least." Caesar stared at him: "Make it ten days. Within ten days I desire that statue to be placed on its pillar in the new Temple of Venus-Genetrix."

And so it was. At the end of September the dedication of the statue of Cleopatra as Venus-Genetrix took place with great ceremony.

It was a gesture of immense significance. Cleopatra, who in Egypt was considered the incarnation of Isis-Aphrodite, was presented by Caesar to the Roman people as a Goddess, in fact, as the emblem of that Venus-Genetrix from whom Caesar himself claimed to descend.

Was it entirely a gesture of love, an exaggerated homage to the beautiful Queen who was the mother of his infant son? One feels reluctant to explain in a simple way such an important act of defiance to tradition. Caesar was not a man to abandon himself to the vagaries of an old infatuated lover. Caesar was, at that moment—the last and most critical phase of his life—on the point of disclosing to Rome that he meant to break with all the past and take the crown and found a new dynasty. It seems therefore certain that in presenting Cleopatra to Rome as a Goddess in the temple that he had erected with great splendour to the very Goddess he claimed as his own Genetrix, Caesar meant to deify the woman with whom he intended to share the crown of the Roman-Egyptian Empire. Indeed, in those same months Caesar made a new issue of coins showing the figure of Cleopatra-Aphrodite holding in her arms the infant Caesarion as Eros.

The opening of the temple of Venus—of which three columns are still extant in the Forum of Rome, only three columns, but so slender, so lithe and beautiful—was followed by great festivities and games in the Circus, that Caesar had recently embellished. For the first time the people were shown a naumachia, a naval battle on an artificial lake. They were delighted.

Caesar's popularity was at its zenith, and the people were quite glad, notwithstanding Cicero's fulminations, to accept Cleopatra as a permanent Goddess: besides, the cult of Isis was capturing the imagination.

Cleopatra was feeling radiant: with her statue Caesar was laying the divine foundations of their joint dynasty.

IX

ROMAN society still regarded with hostility the Queen of Egypt. The statue of Cleopatra as Venus-Genetrix had shocked the aristocracy. Consequently the Villa Trans-tiberina was not the meeting place of all the elegant and influential society that Cleopatra had hoped it would be.

The Roman ladies said that the Queen of Egypt was not the great beauty she was reported to be: she was young and vivacious, agreed, but that was all; a hundred noble Roman matrons had more royal dignity than she had. It was a great pity for the Lady Calpurnia, to have to suffer such a slight in her very city; but of course, what could one expect from a man in his fifties and with his reputation?

The men kept an open mind, and politics entered a good deal in agreeing or disagreeing with their wives' snorting remarks; but those who went to the Villa, and they were a good many, all agreed that the Queen was an exceptional lady.

It was not easy for Cleopatra to find her way through the web of intrigue and greed and ambitions that moved Roman life; and at times she found that Rome lacked the

76

refinement and polish of Alexandria. But she realized that however exalted her rank, it was no little handicap in Rome to be openly the mistress of the Dictator as, in Rome, her " Egyptian marriage " to Caesar counted for nothing. And more than anything else she knew that from the impression she made, from her influence upon the chosen few of the many who frequented her house depended the success of her great plan, the triumph of Caesar's ambitions, the Imperial Crown for Caesar and herself and, one day, for her son Caesarion.

With the unfailing instinct of a Queen and of an intelligent woman, Cleopatra felt that she could impress those obdurate Roman men only with her charm and her exquisite culture.

Her house, therefore, presented an atmosphere not so much of richness and splendour but of elegance and taste. In her dress, usually so rich, she decided to show a simplicity, discarding the " Orientalism " that might cause sarcastic jests in the Public Baths or in the Senate's reading-room, and yet a simpler dress enhanced her incomparable head.

Her vast education, her witty Greek mind, the elegance of her speech which could play so adroitly with both the solemn Latin and the more frivolous Greek tongue, her inborn poise increased by the training of a Court where Royal manners and etiquette had a touch of hieraticism, and all the gifts that the Goddess Isis had passed into her, made her appearance and conversation a joy to the onlooker.

She received in the garden, whenever the weather was suitable, and this gave an air of easier informality to her at-homes; and Caesar made it a point to receive his friends informally at Cleopatra's house, thus giving her an opportunity of taking part, of sharing his thoughts and plans. At the same time, both the Dictator's friends and the not-so-friends could become reconciled with the unassailable fact that Caesar treated the Queen as his official partner in his power.

How far the lissome body, the vivacious eyes, the perfumed aura of Cleopatra's person played upon the visitors? Is there a woman, even an exalted Queen, who is not conscious of her physical appeal over her male visitors?

Many influential Senators became regular guests at the Villa beyond the River—Curion, Sulpicius Rufus, Lepidus. The questions of the day were discussed, the back-chat of the Senate was thrashed out; and the politicians were surprised to find that the young Queen could express clearly and concisely a wise opinion. When she had spoken, she would smile almost coyly, with a twinkle in her shining eyes, and felinely stretch to cause the bracelets upon her lovely arms to tinkle.

The men of letters eagerly sought admission to her salon. Soon the Villa was a little Arcadia. One day she discussed with Sallust his *De Bello Jugurtino,* and the other visitors were surprised at her trenchant comments. Old Asinius Pollio, the famous Orator, brought his speeches for her criticism; and he asked her opinion about the little ironical poems in which he ridiculed the absurdities of his fellow citizens through the mouth of an imaginary shepherd. One day Cleopatra delighted the great Atticus by revealing to that student of antiquities— quite a novelty at the time—an exceptional erudition in his very field: she unrolled before his eyes some delicately illuminated Persian scrolls, and showed him Chinese ivories and carved stones pointing out the spontaneous

78

affinities of Chinese art, as yet completely unknown in Rome, with the Greek art of Alexander's period. Or had they not heard of the new calendar conceived by her astronomer Sosigenes to make the months fall in step with the sun and end the chaos of the different ways of counting the days and years? "By the heavens," exclaimed Caesar that day, "I must have a talk with this man!" And it was indeed Cleopatra's brilliant conversation that brought about the reform of the Roman calendar, and gave mankind the calendar we still use today. Caesar called it the Julian Calendar, and to adjust the current year to the new calendar, Cleopatra's astronomer advised Caesar to make that year—the last year of his life—the longest of all years.

Conversation at the villa was always brilliant; and in Rome the pursuit of letters and arts had never been so fashionable. People were beginning to talk of the new philosophies of Greece; even the Greek language, so much more lively than Latin, was creeping into fashionable conversation. Aristocratic youths went to finish their education at Apollonia, Athens or, best of all, Rhodes. One night Atticus brought a most brilliant youth, by the lovely name of Vergil, just arrived from his provincial town of Mantua, such a delightful poet. The youthful Vergil recited demurely a passage from one of his gracious pastoral compositions. Someone compared it with the Odes of another coming poet, who used quite new metres, Horace by name, himself too a mere youth of twenty.

"It would be a good thing," Caesar said one day, "to have Cicero come to the Villa." Cleopatra spoke to her friend Atticus the antiquarian, for Cicero had now retired to his villa at Tusculum, to brood upon his liberal views and his former association with the Pompey Party—he called it " his honourable exile ", although Caesar said it was plain humbug, for in spite of his obsession for uprightness and liberalism, when he had been Governor of Cilicia Cicero had not disdained to make money like all the rest of them, otherwise how could he have paid for his fine villa at Tusculum and the farm near Naples and the other at Pompeii?

"It had been a matter of great regret for Caesar to lose a man of such distinguished ability as Cicero," Cleopatra nonchalantly told Atticus. " Would he not mention it to his friend? Surely his lofty mind must find insufferable the tiresomeness of a too long rural retirement." And she mentioned her library, which might come useful to the great lawyer and scholar.

Cicero came to the Villa, wrapped rather too solemnly in the toga that his dresser had taught him to drape so beautifully about his shoulders, with one vigorous gesture of his right hand at the very climax of his carefully prepared perorations in the Forum.

Cleopatra received him almost with honour—" Such a long-wished for meeting, the pleasure of hearing the voice of the greatest advocate of all times!" On the table there were some antique manuscripts, rolls of papyri embellished with drawings, depicting the history of the Pharaohs. With her sweet voice the Queen interpreted to Cicero the meaning of the drawings, while Cicero admired the hieroglyphics. " Would he like them as a curiosity for his library? The Queen would be delighted to send them to his villa at Tusculum the next day."

There also came two strange young men. One was called Octavian, a youth of sixteen, who looked as if he had never washed properly, with unkempt light-brown hair and a spotty complexion. Cleopatra never forgot that first impression of the boy, who appeared awkward of manner, staring at her with glassy eyes—did she catch a glint of lust in those eyes? His grandfather, she had been told, was a provincial moneylender, from Velletri, but his wealth had enabled the son, Caius Octavius, to marry Caesar's niece, Atia, daughter of the Dictator's sister Julia; and the boy was now a great protégé of his great-uncle. What premonition, the day he was presented at the Villa, had prompted Cleopatra to keep at her side, almost emphatically, her own child, Caesar's son? Octavian had a learned face; indeed, Cleopatra remembered that Caesar had mentioned to her that soon he would send him to Apollonia to finish his studies.

The other, and even more unpleasant young man, was called Brutus, and he was another great favourite of Caesar's. Brutus seemed quite strange. He was attractive in appearance; a man of about thirty, virile and dignified in his bearing and of proud manners, with an earnest face. But he was such a bore, with his obsession with righteousness! Caesar—she knew it, although he never mentioned it to her—was convinced that Brutus was his son, born of his youthful affair with Servilia (people said that she was a ravenous lover!). But how could this fellow Brutus be really Caesar's son? He had nothing, absolutely nothing, Cleopatra could not help thinking, that could remind one of Julius Caesar, her Caesar, the Caesar she knew so well; nothing of the sunny brightness of his nature, of his superior outlook in life, that was made of cynicism and enthusiasm, as it should be in a man born to conquer and rule, a man who was, like herself, descended from the Gods.

Brutus! When she had exhibited her child, he had peered intently and yet detachedly into the baby's face. Did he see, at least, that he was almost absurdly the image of his father? And then, he had advised her to bring up the child on Pythagorean principles. Pythagorean principles indeed! What good would it be, for Caesarion, son of Caesar, to learn to account to himself each action of his life, each evening of his days, like a shopkeeper reckoning his takings!

Brutus, who was always speaking of the traditions of ancient Rome, (barely seven centuries old, and her Egypt could count in thousands!) and he was praising austerity, and quoting Varro's essay condemning Oriental luxury, he almost looked round in judgment at the luxury of her room.

He was tactless; he was an unbearable prig. He told her that at Pharsalia he had fought against Caesar, on the Pompeian side, merely because he considered Pompey more virtuous and righteous. And be boasted that before the battle he had been busy copying excerpts from Polybius instead of looking at his cavalry squadrons who, anyway, were routed. And Caesar, Cleopatra was thinking, had given orders that he was to be spared in the battle, at all costs. How she hated this fellow Brutus! There was something in him, she could not say what, something fatal in his whole person, that frightened her and made her cringe. Her Oriental premonition, that's all. When she mentioned it to Caesar, the Dictator smiled with his thin lips. He did not say it, but he thought it as he turned his head towards her face—" her Oriental superstition ". Brutus was a good boy; one of the few straight men in Rome. But Cleopatra would not be pacified. Brutus— she hated the sight of him!

X

In the course of that winter Cleopatra had unpleasant news. Caesar must leave Rome, he must go to Spain for war. It will be, he told Cleopatra, a short war; but he must go and end it once and for all with the remnants of the Pompeian Party. They had assembled in the Iberian Peninsula; it was necessary to clear out those pockets of resistance. It was a job that he must do in person; no one else could be entrusted with such a campaign. He would be back in a very few months.

Caesar departed, therefore, for Spain before the end of the year 46; and not being of a humour to tolerate the slightest opposition in Rome during his absence, he took good care to re-appoint himself sole Consul for the following year and asked the people to confirm his Dictatorship for the year 45. The sole Consulship and the Dictatorship gave him autocratic powers; as soon he was away from Rome he would send a message to the Senate with the names of the eight Prefects he had already chosen, who would have powers to rule in his name, a kind of Cabinet that would govern by Orders in Council.

Caesar explained all this to Cleopatra on the eve of departure, as he now told her all he was doing and planning. She should remain at the Villa, her life undisturbed and unchanged, thinking of him as often as she could; and he would write as often as possible; in fact, Caesar added, this would be an excellent opportunity for her to test the ground of Rome without being sheltered by his presence; and they arranged to have a service of special dispatches through which she could keep him informed of all that was going on " behind his back ".

This pacified Cleopatra a little; nevertheless she felt nervous. She was nervous—but how could she say it?—for Caesar's safety. He was still strong and full of courage; but what could withstand a javelin aimed by a strong arm? Moreover, his attacks of epilepsy were now alarmingly frequent. And the convulsions left a terrible mark of weariness upon that emaciated face!

Now Caesar was in Spain, fighting for his very life; and Cleopatra was fighting for him in Rome. Her drawing-room was, in her mind, Caesar's Court. She was growing weary of Roman society and politics, and she was deeply sure that it was a big mistake on Caesar's part always to forgive and forget his enemies. Yet, for the moment, there was nothing else for her but to cajole and watch. Caesar and Cleopatra kept in touch with each other by an exchange of daily couriers, and they both knew that each had planted near the other a net of spies: would the lovely Queen be fascinated by some handsome Roman officer? Or would the far away General find time between battles for some pursuit of love? "What the eye doesn't see the heart doesn't grieve for," Cleopatra wrote to Caesar in every letter; "but she merely was thinking of his health."

The salons of the Transtiberine Villa were now more crowded than ever. The Queen was out to please, to charm, to smooth every path for Caesar. She allowed, indeed she fostered, political discussions. How boring they were; but they helped her to discern how the wind was blowing.

She was rather puzzled by the discussions about political decadence. She had found Rome somewhat primitive as a great city; and Roman life seemed to her rather crude.

What there was of luxury seemed to lack elegance and refinement; one would have described it as a provincial effort to import too suddenly things and manners and ways of life one had seen on travels or in war. The greybeards complained that the City was no longer the stronghold of austere traditions. What did they mean by traditions? Had these Romans no sense of progress? The old religion—they said—was passing: a soldier boasted of having made a fortune by selling bit by bit a golden statue of Diana that he had stolen after a battle! And they deprecated the laxity that had entered into married life: Senators, Consuls, high officers of the State put away their wives on the slightest pretext! Even Cicero, who posed as a moralist, had said to his wife Terentia the cruel words of divorcement " Go hence and take with you whatsoever belongs to you ", and had replaced her with a younger and prettier new wife. (Somebody had whispered to the Queen that poor Terentia had been married to Cicero for thirty years; perhaps it was a release for both sides.) And yet another old bore deprecated the deterioration of manners and morals: it was, the poor fellow was saying, the fault of the immense fortunes accumulated during the recent wars; the newly acquired riches that wiped away the simple habits of former days. Gold was now the only God. Originally used for the decoration of the temples only, it was now displayed in private houses, where everything was of gold or gilded. How right was old Cato to walk about barefooted in a worn-out toga as a protest! But people only laughed at him. And what about the extravagance of women in dress? Encircling their arms, twisted in their hair, clasping their ankles, golden ornaments glittered over them from head to foot!

Cleopatra listened to all this arguing, nonchalantly caressing her long necklaces of rosy pearls. The very eyes of this embittered decrier of such corruption stared lewdly at her marvellous bosom that was heaving calmly under the transparent veils. " Was not this ", she remarked blandly, " the inevitable result of conquests and aggrandizement? The conquerors saw new lands, new peoples, new manners of life. They took them home as part of their booty. The ancient laws could not stand for ever; culture and progress demanded a change. There were other cities in the world where life and culture had reached a different or perhaps higher level than it was yet known in Rome. Maybe the Senate would soon send a Commission to study the various and quite interesting aspects of life and trade and public administration in her capital, Alexandria? They might find practical the centralized system of Egyptian government ... "

The deeper Cleopatra probed into the politics of Rome, the more she mistrusted and felt contemptuous of a form of government that was based on ballot-papers and depended on the favour of a mob that could be bribed and was in fact there merely to be bribed, and yet they chattered glibly of the sovereign rights of the people. Why did not Caesar rise above this mob and rule from the Throne that the Gods had destined for him?

Yet, terrible misgivings assailed her. The men she most distrusted were not considered conspirators against the Dictator, but leaders. And they seemed to fawn upon the one for whom she felt such a dislike—Brutus. One day she was taken by an unsuppressible urge to find out what really moved this man and made him speak with such hostility and bitterness of the absent Caesar. She asked him—and they were alone—whether he was not

86

proud that Caesar believed him to be his son.

Brutus drew himself up, looked at the Queen with fiery disdain, and answered that his patrician conception of family purity could not tolerate the tarnished reputation of his mother, who, now an old woman but still as proud, was living at her son's side.

He spoke these words, and there he stood, staring stonily at the Queen.

From that moment Cleopatra felt that she must protect Caesar from this terrible man Brutus.

XI

In the spring of the following year, 45, Caesar returned to Rome. The two sons of Pompey had been defeated at the battle of Munda, on the 17th March; a terrible battle in which the remnant of the Pompey party lost thirty thousand men. Cneus Pompey, the eldest son, was executed after the battle; his younger brother, Sextus, found safety in flight. Caesar was received outside the walls of Rome by Mark Antony, with whom he had made peace once more. Early in the summer the Dictator celebrated another Triumph, which was not a wise thing to do for it was a victory over Roman citizens, and after the battle of Pharsalia Caesar had wisely abstained from celebrating a Triumph: but now he seemed to think that his personal enemies were enemies of Rome.

How much pressure, in those last few months of Caesar's life, did Cleopatra bring upon Caesar to institute a Monarchy, and how far did Cleopatra's influence coincide with Caesar's own desire to make himself a King?

One has to admit that everything must have seemed to Cleopatra to be ready for the foundation of their joint Monarchy. Caesar was now the sole ruler of Rome. The people had voted him Consul for a period of ten years, and a decree proclaimed Caesar Dictator for life. The Senate became a mere instrument for the execution of his orders: at times even the long-honoured tradition of calling the decrees " in the name of the Senate and of the People "—*Senatus Populusque Romanus,* which was the opening formula of all decrees—was abandoned for the Orders-in-Council of the Dictator. In the intimacy of the Transtiberine Villa Caesar discussed the unavoidable necessity of taking the Crown. Even his plans of completing the conquest of the East made it necessary, for according to an ancient prophecy, the Parthians would submit only to a King.

As a first step, Caesar made the people grant him the title of Imperator and not only for life but as an hereditary title. In itself the title did not mean very much, as it amounted to no more than Commander-in-Chief and did not imply any monarchical meaning. But the hereditary character increased and transformed enormously its significance. The Senate who voted the title on behalf of the people must have realised that one day this title would pass to Caesar's heir: and the only known heir of the Dictator was the child that was nursed at the side of his Royal Mother within the precincts of the Transtiberine Villa. Nor was it a mystery that Caesar had expressed his intention of officially marrying Cleopatra. Indeed, a rumour was carefully spread that a Law was soon to be presented by the Tribunes of the people authorizing the Dictator to have, if no demise should occur, two legal spouses, one of whom might not be necessarily of Roman birth—i.e. Calpurnia and Cleopatra. It was explained that Ceasar would thus become King of Rome with Cleopatra as his official consort, and the marriage to the

Egyptian Queen would add to the territories of Rome the vastness of Egypt without any recourse to arms, the only great and ancient Kingdom yet independent of Rome, and whose immense wealth would constitute an unsurpassable appanage for the Roman Throne.

To the seven effigies of the ancient Kings of Rome, which were preserved in the Capitol, was now added the statue of Caesar, dressed in Royal robes. Soon he took to appearing in public dressed in the embroidered tunics and vestments of the ancient Kings of Albalonga. On the new coins his head was shown as the head of a King. A throne of gold was placed for Caesar in the Senate House. Equally, his seat in the Courts when he presided as Supreme Judge was like a throne. To the official ceremonies he rode now upon a consecrated chariot, designed like the chariots of the Egyptian Kings; and he rode in the chariot with a crown of golden laurel upon his brow and holding in his hand a stick of ivory that resembled a sceptre. The Senate, upon his request, granted him a Royal Escort of German Cavalry. The privilege was granted to him to be buried within the city walls: most ancient patrician families had their tombs along the Appian way; but Cleopatra had pointed out to Caesar that Alexander's tomb in Alexandria stood close to the Royal Palace.

Cicero, still in exile, prepared a long epistle exorting the Dictator to renounce any idea of a Monarchy; but his friends advised him not to send such an inopportune letter. In Rome, a former Consul, Lucius Cotta, proposed to elect Caesar King of the territories outside the city; but the suggestion did not arouse enthusiasm either in the Senate or in the Villa across the Tiber.

Caesar's pride had now passed all limits: one day, to

test the people's feelings, he publicly proclaimed his divine descent from Venus: and the people acclaimed him and his image was carried in the Circus, in the *pompa circensis,* among the images of the Gods. A new temple was opened by Senatorial Decree to Jupiter-Julius, and a statue with Caesar's features was erected in the temple of Quirinus, with the inscription " To the Immortal God ". In Caesar's honour was instituted a college of Priests of the Luperci; in every temple of Rome a ceremonial couch was placed for Caesar; and the words " Genie of Caesar " were added to the political oath by which Jupiter and the Penates were called as witness. By the end of the year 45 no one in Rome had any doubt about the intention of Caesar to step upon a throne. The appellation, may be, might not be that of King, for Caesar had let it be known: " I am Caesar, not a mere King." Or maybe, people said, it would happen after the Indian campaign.

Still Caesar postponed his decision. One day he repeated to Cleopatra: " There is an ancient prophecy which says that the Parthians will surrender only to a King," and he smiled with bitter sarcasm. Cleopatra answered: " Why not be the equal of Alexander the Great? "

She knew she was touching the sorest spot in Caesar's mind. The shades of Alexander! Had she not seen Caesar tremble from head to foot when with her he had stood gazing upon the crystal bier of the Great Conqueror? The pattern, the hero, the God of his own youth.

Suavely, lovingly, inspiringly Cleopatra now spoke to Caesar of Alexander. And he listened, with his face transfigured, for her words were the echo of his own thoughts. His face looked every day more emaciated and marked by the fateful illness; but in the tension of those talks it was transfigured by the fire of his ambitions. And Cleopatra was saying: "Do you remember our desert ride to consult the oracle of Amon? It was the same desert ride that Alexander took to hear the same oracle of Amon. You stand at the threshold of your divine destiny, O Caesar! If it is true, as you say, that Rome will not countenance the overthrow of the effete Republic unless the Dictator shall enter the city covered with the glory of an unparalleled victory and conquest, why not prepare a campaign to the Indies? Alexander's dream fulfilled by Caesar! Follow Alexander's yet untrodden route; repeat in Persia the scene of Alexander's triumph; go to recapture the standards and eagles left there by old Crassus with the bodies of the slain; then march through Hyrcania; cross the mountains into the fabulous Empire of Golconda! My treasury is yours for this expedition."

Caesar listened. He turned his face towards Cleopatra, and saw the spirit of this Amazonian Queen mingled with the devotion of his own son's mother; and he stretched an arm to press—in an accustomed gesture—her lissom body to his spare frame.

The preparations for the Indian campaign went on. Actually, it would be an altogether different campaign: Caesar, whose mind in those last few months of his life seemed to work more feverishly, was planning to reach as his goal not the too distant Euphrates nor the Indies, but to repeat Alexander's victories in Persia, and then, through Hyrcania, march to the Caspian Sea, cross the Caucasus into the land of the Scythians and then, attacking the Germans, he would return to Italy by the way of Gaul, so that the Roman Empire would be bounded North, West, and South by the ocean and the seas. For this vast campaign he would establish depots of arms in all the Mediterranean ports, and to the generous offer of Cleopatra he would add another great store of gold raised by the sale of public land. Indeed, the whole of Italy was soon astir with these great plans; and Caesar spoke of entering a contest with himself " to make his future outshine his past ".

But at night, after the din and bustle of the Senate House and the conduct of so many affairs which he insisted in conducting personally, he would repair, haggard and careworn, to the Villa across the Tiber and pace restlessly the room listening to Cleopatra's beautiful voice, and catch the golden glance of her eyes, and suddenly stand in front of her and inhale the perfume of her dress and her body; and his thin mouth, ever a line across the emaciated face, would say wearily: " I have lived too long already; better die once for all than be always waiting for death! "[1]

XII

AFTER his return from Spain, Caesar had introduced Mark Antony to Cleopatra. The young and handsome Antony mentioned that he had the privilege of meeting the Queen ten years before, at the banqueting table of her father; but Cleopatra did not remember. And Caesar, who knew only too well the fascination his spectacular friend exercised upon the ladies, smiled sardonically.

Mark Antony, related to Caesar on his mother's side—Antony's mother was Julia of the Julian family—was then thirty-eight, and a most handsome man. He had a re-

[1] Cicero and Appianus.

markable stature, and the rather exaggerated physique of a gladiator. With his heavy and curly dark hair and his broad forehead, the aquiline nose and his well moulded mouth above a massive chin adorned with a graceful beard, he looked like a living statue of Hercules: indeed, Antony was very fond of saying that he descended from Hercules. He was well aware that his appearance roused great enthusiasm among the ladies, and he used his charms immoderately. He was also a colossal child. Cicero, who had reasons to hate Mark Antony, said that he was nothing but a butcher or a boxer with a tough neck and formidable loins; but his soldiers adored him to the point of valuing his praise higher than their life; a devotion due to his noble descent, his manners open and frank, his splendid generosity, his delightful yet dignified friendliness with anyone, and his kindness and interest for all his men. After a battle he would go from tent to tent visiting and comforting the wounded, and the sincere grief he felt for them prompted the soldiers to kiss his hands and call him their beloved General.

Antony was also peculiarly simple in his mind, almost an eternal child. There was nothing of the genius in Mark Antony; only a giant of a man, who enjoyed life immensely. In war he was an officer of exemplary courage; in public life he loved or hated without measure or prudence; in private he admitted no obstacle to his pleasures. (Cleopatra had heard from Caesar that one morning when Antony was to deliver a speech of the highest importance in the Forum, feeling embarrassed by the excessive potations of the previous night at the wedding-feast of a friend called Hippias, he had simply vomited before the crowd and resumed his speech.) At private banquets or official celebrations he drank with

CLEOPATRA

enthusiasm, challenging anyone to beat him: and he could drink all night and still be sober, joking noisily. He was fast and strong with women; boasted like a school-boy and laughed uproariously. In those very weeks all Rome had enjoyed the rough childish joke he had played upon his wife Fulvia on the day Caesar returned to Rome from Spain. Rumours had gone through the city that the enemy was at the gates: Antony, who had gone to meet Caesar, dressed himself as an itinerant merchant and returned to his house where he said he was the bearer of a most urgent message from Mark Antony; he got admission before the lofty Fulvia, and while she was breaking the seal of the fateful message, he threw back his cloak, seized her by the neck and kissed her on the mouth, and without more ado he flew back to Caesar, to enter Rome in great pomp, upon the same chariot as the Dictator.

His sense of humour was unequalled: to recompense his chef for an excellent dinner he made him a present of a beautiful house that did not belong to him!

One day the citizens of Megara in Greece were pointing out to him their small but ancient Senate House, which was an architectural gem, he remarked, " Not very big, but in fine state of ruin ". He had a good deal of the actor in him; a taste of the stage and a love of the effect. When he spoke in public—and Antony was an excellent orator—his voice, his gestures, his delivery never failed to impress or to move the audience. His eloquence, trained at the Eloquence School of Athens, had a touch of what was called the Asiatic style, florid, full of imagery, some-what pompous, but highly impressive; and Antony loved to increase the impression upon the audience by dressing his Herculean body up to the occasion, with his tunic

94

belted low upon his hips, a short broad sword at his side, and upon his shoulders a scarlet chlamys. Later in life, his fondness for dressing-up made him appear in public dressed like Bacchus or wrapped in a purple mantle held by brooches set with enormous gems.

He was—the courtesans said—" supercharged with virility "; and contemptuously he trampled all moral principles, enjoyed scandalizing the grandmothers and acted more than often as an irrepressible playboy.

Like many other men of colossal stature, Antony was completely ruled by Fulvia, his second wife. Fulvia, who was to play an important part in the drama of Cleopatra, was a most remarkable woman. Antony had married Fulvia after the Tribune Dolabella had deprived him of his previous one, Antonia; but Fulvia had herself two previous husbands, the second one of whom was Durio, a bosom friend of Antony, to whom he had lost first a fortune at dice and then his wife in the game of love. Now, well into her mid-twenties, Fulvia had political ambitions and spoke airily of succession to a sovereignty —" a mere burgess daughter! " thought Cleopatra disdainfully.

At the time Antony was Caesar's best friend. He had, on and off, always been one of the staunchest supporters of Caesar's Party, for Antony had been an officer with Caesar in Gaul, and aferwards Caesar had rapidly raised him to the offices of Questor, Augur and Tribune of the Plebs; and Antony had been expelled from the Senate House when the civil war broke out. He had been Deputy-Governor of Italy during Caesar's first absence in Spain in the year 49, and second in command in the decisive battle of Pharsalia, when he led the left wing to victory; and again Deputy-Governor when Caesar was in

Egypt and then in Africa. In 46 he took offence because Caesar had insisted on payment for the property of the defeated Pompey which Antony had appropriated; but reconciliation took place after the second and final campaign of Spain: Antony went to meet the victorious Dictator at Narbo, refusing to join the conspiracy of Trebonius; and Caesar showed him his gratitude by making Antony joint Consul with himself for the year 44—the last of his life.

Antony was therefore the most zealous supporter of Caesar's Party and a fanatic for the restoration of the Monarchy with Caesar as King-Emperor.

At the Villa Transtiberina Antony was considered a most useful ally.

XIII

CLEOPATRA was feeling most uneasy. The year 44 commenced in an atmosphere of uncertainty and political misgivings.

Caesar had fixed his departure for the Persian campaign for the 17th of March, two days after the reopening of the Senate, which had been summoned for the Ides of March. The marriage with Cleopatra—for which a special law was passed the previous year—would be celebrated after his return from the campaign about three years hence.

The Queen's uneasiness was great and understandable. The prospect of a three years' campaign alarmed her, both as Queen and a mother. Caesar's health was rapidly deteriorating: as long as he ruled in Rome, she had something more valuable than a mere alliance in her hands; she had the boy Caesarion. But with Caesar away, absorbed in a long and distant campaign, anything might happen.

Cleopatra, therefore, had planned that soon after Caesar's departure she would return with her son to Egypt. There she would devote herself to the education of Caesarion, and it would also be easier for her to give full financial assistance to the campaign and keep in touch with Caesar by means of the Syrian troops and dispatch-bearers that she would supply.

But Cleopatra was seriously disturbed by Caesar's latest public attitude. Day by day his arrogance was becoming more marked. One day, on entering the Forum, he reprimanded one of the Tribunes, Pontius Aquila, for not having risen from his seat when Caesar had passed the Tribunes' chairs: for a few days he was petty enough to repeat the sarcastic remark "with the kind permission of Pontius Aquila we will do this or that ". On the other hand, one day that a delegation of Senators came to offer him some new honours he remained discourteously and tactlessly seated in receiving them. Even his most intimate friends had to wait for an audience. When somebody during a debate remarked that a new order had not yet been passed as Law, Caesar flew in a rage and cried: " My word is the law." And yet, there was a growing number of people who did not consider his words as constituting law. And he no longer made any attempt to hide his intentions to take the crown. At the prompting of Mark Antony, some enthusiasts placed the Royal diadem upon several of the many statues of Caesar in the city; quite correctly the Tribunes Marullus and Caesetius ordered the Royal attribute to be taken away: Caesar rashly said that he considered this as a deliberate insult. On the 26th of January, while he was taking a

walk with some friends, some passers-by saluted him as
King: the over-zealous Tribunes of the Plebs had the
demonstrators arrested and put into prison. Caesar
caused such an uproar in the Senate that the Tribunes
were expelled from the House.

And the Villa across the Tiber was getting on the nerves
of many influential people, not to mention the resentful
and jealous Roman ladies. The Villa was plainly a Royal
Palace; it was indeed the Palace where only a second
throne needed to be installed. At the side of the Queen,
Caesar held his Court, and Cleopatra took great care
that the ceremonial was no less solemn and august than
it was at the Bruchion in Alexandria. The army of
chamberlains, dignitaries, eunuchs and lords and ladies-in-
waiting was incensing the Roman aristocracy. In a letter
to his friend Atticus, Cicero minced no words in saying
that he detested the Queen, and called a plain scoundrel
the chamberlain Serapion by whom the Queen had sent
him a letter.

One day Caesar rode through Rome in an Egyptian
chariot with a crown of golden laurel on his bald head:
the populace asked with irritation, was a Roman chariot
no longer good enough? What was indeed this Egyptian
style coming out in sudden fashion? A new curule chair
was made for Caesar, copied from the throne of the
Ptolemy Kings. Artists from Alexandria's mint were de-
signing the new coinage; Alexandrian experts were reorganizing the financial system of the Roman treasury;
even the Circus Games were now entrusted to Alexandrian
impresarios! Nor were the people particularly fond of
the newest reform of the calendar—what was wrong with
the old one? For so many centuries the Roman months
had disagreed with the natural revolution of the year, so

much so that the festivals and days of sacrifice had, little by little, fallen into seasons quite opposite to those intended by the festivals; but who cared? The Priests, who were the only persons that knew anything about it, used to insert, all at once and in the most unexpected and inconvenient way for business people, an intercalary month called Mercidonius, of which old King Numa was the inventor: and Numa had been a King who used to have palavers with a gentle Nymph called Egeria who inspired him to do great things! And now Caesar, with the aid of Egyptian mathematicians and astronomers, had changed all this ancient way of reckoning the dates when rent and interest fell due! "Ah," Cicero had not lost time in saying, "Lyra will rise tomorrow in the sky, by the Dictator's edict."

Even the great public works promoted by Caesar came to be ridiculed or spurned. Perhaps there were too many plans, as if Caesar was forgetting that Rome was not built in a day; or was the "Egyptian woman" putting the devil in the old boy? True it was that each day Caesar laid before the Senate some new plan or new law. The River Tiber was going to be diverted from Rome to Circei by means of a canal and go into the sea near Terracina; the isthmus of Corinth in Greece was to be cut; a new great road was going to be built across the Apennines; a great port was to be created at Ostia, to speed up the supplies to the City. And vast public buildings were going to be built in Rome; new public libraries to be opened in the various districts of the Capital; the marshes would be drained from Nomentum to Setia, by which ground enough would be gained from the water to employ thousands of hands in tillage: a long list of other plans were designed, which did not take effect.([1])

Now, oftentimes, Caesar spoke with Cleopatra, in the presence of Antony, of his disappointment and resentment that the people did not offer him the Crown straight-forwardly and spontaneously. Also, he said, he was deeply concerned for Cleopatra's situation, as without her the creation of a hereditary monarchy would be meaning-less. His legitimate wife, Calpurnia, had clearly proved unable to give him an heir; his only and real heir was Caesarion. But how to discard all at once Calpurnia without shocking further public opinion?

Cleopatra knew that Caesar's passion for her was now becalmed; but she loved him all the better for his finding pleasure in her company, for this comforting and re-assuring companionship that rested on the memories of their Alexandrian days, and the reliance and harmony of their similar minds, both enflamed by their ambitious dream of immortality. And between them and above them was their son.

On the 15th of February fell the festival of the Luper-cals. It was a great popular holiday, although the people had forgotten both the origin and the meaning of the feast, that was identified with the God Lupercus, vaguely connected with Faunus or Pan, as the God of the fecundity and fertility of men and earth. For the feast-day the Honourable College of the Luperci chose two young men who, in the morning, opened the ceremonies sacrificing one dog and one nanny-goat. Afterwards the College of Physicians drew blood from the two young men who were expected to laugh and not wince. Then the sacrificial

---

[1] Plutarch.

Priests skinned the two offerings, cut the skins into long strips, which were called *februa;* and the two young men, running through the main streets completely naked, whipped with those strips of skin all the women they met: in fact, any sterile woman desirous of having a child, would place herself along the route and offer her flanks to the generous touch of the sacred whips, which were supposed to give her fertility. A similar cult existed in Egypt, and the whip of the God Amon, the Pan of the Nile valley, had in due course touched the flanks of Cleopatra, thus making her the re-incarnate Goddess of fecund voluptuousness.

Caesar took a special interest in the Lupercalia of the year 44: not long before he had re-organized the College of Luperci and given to it the new name of Luperci Julii, thus identifying himself also with the God of Fertility. Mark Antony was, that year, the principal manipulator of the *februa*. Pale, emaciated, in a gorgeous robe, Caesar was seated upon his golden throne in the Forum, when Antony, naked and perspiring from the strenuous run, suddenly jumped the fence that surrounded the Dictator and his attendants, and distributing right and left vigorous strokes with his whip, he advanced towards Caesar and proffered him a diadem interlaced with laurel, asking him in a clear voice to accept the Royalty of Rome. As soon as Antony spoke these words, loud applause broke from Caesar's supporters posted in all parts of the Forum. But a vast booing rose from the crowd. Caesar pushed away the diadem with his hand, and the crowd applauded him with delight. Mark Antony repeated his offer holding the crown above the Dictator's head: again the isolated applause was drowned into the booing of the crowd. At the end Caesar made a gesture of definite protest, and Mark Antony, splendid in his herculean nakedness, departed with great bounds shaking his ferine whip. Caesar ordered that the proffered and repulsed crown be placed in the Capitol and the official diary be inscribed with a note that " Julius Caesar had that day refused the crown offered him by the People ".

Two days later Caesar made a new will—and of this testament Cleopatra had no knowledge.

XIV

On the eve of the Ides of March, Cleopatra received a message that Caesar would dine with his friend Marcus Lepidus and would afterwards return direct to his house.

Thus was Cleopatra left, on that fatal eve, distraught with fears and premonitions. For the rumour of a conspiracy had been rife in Rome for many days. Cleopatra had been told of the bad omens: the sky had become suddenly lit at night by mysterious light; strange noises were heard during the night in various districts; solitary birds had appeared in the Forum; people said that men of fire had been seen in the sky fighting each other; a great flame was seen to issue from a soldier's hand and yet his hand was not burnt.([1]) It was a dreadful atmosphere of disaster.

And Cleopatra could not chase from her mind the names of the two chief conspirators—Cassius and Brutus: the first obsessed by a maniac's hate of all forms of autocracy; the second, nursing his high principles as he would have nursed a wound. Of the two, Brutus she considered the most dangerous. She remembered that one day Caesar, on listening to a harangue by Brutus, had murmured: " I do not know what this man wants in

---

[1] Strabo, quoted also by Plutarch.

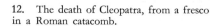

life, but whatever it is he wants it vehemently." And it had been reported to her that Cassius had put this question to Brutus: " What shall we do if at the Senate meeting Caesar will be proclaimed King? " And Brutus had answered: " In such case it will be my duty to rise and die for the freedom of my country." Such was the man that Caesar believed to be his own son: the man that Caesar had ordered to be spared at Pharsalia at all costs. And the other conspirators plied upon his principles, and placed pieces of paper on his official seat: " Awake, O Brutus! " or " You are not a true Brutus! " and upon the statue of his ancestor Junius a hand had scribbled " Oh, to have today a Brutus among us! "

Caesar dined with his friend Lepidus, who was his Master of the Horse. After dinner, while Caesar signed some urgent letters, the conversation turned upon what was the best kind of death. Caesar swiftly raised his head from the papers and answered: " A sudden death."

That night, while he was resting upon his bed in the same room as his wife Calpurnia, the doors and windows of the room flew suddenly open. Disturbed by the noise and the preternatural light in the sky, he saw that Calpurnia was in a troubled sleep. All at once Calpurnia uttered some strange words, then she wept loudly and convulsively, and on being awakened she told Caesar that she had dreamed she was holding his murdered body into her arms. He soothed her; yet, in the morning Calpurnia begged him not to go out that day and to adjourn the Senate: " If he had no regard for her dreams," she said, " let him have recourse to some other kind of divination or sacrifices." So impressed was Caesar that he offered a number of sacrifices, and the diviners found many unfavourable signs. Caesar was on the point of sending Antony to dismiss the Senate, when Decimus Brutus surnamed Albinus came in. He was one of the conspirators, but Caesar placed much confidence in him; and this man, fearing that if Caesar adjourned the Senate the plot might be discovered, laughed at the diviners and told Caesar he would be highly to blame if by such a slight he gave the Senate an occasion for complaint, " for the Senate is meeting at your summons, and is meeting prepared with one voice to honour you with the title of King in the Provinces and to grant that you should wear the diadem everywhere outside Italy ".

At this Caesar entered his litter with Decimus, and was borne to the Senate. While he was on his way to the Senate, one of his intimates, a Greek philosopher by the name of Artemidos, who had learned of the conspiracy, ran alongside Caesar's litter and trust into his hands a roll of paper telling him with urgent words and signs to read it at once; but Caesar merely nodded his thanks and kept the roll in his hands: it contained the names of the conspirators!

That day, some games were being held at the Theatre of Pompey, and the Senate had assembled in one of the adjoining buildings. Marcus Brutus and Cassius had arrived quite early at the portico in front of the Theatre, engaging in public business as Praetors. But they were alarmed by the rumours of fresh bad omens at Caesar's house. At that moment, a man took aside another of the conspirators, Senator Gaius Casca, and said to him in an urgent manner: " You kept the secret from me, but Brutus has told me all." Casca shuddered with fright, but his friend, smiling, only added: " Do tell me, where shall you get the money to stand for the Aedileship? " Casca recovered himself, but while Brutus and Cassius were conferring in whispers another Senator, Popilius Laena, drew them aside and said that he " joined them in his prayers for what they had in mind ", and urged them to make haste. They remained silent with terror.

When Caesar stepped out of his litter, Senator Laena accosted him and engaged him in earnest conversation. Again terror struck the hearts of the conspirators; but Laena merely appeared to be pressing some personal petition.

It was customary for the Magistrates, when about to enter the Senate House, to take the auspices at the entrance: the first bird that was slain was without the upper part of the entrails. The augur said it was an omen of death. Caesar laughed and said that the same thing happened to his own entrails while he was beginning his campaign in Spain. The augur replied that he was truly foreseeing a very great danger; at which, Caesar ordered him to sacrifice again. Again the omens were bad; yet Caesar turned to another augur who had once warned him to beware the Ides of March, and jestingly he asked him: " Where are your prophecies now, Spurinna? " And the diviner answered: " Yes, but the Ides are not yet past."

Caesar then entered the House: in his right hand he was still holding the roll that Artemidos had so urgently entreated him to read at once. And another bad omen was that the golden chair of Caesar was not in readiness, for the attendant, as Caesar was late in coming, had already carried it away thinking that the Senate would not be sitting that day.

When Caesar entered the House, the Senate rose to do him honour.

The conspirators had left Trebonius, another of their number, to engage Mark Antony in conversation at the door. The others stood around Caesar like friends as he was about to sit in his chair. Tullius Cimber came forward and pretended to intercede for the recall of his brother from exile. When he was seated, Caesar gave an emphatic denial; and as the group continued their importunities with an air of compulsion, he grew angry. Suddenly Cimber seized with both hands Caesar's purple robe and pulled it from his neck: this was the signal for the attack, and Cimber cried: "Friends, what are you waiting for?"

Casca gave the first blow with his sword, striking Caesar at the neck; but the wound was not serious. Caesar turned upon him, and seizing Casca's sword with both his hands cried: "Casca, great villain, what dost thou mean?" Then he added, in Greek: "Brother, help!" But Casca's brother pierced his side, and Cassius, the man that Caesar had pardoned after Pharsalia, wounded him in the face.

Caesar fought like a stag at bay. But every hand was raised against him, every face monstrously eager to taste his blood. Decimus Brutus smote him in the thigh; Buculianus in the back; Marcus Brutus planted his dagger in his chest. At this Caesar looked up in utter surprise, and crying "*Tu quoque, fili mi*", he pulled the hem of his toga over his head, to shroud his face and conceal any sign of horror, and drawing the skirt of his robe around his legs so that he might not appear undignified in falling, he fell on the ground, either by accident or pushed by the attackers, at the foot of the statue of Pompey, his great enemy.

The conspirators continued to stab him wildly after

he had fallen, until he had received twenty-three wounds. In their fury they wounded one another.

Caesar was dead. Marcus Brutus advanced to address the Senate; but no one was there to hear him. The Senators were running out of the House; there was a general flight through the Curia and the whole City. In the stampede several Senators were wounded and many citizens were killed by the mistakes of those into whose hands they fell. The neighbouring Theatre emptied in great haste and panic; the markets were plundered; the gladiators, who had been armed early in the morning for the day's shows, ran out of their dressing-rooms and abandoned themselves to attacks and robberies. The citizens barricaded their doors and prepared for defence on the roofs.

Brutus and the other conspirators wrapped their togas around their left arms to serve as shields, and in great fright and perplexity, brandishing their swords and daggers still dripping with Caesar's blood, they ran along the streets shouting that they had slain the tyrant. One of them carried aloft on the end of a spear a cap such as was given to enfranchised slaves and ransomed captives as a sign of liberty; and he urged the citizens to restore the government of their fathers in memory of the elder Brutus. But as no one seemed inclined to follow them, the conspirators felt disconcerted and alarmed; and fearing Lepidus and the army under him in the City and also Antony in his capacity as Consul, they hastened up to the Capitol, taking with them as guards a band of gladiators.

Towards the end of the day, the murderers sent an emissary, Dolabella, to learn of what Mark Antony and Lepidus intended to do. Antony—who had run to his house through some narrow lanes—replied that he would consider the matter with the conspirators in the Senate and take as propitious for the City whatever they would approve in common.

Torches were lit during the night at all crossroads to avoid disorders; and thus the friends of the murderers were able to go to and fro during the whole night, visiting the houses of influential Senators and beseeching them on behalf of those men. The leaders of colonial troops ran about uttering threats in case they should be deprived of the land that had already been assigned or promised to them by Caesar.

And the more honest citizens began to regain heart when they learned how small was the number of conspirators; and when they remembered Caesar's merits, they became divided in opinion.

In the meantime Caesar's body remained on the floor of the Senate until three of his slaves went there and laid the body on a litter, and carried it home, with one arm hanging down over the side. Caesar's doctor Anstistius declared that among so many wounds there was none that was mortal, except the second which Caesar had received in the breast. The conspirators let it be known that they meant to drag Caesar's body to the Tiber; but they were deterred by fear of Antony and Lepidus. That same night all Caesar's money and papers were transferred to Antony's house, either because Calpurnia thought that they would be safer or because Antony ordered it.

And to the Villa across the Tiber the tragic news was brought by a humble and faithful slave of he who had been Caesar.

XV

NIGHT had fallen again when Cleopatra received Mark
Antony at the Villa. The Consul and friend of the
murdered Dictator had come to acquaint the Queen of
Caesar's will—the testament that Caesar had made a few
weeks before, and of which Cleopatra knew nothing.

The will—Antony said—was made by Caesar at his
Lavican Villa, and committed, as was customary, to the
custody of the Abbess of the Vestal Virgins. It had been
opened in the house of Antony, at the instance of Lucius
Piso, Caesar's father-in-law.

In this testament, foreseeing the eventuality of dying
before his elevation to the throne, Caesar had divided all
his possessions between the people of Rome and his direct
relatives, personally naming three heirs: the two grand-
sons of his sister, namely Gaius Octavian for three-
quarters of the estate, and Lucius Pinarius and Quintus
Pedius for the remaining fourth. A codicil added that
Gaius Octavian, at present a junior officer in Apollonia,
was to assume his name as an adopted son. To the people
of Rome he bequeathed his gardens near the Tiber, including the Transtiberine Villa, and three hundred
sesterces to each man.

Neither Cleopatra nor the child Caesarion were mentioned in the will. " You are sure that there is not another
will? " " There is no other will."

Thus was ending Cleopatra's dream as Queen-pre-
sumptive of the World. Her love, her splendid devotion,
the divine gift of a real Heir to Caesar—all was crushed to
nothing. And all because of one fatal day: for it might
well have been true that the Senate really intended to
offer the throne to Caesar, the throne that he would have
shared with her.

What, oh what, had made Caesar make that unjust, unfair and cruel will? Had Calpurnia destroyed a later testament? And what, oh what had pushed Caesar to prefer a nephew, that pale and furtive and sly man Octavian, to his very own son Caesarion, who was the unmistakable image of his father?

Why did not Antony and Cleopatra produce a later testament written and sealed that very night with Caesar's seal that Antony was wearing at his finger? And yet, during the next few days Faberius, Caesar's private Secretary, forged for Fulvia scores of papers in Caesar's name, and at the request of Antony fabricated amnesties and notes-of-hand transferring and acquiring fortunes! Both Antony and Cleopatra had everything to gain from a new testament: yet, it was not done, and Caesar's cruel will was let to stand.

From that act of sublime respect for the will of their great dead Caesar came all the course of history as we have come to know it.

Antony advised the Queen to remain, for the present, in Rome, keeping however, for her own sake, to the Villa. So Cleopatra was now a hostage to fortune—the prisoner of the dead Caesar.([1])

That same night Antony went to the Forum, where Caesar's body had been removed, and looked at length into the imperious face of his old master and friend. It was a clear moonlit night.

The following day notice of Caesar's funeral was

---

[1] A few days later Antony tried to rescue the fortune of Cleopatra, declaring to the Senate that Caesarion had been recognized as a legitimate son by Caesar; but Oppius, a partisan of Octavian, challenged him to produce the evidence, and subsequently even denied this assertion in a book.

solemnly proclaimed. A pyre was erected in the Campus
Martius near the tomb of Caesar's daughter Julia. Before the Rostra in the Forum was placed a gilded taber-
nacle, modelled as the temple of Venus-Genetrix, and
within this was an ivory bed, covered with a cloth of
purple and gold. At the head of the bed was a trophy
made with the bloodstained robe in which Caesar was
slain. As it was thought that one day would not suffice
for carrying the funeral oblations in solemn procession
before the corpse, directions were given for everyone to
carry them from the City into the Campus Martius by
what way they pleased.

Before the funeral, however, Antony had sent during
the night notices summoning the Senate to meet at daybreak at the temple of Tellus, which was very near his
own house, because he did not dare to go to the Senate
House at the foot of the Capitol, where the gladiators
were still aiding the murderers; nor did he wish to disturb
the temper of the City by bringing in the troops. But
Lepidus did that; and it was a wise move, as some of
Caesar's veterans were growing indignant, and when the
Praetor Cinna commenced to make a speech abusing
Caesar, they threw stones at him, compelling him to take
flight, and pursued him and nearly set fire to a house
where he had taken shelter, had not Lepidus's troops prevented it.

In the Senate, the House was divided, and many sought
to aid the conspirators in various ways. It was then that
Antony as Consul called for silence, and thus he spoke:
" It comes to this, that either the Senate will admit that
Caesar was the First Magistrate and the elected ruler of
the Republic, and therefore all his acts and decrees will
remain in full force. If, on the other hand, it is decided

that Caesar usurped the government, his body must be cast out unburied and all his acts annulled. But his acts embrace the whole Earth and Seas, and most of them will stand whether we like it or not. And if you want to judge Caesar, you must first resign the offices which you received from him."

It was a shrewd poser, and Antony knew very well what he himself stood to gain, for before his death Caesar had assigned the Province of Syria to Dolabella and Macedonia to Mark Antony. The Senate had already expressed their intentions of giving Syria to Cassius and Macedonia to Marcus Brutus.

A great crowd had collected in the meantime outside the temple of Tellus while the Senate was sitting; and some shouted for peace for the Republic and others called for avenging Caesar. At last Antony dismissed the Senate, and at night the whole people of Rome crowded into the Forum for the funeral of Caesar.

To incite indignation for the murder, during the play that it was customary to act at a State funeral, a passage was sung from Pacuvius's tragedy entitled *The Trial for Arms,* and some lines from Attilius's tragedy of Electra. Instead of the customary panegyric, Antony ordered a Herald to proclaim to the people the Decree of the Senate by which the People had bestowed upon Caesar all honours human and divine. Then, sizing the temper of the people, Antony spoke the most wonderful funeral oration in history, which ended thus: "I stand ready to avenge him as I have sworn and vowed." But at this the Senators showed signs of commotion and Antony soothed them and recanted: "It seems to me, fellow citizens, that this deed is not the work of human beings, but of some evil spirit. It becomes us to consider the present rather than the past, lest we be drawn into evil commotions. Let us then conduct this sacred one to the abode of the blest."

At this Antony gathered up his robe, girded himself so that, whatever happened, he might have the free use of his hands, took his position in front of the bier as in a play, bending down to it and rising again, and he began the exaltation of Caesar.

Antony was a wonderful actor; and he uncovered the body of Caesar, lifted his bloody robe on the point of a spear and shook it aloft, pierced as it was by the dagger-thrusts and reddened with Caesar's blood. And the people, like a vast chorus, moaned and cried with him, and became filled again with anger. While they were in this temper, somebody raised above the bier an image of Caesar modelled in wax. The body, as it lay on its back on the couch, could not be seen; and the image was turned round and round by a mechanical device, showing the twenty-three wounds in all parts of the body and on the face that the people had known so well. At this the people groaned; and some set fire to the Senate House where Caesar had been murdered, and ran hither and thither searching for the murderers, who had fled. Then, the people returned to Caesar's bier, and bore it as a con-secrated relic to the Capitol, intending to bury it in the maximum Temple and place it among the Gods. But being prevented from doing so by the Priests, they placed it again in the Forum, on the spot where was the ancient Palace of the Kings of Rome. And while some pro-posed that Caesar's body be burnt in the sanctuary of the Temple of Jupiter Capitolinus and others in Pompey's Senate-House, suddenly two men, with swords by their sides and spears in their hands, set fire to the bier with lighted torches. And the crowd and the veterans of all Caesar's campaigns broke up the tribunals and the benches of the adjoining Courts and anything else they could find in the Forum; made a huge pyre throwing upon it the adornments of the procession, some of which were very ancient and costly, and set fire to it. The musicians and players stripped off the dresses they wore for the occasion, taken from the wardrobes of Caesar's Triumph, rent them and threw them into the flames. The legionaries cast in their breast-plates and armours which they had worn in honour of the funeral; most of the ladies did the same with their ornaments, casting on the pyre their necklaces and the golden bullae of their children; and the whole people of Rome remained by the pyre throughout the night.

This was the funeral that the people of Rome gave Caesar; and afterwards an altar was erected on the spot, that is the very site where the remains can be seen of the Temple of Caesar himself.

Yet, in a few days civil war appeared to be inevitable. In view of the situation, Mark Antony advised Cleopatra to return to Egypt with her son and to await there the end of the conflict. The Queen accepted the advice. Many signs had already convinced her that Caesar's death was a portent: a great comet had appeared in the heavens, which shone bright for seven nights after Caesar's death and then disappeared; and the sun seemed to have lost its splendour, for its orb looked pale and so it did all that year, and it was as though the sun was eclipsed by the approach of the star of Caesar now in the heavens.

On the 15th of April Cleopatra sailed from Rome: her eyes stood fixed towards Alexandria and her kingdom.

Antony had promised that he would be the champion of the boy Caesarion.

Before her departure, Cleopatra saw the Priests and the High Officers of the Republic proclaim Caesar a God: certainly he would not desert his Queen and his Sister-Goddess, nor abandon his own child.

BOOK THREE

CLEOPATRA AND MARK ANTONY

I

I T was the festival of Serapis, two years after the
return of the Queen from Rome.

The news of Alexandria's Festival always spread far
and wide. People came from Boubastos and Memphis
and Hermonthis, from Pelusium and from the towns along
the Syrian and Cilician coasts. For many days the
throngs of visitors swarmed nosily along the Canopus
admiring the splendid buildings, or visited the bazaars
and the amusement booths of the old Rhakotis. Men
from all countries and of all races; Greeks dressed in the
pallium; Roman soldiers with cothurns of bronze; Gauls
with blue eyes; and a medley of Asiatics, noticeable for
their heavy lidded eyes and their flowing robes.

On that day the Royal way was kept clear, for the
Royal Procession was due to pass.

The procession was opened by a fanfare of trumpets
and cymbals. Solemn, unending, the cortege was headed
by several sets of musicians, each set distanced from the
preceding one, the players of cymbals, the players of
citherns, that were rings strung on metal bars, the players
of drums which the drummers carried hanging from their
necks and beat with sycamore sticks. Then came the
Priests: first the magicians that could tell the future;
then, the readers of hieroglyphics; the prophets with very
long beards and the bearers of the Gods' images held
high on gilded staffs, or carried upon chariots. The

ancient Gods of Egypt passed between the exulting people: the mysterious figures of Apis the Bull, the hawk-mask of Toth, the jackal head of Anubis God of Death. As each image passed, the crowd shouted their prayers and requests, for the Gods could confer strength and blessing upon the suppliants.

The High Priest advanced between two rows of soldiers. The High Priest was a very old man and leaned on a staff. His face was covered with a long veil, the colour of hyacinth, for no profane glance was allowed to desecrate the High Priest's face before he would commune with the God and receive the oracle.

Behind the High Priest came the priestesses, who were young and dressed in white, and held with their delicate fingers stems of lotus flowers.

Then followed the bell-ringers; the bird-catchers who held on their staffs daubed with glue the sacred fowls. Then came the vendors of amulets and images and scarabs; and the beggars exposing their infirmities.

And all marched to the temple of Serapis. There, the students from all the Colleges were already assembled under the portico, each group in its appointed place.

Although built in recent times, the great sanctuary was in the style of the ancient Egyptian Temples or " house " of the God. The approach to the sanctuary, was by a paved road, flanked on both sides by Sphinxes. In front of the temple stood the so-called pylons or great gates flanked by two towers with coloured walls and high flag-staves and obelisks graven with the hieroglyphics which the common people could not read.

Immediately beyond the pylons was the great court, surrounded by a colonnade of mighty pillars. In the further wall of the court was the entrance into the hypostyle, a gigantic hall whose roof was supported by pillars and lighted only by small windows set close under the roof; this gave to the hypostyle an atmosphere of mystery, increased by the dense smoke of the incense and cinnamon burning in the huge burners of shiny brass.

The festival was celebrated in the columned court and the hypostyle; but these were not the " house " of the God.

The God dwelt in the central one of the three dark chapels that stood behind the hypostyle. In that chapel was the divine bark with the image of God: the two adjoining chapels were the abode of the God's consort and of his son. Upon the doors of these chapels was written: " He who enters must purify himself three times."

The walls and pillars of the outer temple were covered from roof to floor with representations of the life and virtues of the God; the blank spaces between the panels shone with bright colours.

Suddenly in the vast crowd along the roads there was a commotion. Far away at the top of the Canopus, above the turreted magnificence of the Royal Bruchion a light shone. The heralds announced: " The Queen! "

The Royal procession had moved from the Palace. Runners with long staves hastened figuratively to clear the way for the Queen's carriage. Then the chariot advanced, drawn by fiery white horses, richly caparisoned and held at the bridle by grooms. On either side of the chariot ran the Queen's bodyguards on foot; behind it came Egyptian soldiers and Asiatic mercenaries armed with all kind of weapons; their regimental badges were carried before them; behind them came their officers upon light chariots. After the Queen's carriage came two young Princesses

121

who drove together, the elder holding the reins, while the other leant tenderly on her sister.

Behind the Royal carriages came six other carriages with the Court ladies, and on either side six more with the Lords of the bed-chamber. Runners and servants ran along swinging their gilded staves.

The Queen's carriage was shaped like a shield of gold, upon which the Queen appeared to be borne aloft, seated on a miniature throne. She seemed to be sheathed in silver, a stiff dress that encased her as though she were a graven image, with her knees bent, her elbows pressed to her sides, her eyes turned to the sky. The Queen wore the robes of a Goddess, and around her head was set the divine diadem or uraeus adorned with the snake, and in her right hand she carried the divine sceptre. The crowd knew that each garment had been put upon the Queen, that day, by the Lords of the Royal Vestiture: the Washer of Pharaoh had attended to the washing of the Queen's hands and feet; the Chief Bleacher had inspected the transparent tunic before it was passed over the Queen's body; the Keeper of the Diadem had carried and placed upon her head the diadem, and afterwards the Keeper had boasted that he had " adorned the brow of his Goddess ".

Thus dressed, the Queen was no longer a woman, but the divine daughter of the Pharaoh Kings; a Priestess who would soon be in the presence of the God Serapis. Four slaves waved fans of peacock's feathers above her head.

On the threshold of the temple a herald chanted upon a zither the psalm of the many titles of the Queen: " In the third year of His Majesty Horus: the strong Bull, beloved by the Goddess of Truth, the Lord of the diadem of the Vulture and the Snake: who protects Egypt and subdues the Barbarians: Isis the daughter of Amon, shining daily on her throne as her father Amon did: Young in years, great in victories, the Queen of Upper Egypt and the Queen of Lower Egypt, Cleopatra, the chosen of Osiris, from the loins of Amon, the Queen of Queens, the daily giver of eternal life like her father Amon ... "

The moment of the burnt-offerings had come. Erect, her shoulders covered with the mantle of Isis, that was white as the whitest of flour, symbol of the great crop of blessed Egypt, Cleopatra stepped from the golden shield over the sill of the temple. The great door was closed again, the door behind which was the watch-dog of black granite, with its triple head of lion, wolf and jackal. And behind the tall columns of the central chapel, flanked by hieroglyphics which told the destiny of the human soul, rose the statue of Serapis, modelled in marble and gold.

Serapis, the Omnipotent God. Serapis the dispenser of Glory, of health and of riches; the controller of the mighty wealth dispensed by the waters of the Nile. Serapis who was three times the height of man and serene as no man could ever be. Serapis whose long curled beard reached down to his knees; the seal of Kings was upon his forehead. Serapis whose hands were extended with a gesture that embraced the whole world. The light from the small windows near the roof fell on his enamelled lips; and the enamelled lips seemed to tremble in a kiss or in a word of promise.

The sacrificial table stood before the statue. Upon it were engraved the signs of the Zodiac; in the centre of the table the oil was burning, and side by side with the blood of the victims were golden vases holding the wine and the wheat, the water of the Nile and the seven perfumes of Arabia.

The High Priest lifted the hiacynthine veil from his face and bent towards the flame, pouring upon it the wheat and the wine, the water of the Nile and the perfumes of Arabia.

Cleopatra prostrated herself before the God. Outside the temple every heart beat furiously, communing with the mysterious rites in the holy of holies. It was the solemn moment when the omens become visible; when the multitude had one single voice and one single soul.

The High Priest uttered the prayer of the people of Egypt: "O God Serapis, God whom the winds obey, liberate the still waters of the sacred River!" And Cleopatra prayed silently.

The smoke cleared, the great door re-opened, revealing the terrifying watch-dog with the triple head; and the Queen reappeared. Under the sparkling jewels her wonderful bosom was heaving. Three blasts of trumpets announced that the Queen was about to speak. She advanced to the edge of the step, and her voice pronounced these words: "The mercy of the God Serapis has promised glory and progress to Egypt. The Nile will spread its blessed waters upon the fields for our wheat to swell!"

The multitude responded with a cry of joy. The Queen stepped again upon the shield of gold, and with the fans of peacock's feathers waving lightly around her head, was carried back to the Palace.

She felt happier. For Serapis had answered her secret prayer that Mark Antony would range himself by her in defence of her child Caesarion.

II

THE last two years had been a period of continuous worries for Cleopatra. Her Ministers and the great merchants and bankers of Alexandria had begrudged their welcome on her return: the Queen had spent two years out of Egypt—where was the Treaty of Alliance with Rome? Where was the ritual parchment with its great seals? What had the Roman Senate actually promised the Queen after the assassination of Caesar?

And what could Cleopatra reply? The satisfactory trade of Egypt with Rome? Or the legitimization of Caesarion by the Senate? But this she could not believe herself, for it had been a feeble though chivalrous attempt on the part of Mark Antony, soon dropped in the general turmoil and chase after personal safety and advantage. She knew that Fulvia, that determined virago who shamelessly and unendingly forged documents with Caesar's seal so as to acquire friends and wealth, would never countenance her husband Antony supporting anybody's claim but his own.

For two years Cleopatra had been full of doubts and indecision. The loneliness in the vast Palace appalled her: it was too full of memories—it was there she had appeared to Caesar out of a rolled carpet; there Caesar had taken her with the urge of an impetuous lover after his safe escape from the galleon in the Port (and she was sure it was that day that she conceived Caesarion); and there, at that great table, she had sat at banquet with her father and Mark Antony eleven years ago; and her father, the drunken and dreamy flute-player, had given her one advice, only one, but he had urged her to adhere to it, at all price, if she wanted to keep her throne: " Never against Rome! "

But which Rome? Rome herself had been again in the flames of civil war, and no one could forecast who would, at the end, be the real ruler of Rome.

Her couriers, agents and spies brought to her, by each ship, extraordinary and horrifying news from Rome; and on this news her very fate depended and the future of her son.

Calpurnia, the unhappy widow of Caesar, had entrusted Antony with her treasure, which amounted to four thousand talents, and all Caesar's papers, which contained notes of all his designs and plans; and of these Antony, aided by his wife Fulvia, had made a most clever use, for, by inserting in them what names he thought convenient, he had appointed many of his friends Magistrates, others he had recalled from exile, others he had freed from prison, on pretence that all these things had been ordered by Caesar. It was such a transparent ruse that the people called these favoured persons the Charonites, that was the name given to the slaves enfranchised by their masters' last wills.

But in this way Mark Antony's power seemed assured: he was Consul, his brother Caius was Praetor, and his brother Lucius a Tribune of the people. So powerful indeed Antony considered himself, that when a few weeks later Octavian had arrived in Rome from Apollonia to take up the inheritance of his uncle Caesar, Antony had treated him in a cavalierly way, and told him that it was absurd at his age to pretend to assume the succession of the great Dictator. (And Cleopatra had smiled when she had heard this report, for she still carried in her mind the impression the young man had left in her, so thin and pale, with a spotted face, always badly washed and with his hair uncombed.)

But Octavian was not to be repulsèd so easily; he insisted on the money, and assumed his uncle's name as it was his right by the will. Antony opposed him in the Tribuneship; and when Octavian made use of the golden chair which had been granted by the Senate to his uncle —almost a Throne—Antony promptly told him that unless he desisted to solicit the people, he would have him locked up in prison. Soon the rupture between the two men was complete; Antony called Octavian a vulgar adventurer, accused him of having cadged the adoption of his uncle through their immoral relations, and proclaimed himself avenger of Caesar, ready to support the legal rights of Caesar's only son, Caesarion.

But when Octavian joined Cicero and the rest of Antony's enemies, and the veterans seemed inclined to stand by this heir and adoptive son of their beloved Commander, Antony thought it better to accommodate, and at the end of October of the year 43 he arranged with Octavian a meeting in the Capitol: a meeting of mutual distrust, for, when the two adversaries exchanged the kiss of peace, they carefully felt each other to make sure that neither carried a dagger in the folds of his robe. By that arrangement, Antony and Octavian formed a compact with a third man of no great importance, Lepidus, and called this a Triumvirate and had it approved by the Senate. The three men were to govern jointly Rome and Italy and the outer provinces for a term of five years, till the 31st December of the year 38, all three administering Rome and Italy jointly, and each ruling on his own a definite part of the outer territories. Antony and Lepidus chose the control of the most important provinces, Africa and Numidia; the Isles were assigned to Octavian.

Then, they drafted a long list of proscriptions and

murders; one hundred Senators and some two thousand other influential citizens were savagely " liquidated ". Octavian surrendered to Antony Cicero, who still spoke of " restoring the ancient liberties "; and Antony sacrificed his uncle Lucius Caesar to Octavian, while Lepidus had the privilege of putting to death his own brother Paulus.

Cleopatra had smiled bitterly when she heard the news of Cicero's death; the old weathercock, who the day after Caesar's murder had written that his only regret was that he had not been invited to this banquet of the Gods, and only a month later had sent a most emotional letter of homage to the genius of Antony! Cleopatra had not forgotten the letter Cicero had written to Atticus —and which had been intercepted and copied by Caesar's Police—in which he said that " he deplored her staying at the Transtiberine Villa, that he detested the Queen and did not want to have anything to do with the Queen and her band ".([1])

But the murderers of Caesar, Cassius and Brutus, were alive and free in Macedonia, where they had assembled an army: Cassius was contemplating the invasion of Egypt, to seize Cleopatra's treasury and fleet. (But Cassius had discarded the idea, merely upon the information that Cleopatra was ready for war.)

Antony and Octavian, whom the people already called with his new name of Caesar, went together into Macedonia against Brutus and Cassius, and the government of Rome was left to Lepidus. Antony encamped opposite to Cassius, and Octavian opposite to Brutus; and Antony's efforts were successful. But the turmoil in Rome flared up once again, for Dolabella, now an enemy of Antony and of Brutus and Cassius as well, intimated to

[1] Cicero—*Letters to Atticus.*

Cleopatra to send back the Legions that Caesar had left in Alexandria; and the same request was addressed to her by Cassius. Cleopatra had answered favourably the request of Dolabella, and replied to Cassius with a *fin-de-non-recevoir*: how could she send the Legions to help the men who had murdered Caesar? Cassius obtained some ships from the Viceroy of Cyprus, Serapion (who was soon to pay for his deception), and Dolabella was defeated by Cassius, a defeat that did not affect Cleopatra, for the Legions had been sent belatedly, and did not arrive in time for action.

In October of the following year, 42, the great battle of Philippi took place, and Caesar's murderers were finally defeated by Antony and Octavian. Cassius was killed in battle, and Brutus committed suicide. Octavian was sick on the day of battle, so that the honour of the victory fell entirely to Antony. As Antony stood over the dead body of Brutus, he threw his purple robe over the body, and ordered one of his freedmen to give it an honourable funeral: and later, when he was informed that the freedman had not burned the robe with the body and had been mean with the money to be expended on the funeral, Antony commanded him to be slain.

After the battle of Philippi, Octavian was conveyed to Rome and it was expected that his illness would soon take him to his grave.

Antony seemed now the real master of the Roman World. He decided to visit the East, to raise funds and affirm the authority of the Triumvirate, and his own. To Octavian was left, at Antony's suggestion, the administration of Rome and Italy: and this was an enormous and fatal mistake, for Octavian did not die, and consolidated his rule in Rome.

Yet, Antony was at the peak of his success; and he traversed some of the Asiatic Provinces raising money everywhere; he passed with a large army into Greece, where he was acclaimed as Dionysus, attending the disputes of the logicians, the religious ceremonies and the public games; amused the Greeks by walking through Athens in white shoes; visited Ephesus, and there the women marched before him dressed as Bacchantes escorted by men and boys in the costumes of Pan and Satyrs, and the whole city was garlanded with ivy and everybody played harps and flutes and pipes while the citizens hailed Antony as Bacchus—" Bacchus! ever kind and free! "

At the end Antony went to Tarsus, on the Cilician coast, and there he set up Court, and summoned Cleopatra to appear before him. And yet Cleopatra was not obeying the summons.

These were the events of the last two years, which Cleopatra had followed from her Palace, with growing alarm. What would the future portend?

But in the vastness of the Bruchion the Queen was lonely. She would have been loth to admit it; day after day she repeated to herself that nothing mattered but the political situation and the safety of her throne; but she was lonely. And maybe she was lovesick, as any woman can be. It was not glory that she was missing; not Rome that she was missing, for the memories of Rome were now repelling to her; it was not splendour and pomp that she was missing, for splendour and pomp she could evoke by merely clapping her hands. What she was missing was the elderly Caesar who had been such a lover and inspirer of the greatest dreams—and the dream that was Caesar could be fulfilled only with a man at her side.

Through the halls of the Palace pattered the little feet

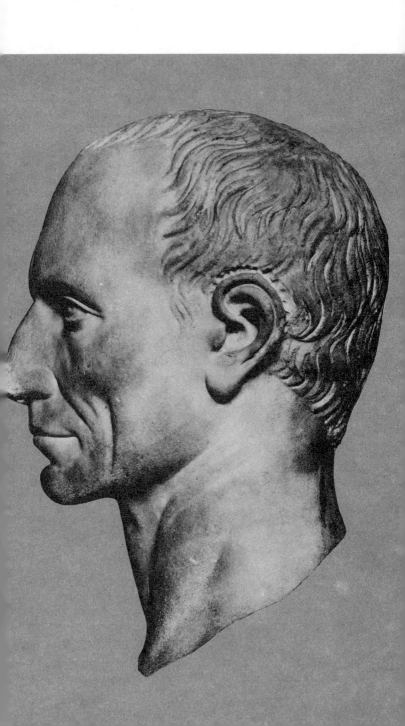

of Caesarion—" so ridiculously like his father ".

Six months after the battle at Philippi, an Ambassador arrived at the Palace in Alexandria, an Ambassador from Mark Antony.

The Ambassador that Mark Antony had chosen was Quintus Dellius, a most charming and elegant man—the Dellius of Horace's Alcaic Ode " Enjoy the fleeting hour, *moriture Delli!* " And Dellius was indeed keeping the even mind and the restrained spirit that Horace advised him for a happy existence. He was a wit, a well-read and well-informed man, and possessed an adaptable disposition that had made it easy for him to follow successfully every man in power, and to quit his service on the instant that his star set and pass to the next one in command. Before the battle of Philippi he had been a friend of Cassius, and now he was the Ambassador of the winner, Mark Antony.

Dellius was also something else—he was a disreputable creature who acted as a paramour and procurer to Antony and at the same time kept Fulvia informed of her husband's campaigns, in the alcove as well as in the field.

Cleopatra knew this quite well, and she felt indeed that Dellius was an ideal Ambassador.

She received him seated upon her throne, surrounded by her Guards, making a colourful picture against a Persian tapestry of birds and flowers. Dellius was short of stature, with refined features, and a gracious manner. After saluting in the Roman fashion, with his right hand upraised, he remained motionless looking at the Queen, as though absorbed in an overwhelming rapture.

" Why have you come to see me? " the Queen asked with playful dignity. And as Dellius answered that Mark Antony's happiness would never be complete until the

Queen would honour him with her gracious presence, he began to understand what an exceptional creature Cleopatra was, and why Antony should grow impatient of having her at his side.

The Queen dismissed her Guards and attendants, and conversed affably and lengthily with the Ambassador. She was fully informed, she said, of the political situation; and she was also quite aware of the Triumvir's new mode of life after his great victory. " Was it perchance a passing whim of the great General that had prompted him to seek her out through a special Ambassador? Did he not find sufficient the homage of so many beautiful Queens and Princesses? "

" Oh, your Majesty means Glaphyra, Eutrope and the others! Beggars already dethroned, vassals who threw themselves at the Conqueror's feet . . . " Ambassador Dellius paused and gazed at the Queen with meaning; and an indefinable fear made him halt. Cleopatra looked at him icily from the height of her ivory throne, as though to stop the lowly comparison that had escaped his lips. But then, after a meaning pause, she opened her lips, and laughed—an innocent and girlish and yet wicked laugh. And Dellius felt her animation, her captivating changeful mood, her sensuous languor, her incomparable feminine appeal. He divined in that instant the terrific influence such a woman would have in the life of Antony. And Dellius repeated: " Mark Antony wants you to come to Tarsus."

And in the reticence of the worldly Dellius Cleopatra read that by deferring her visit she had wetted Antony's desire to see her.

She answered: " Yes, the Queen will go." A new vista of hopes and possibilities suddenly opened to her.

132

She would renew her acquaintance with Antony: she would turn him into her friend. She would treat him as the avenger of Caesar, the natural supporter of the Queen of Egypt and of Caesarion.

She added: " The Queen will set out before the days begin to shorten."

That very day she ordered her personal fleet to be made ready. She gathered gold and slaves, jewels and treasures; in hundreds of chests, jewels and gold and treasures were carried down the steps of the Palace into her ships: twelve triremes were filled with them.

She prepared for the visit like an expedition. It was, indeed, an expedition, Cleopatra told herself: she was setting out to conquer Mark Antony.

III

AT forty, Mark Antony was at the peak of his success: but in his greatness there was a streak of comedy and ridicule. For Antony, now the undisputed ruler of the East from Greece to Judea, liked to think of himself as a kind of new Jupiter. In fact, being a young man and a most handsome man at that, he prepared to consider himself the son of Jupiter. Hercules was now discarded as too commonplace.

This somewhat absurd side in Mark Antony is very important in assessing the part he was to play in Cleopatra's life. Mark Antony was a colossal child; capable of conquering the world at the head of an army; but he was equally capable of losing it all rather than resist a pleasure. He had nothing of the genius; he was, on the contrary, an enormous commonplace. Yet he was saved by his magnetism, or rather by the contagious force of his impulsiveness and his sheer vitality.

He could not make great decisions, for his passions carried him away. And his life was torn between ambition and sensuality. Now, after the political battle and the astounding victory at Philippi, sensuality was rapidly taking possession of his life.

The fatality was that the satisfaction of his sensuality appeared now as the summit of his success. For Mark Antony was, in essence, a gross man, for whom the pleasures of the flesh were more tangible and satisfactory than the pleasures of the mind. He was an educated man, but not a cultured one; and Art was to him only the means of enriching the pleasantness of life. He was capable of impressing his soldiers with his endurance in the field, with his disregard for rough conditions, and could, with them, live on roots and drink stagnant water and sleep on the hard ground; but when the battle was over and won, his senses demanded their fill, and Antony's orgies of eating and drinking and love-making were famous.

So that after Philippi he had been fully alive to the necessity of visiting the new Provinces that had come under his care, and had eventually set foot on the soil of that East which was to be his triumph and his undoing.

His domain offered him two shores: on the side of the snow-capped Ossa and Pelion lay the calm fascination of Greece; on the coast of Asia Minor were the ancient cities, one more famous than the other: Pergamus, Ephesus, Smyrna; there was Syria, Lebanon and Judea, and beyond all that was Egypt, the fabulous kingdom of the beautiful Queen Cleopatra.

Antony first visited Greece: he already knew Delphi, Corinth and Olympia from the days he had trodden the fields of Thessaly as a young Commander fighting on the side of Caesar against Pompey.

The Greeks, by now accustomed to foreign rule, found this new Roman overlord as handsome as Alcibiades and as full of warlike virtues as Themistocles. They liked his physical bearing and strength; they called him son of Hercules, and in his god-like way, Antony showed his generosity in restoring the theatre at Megara, rebuilding Thebes and Larissa and the temple of Venus Pandena at Corinth. He did not think too much of Athens, with her narrow streets and irregular squares; but the monuments of the Acropolis were left undisturbed; the Porticus of Pericles still held its brilliantly coloured decorations, and the magic sunsets on the rose-coloured Pantelicus still had a charm.

Antony had the good sense to enter Athens on horseback, clad in cuirass and helmet, which pleased the descendants of Themistocles; and he partook with dignity the frugal hospitality that was offered him in the ancient house of the Archontes: recalling the example of Caesar, he put on a woollen cloak and, preceded by a single Lictor, climbed on foot the hill of the Acropolis.

As it was the season for the Festival of Adonis, he consented to celebrate it with the Athenians, and joined graciously in the rite of the quickly fading flowers which symbolized the early death of the son of Myrrha: the mourning women sang elegies weeping for the young God, and on the following day the girls crowned with roses filled the air with songs of joy for his resurrection. Antony presided over the competitions held in the Pnyx, distributing the prizes to athletes and orators; gave just judgment in the Tribunal; and won over the Greek people completely.

But he had soon tired of such simple life, and had

135

crossed the sea to the shores of Asia. The cities of Asia Minor offered him more than his fill of pleasure. Antony commenced his tour with Antioch, and this splendid metropolis—the third in importance in the ancient world —was equally unrivalled in corruption. Antioch seemed to hang from the sides of the Coryphean mountains; long before entering the harbour, the travellers saw the gigantic forts cut in the rocky slopes and crowning the summit of the walls. The city was gleaming white, on the banks of the Orontes and surrounded by the deep-green of cypress groves. Since the decline of Athens many business people had settled in Antioch, and such foreign population had yet no parallel in Rome.

Antioch's commercial power was equal to Alexandria's; and the laxity of life made Antioch the most depraved city between Paphlagonia and Palmyra. The most beautiful courtesans flocked to Antioch from Susa and Ecbatana; some even came from as far away as India; and when the feast of Maia was celebrated, bands of naked girls ran through the streets with flowering poles and torches, inviting all men to celebrate the day of fertility in the groves and in the pools.

The moment Antony breathed this new atmosphere in the Seleucides Palace, which had once belonged to Sardanapalous, he cast away the disguise of Athenian simplicity and became his natural self. The life of an Asiatic Sathrap suited him to perfection. And in each city he performed it with the utmost relish.

His stay at Ephesus became famous—and it marked his outlook on life for ever. The celebrated city was dissolute in a kind of mystical way. Fantastic liberties and orgies took place at the shrine of Diana under the guise of worship. In Ephesus, Diana was no longer the chaste Goddess of Delos. Her magnificent festivals attracted crowds of visitors who come not in pilgrimage, but to enjoy themselves. The Priests and a mass of magicians and charlatans helped to transform the feasts in wild revels. And when the Ephesians heard that Mark Antony was on his way to visit their city, they decided to welcome him as Dionysus. Young Bacchantes preceded his garlanded chariot; youths dressed as Satyrs and Pan followed it to the accompaniment of flutes and pipes. They called him Hercules and Bacchus. Antony found that in Ephesus his whims and desires could be limitless.

At last he chose Tarsus as his seat of residence, and summoned Kings and vassals to present themselves to do him homage. Tarsus was a flourishing port on the Gulf of Alexandretta, at the eastern corner where it joins the Mediterranean, on the mouth of the river Cydnus, at the foot of Mount Taurus, opposite the island of Cyprus and the city of Antioch. It was a keypoint, from which had marched the armies that had sought to conquer, from the Syrian base, the kingdoms of Armenia, Media and Persia —what the Romans called the land of the unconquerable Parthians. Strangely, the river Cydnus was full of papyrus reeds. Towards its mouth, the river spread out forming a lake, that gave an idyllic aspect to the city.

From Tarsus Mark Antony sent out his summons: and the Kings of Antioch and Sysima, the Satraps Palemon and Herod who reigned in Judea, and Adallas of Sidonia, and the Tetrarchs of Lycaonia and Pontus, and the rulers of Thracia and of Arabia, all duly came, along the dusty roads, on horseback or by litters, on elephants or on chariots drawn by oxen, and followed by long files of dromedaries carrying the luggage with Oriental pomp; and all came to render homage to Mark Antony on whose pleasure depended the continuance of their domains. Installed in a luxurious tent, Antony received the suppliants with great ceremony and dealt out his favours. Soon the Kings and Satraps learnt the advisability of being accompanied by their wives and daughters, or better still, of sending them alone. The beautiful Glaphyra secured the throne of Phrygia for her son; the young widow of Aristobulus was confirmed on the throne; even Mariamne, the devoted wife of Herod the Great, succeeded, in spite of her reserve, in winning what she desired for her husband. But Cleopatra had not come.

Ever since their last encounter after the fateful Ides of March, Mark Antony had dreamed of the beautiful Queen of Egypt. What was she really like? What were her real feelings towards him? In the old days she had always been discreet, perhaps careful not to give Caesar grounds for jealousy. But she had not answered his repeated summons and he had been forced to send Dellius as an Ambassador.

And now Dellius had brought back the promise that the Queen would arrive " before the days will shorten ".

IV

MARK ANTONY was seated on his curule chair in the Tribunal, in the public market, when the clear air of the morning was suddenly filled with the clamour of a crowd coming from the port. A strange tale was passing from mouth to mouth that Aphrodite had arrived. The daughter of Zeus, the crowd was saying, was sailing up river on a golden galley.

The whole city was soon on the quay shouting with wonder and acclamation to the approaching vessel.

It was indeed a marvellous sight. Having cruised

slowly up the coast of Syria, along Ptolemais and Tyrus and Berytus and on to Heraclea and across the gulf of Issus, Cleopatra's royal galley had entered in the suitable hours of the morning the mouth of the river Cydnus, and was advancing majestically into the pool.

The magnificence of the Queen's ship and of all the fleet was beyond imagination. Sails dyed in the scarlet of Tyre adorned the Queen's galley—the famous " purple sails " that were spoken of in wonder in all ports of the Mediterranean—and upon the riggings the crowd from the shore could distinguish little Nereids, waving fans and scattering roses. The very sails appeared to be made of stout silk, and purple draperies covered the decks. Fifty oarsmen rowed rhythmically, to a measure of music, and the three banks of oars were tipped with silver.

From the bridge rose a golden shell, under an awning of gold embroidery; and upon the shell reclined the Queen herself surrounded by the symbols with which the painters and sculptors had always depicted her. From the galley wafted a light smoke, and the breeze carried to the shore the perfume of incense and cinnamon. And the crowd shouted: " Venus has come to visit Bacchus! "

Antony sent Dellius to welcome " the Queen of Beauty " and convey an invitation to dine with him in the evening. Dellius returned with the reply that the Queen warmly appreciated the invitation from the Triumvir, but she wished, on this first evening, to have him as her guest. It was more than proper etiquette; a kindly worded acceptance was conveyed to the Royal ship, which had, in the meantime, cast anchor in the pool, and stood in full view of the people of Tarsus.

Many hours before sunset, Cleopatra began her toilette.

The hour of her bath was the hour when Cleopatra adored herself. The water in the marble basin was just deep enough to cover her as she lay in its warm and clear embrace. All parts of her body she could thus contemplate and caress. Her skin had the glow of blond tortoiseshell; the lines of her supple legs seemed longer in the azure transparency of the perfumed water. Her entire body was so firm and light, that she could raise it in the water on the pressure of two fingers. It floated gently, and then it fell back upon the marble with a soft splash of water that mounted upon her breasts and touched her rounded chin. She examined, almost appraised with the expert eyes of a beautiful woman every limb of her body —the mother-of-pearl translucency of her skin, the smooth firmness of her breasts, the suppleness of her stomach, the roundness of her thighs, whilst her mirror told her the beauty of her face, of her eyes and her mouth that could be as ardent as a flame.

She played with her hair and her breasts like a young girl. Then she rose from her bath, and her rosy feet shone upon the floor. A Nubian slave gave her a vigorous rubbing: this massage gave her skin a fresh glow, that made it almost transparent. Two other slaves rubbed all her body with oil of nard from Sidon.

Cleopatra reclined upon a couch, and one maid blanched her dainty hands with lotion of hissop; another polished her rosy nails with powdered mother-of-pearl; and another touched with carmine the toes of her tiny feet.

Then the Queen went to her dressing-table. Her hairdresser passed a large sponge over the silky hair that was the colour of amber, and dried it between two towels. Then plunging the sponge into a jar of perfumed oil, she caressed the shoulders and back of the Queen before rubbing her with a rough cloth.

In the sunny light, the chevelure still damp and heavy shone like a shaft of rain traversed by the sun-rays. The dresser held it in both hands and twisted it. She gave it two twists, that turned it entirely; fixed it with straight golden pins, and enclosed the coil in a large green ribbon which she crossed three times over to give relief to the sheen of the silk.

Cleopatra followed the swift work of her dresser in a round mirror of polished silver that a slave held in front of her. She saw the dark hands of the girl moving within the glossy depth of her hair, modelling her tresses with a deft touch. The dresser had come from Persia, Iras by name, and none had been more skilful with the Queen's flowing tresses. Iras invented a different style each day and the change always made a subject of conversation between the Queen and her favourite Iras. Today the hair must be dressed suitably to hold the plain diadem, for the Queen must appear both majestic and seductive to Antony.

When the hairs were satisfactorily dressed, another attendant brought a large box of chased gold lined with rosewood, which contained all kinds of rouge and cosmetics. With a tiny brush of camel-hair, the beautifier took from one compartment of the box a small amount of dark paste, and passed it over the Queen's eyelids, long and curved, so that the eyes appeared a deeper blue. Two swift strokes of a dark pencil made them longer and more languid; a bluish powder made the lids heavier; two touches of vivid vermilion accentuated the corners of the eyes, where tears descend sometimes.

Then the attendant passed, very lightly, the rouge over

the Queen's face and over her breasts; with a feather of the softest camel-hair, that she plunged into ceruse, she traced white lines along the arms and round the neck; and with a little brush charged with carmine she touched with scarlet Cleopatra's lips and the points of her breasts. Her fingers, which had spread on the cheeks a light cloud of red dust, marked now at the level of the hips the three deep folds of the waist, and in the rounded back she marked two dimples that seemed to move. Then, with a leather puff soaked in rouge, she touched delicately the elbows, and gave brilliance to the fingernails. The make-up of the Queen was finished.

The women in charge of the robes came in. They brought a great chest in which the robes lay without a crease. They laid the robes out, for the Queen to choose. She chose an emerald-coloured tunic, fastened at the shoulders by the clasps of rosy pearls. It was made of Sidonian silk worked in a very close weave, and afterwards transformed patiently in an open-work pattern by the Nile's craftsmen who released the threads by pulling the tissue.([1]) The tunic left bare the arms and the bosom. Over the Queen's breasts was hung a transparent veil, made by the women of the island of Cos, so light and transparent that it was said to be woven of morning mist. Then another attendant fixed on her bare feet sandals of the whitest and softest kid, with soles of thin gold and held by a fastening in the shape of a winged scarab; and the lady-jeweller adorned her arms with precious bracelets and placed at her ears the famous and huge pear-shaped pink pearls.

At sunset the golden galley traversed the calm water

---

[1] Lucan's—Description of Cleopatra.

of the pool, manœuvring silently, her huge purple sails hanging loosely at the masts, only the silver-tipped oars quivering in and out of the water that the setting sun made opalescent. Two rudders shaped like sculls steered the ship, and the pilot held himself stiff and straight on the poop, under a canopy cut like an elephant's head made of gold, with the trunk turned up in the air. On the deck musicians played a slow sensuous melody upon flutes and harps.

The Queen rested on a couch of purple, shaded by a canopy of golden tissue. At her sides four Cupids fanned her with flabella of ostrich feathers that were reserved for the Egyptian Queen. From the censers and burners rose a scented smoke.

The ship came to rest alongside the quay, and Mark Antony, dressed in a light silver breastplate beautifully chased to represent Vulcan beating upon the anvil the arms for Achilles, his head erect, his beard and face perfumed, every nerve alert in his impatience, went on board, followed by his most brilliant officers.

The first meeting with the Queen was full of amiabilities. It was certainly not the encounter of the Triumvir of Rome coming to ask this reluctant Queen to render account for her absenteeism during the war. If any such intention was ever in Antony's mind, the Queen gave him no opportunity.

Cleopatra received Mark Antony as a demi-goddess, and Antony was too much of an actor not to enjoy the decor.

The decoration of the deck and riggings, the subtle music, the perfumes, the enchantment of the crepuscular hour, all made an exquisite setting to Cleopatra's beauty. At once Antony thought of her as both frightening and adorable—never had he beheld a more extraordinary and desirable creature!

The Queen took him by the hand, and together they descended to the banqueting hall, followed by their Court and suites. Twelve double couches were laid, encircling the raised couch of the Queen and her guest. The couches were covered with rich silken carpets, the cushions were embroidered in gay colours; each table was laid with golden vessels encrusted with gems; the goblets were of gold and of exquisite workmanship. Tapestries of golden tissues hung on the wall; the floor was spread with roses.

Antony could not restrain his impulsive admiration of the magnificent reception; and Cleopatra, declaring her hospitality utterly unworthy of her guest and friend, begged him to accept all the vessels that were used at the banquet—plates and platters and urns and amphoras, goblets, bowls and vases and the couches and tapestries as well.

When they returned on the bridge, Antony and his suite let themselves go in a joyful applause. A display of lights decorated the whole ship, lanterns of varied colours were suspended in circles and stars amidst a pergola of branches in bloom; the elegant dresses and costumes of the guests transformed the scene into a wonderful masque. From the shore the crowd enjoyed the view and acclaimed Antony and Cleopatra a Royal pair.

Full of wine and desire Antony invited the Queen to dine with him in his residence the following night; but very subtly Cleopatra convinced him to sup again with her and bring his military court.

The second banquet was of such splendour that none of the Roman officers had ever seen or imagined the like.

Not only did each guest receive as a gift the vessels and their couch, but the Queen gave them, as a souvenir, the litters which had called for them at their quarters and conveyed them to the ship, and to the litters she added the slaves that carried them and two beautiful Ethiopian boys to act as pages and torch-bearers, and to the highest in rank she made presents of splendid horses caparisoned in gold.

On the third day Cleopatra deigned at last to dine with Antony, who had ransacked the city of Tarsus to organise a banquet worthy of the Queen. But it was so inferior that Antony was the first to ridicule the meanness and vulgarity of his treat. Whereas the brilliant conversation, that Caesar used to enjoy, had enlivened the receptions on board the Royal ship, the rustic humour that marked Antony's feast savoured more of the camp than of the Court. But the Queen was quick to fall into the same vein, and played upon Antony without the least reserve. And thus was Antony completely seduced, until his love and concupiscence for Cleopatra knew no bounds.

Those days at Tarsus became famous in history as a series of revels of unsurpassable splendour.

The fourth night Cleopatra gave a banquet to all the Roman officers. The guests reached their places marching upon a carpet of roses, a mattress of soft petals, kept in place by a net held tight to the walls: the historians have recorded that this floral carpet cost more than the equivalent of ten thousand pounds.

Day by day the fantastic merry-making went on. Cleopatra stopped at nothing to display before Antony her opulence and her charm. Her purpose was to bring him to conclude with Egypt an alliance against Octavian as usurper of the rightful succession of her son Caesarion.

If by now Antony had lost his reason, Cleopatra had kept hers. Her mind was stronger than her emotions. Entirely Mark Antony was forgetting to discuss the political problems; it was Cleopatra who brought them to the point between revels and flirtations. Her sole aim was to bring about a rupture between Antony and Octavian, to make them stand one against the other, and to use Antony as the mighty warrior to defeat in open conflict his opponent and be the sole ruler of Rome and defender of Caesarion. Even now, in the otia of Tarsus, her couriers brought her informations that, as a result of the cowardly conduct of Octavian at Philippi, the Roman army was solidly behind Mark Antony.

She used every artifice, every feminine ruse, every seduction to make of Antony an ardent and submissive lover. The delicacy of her person, the vivaciousness of her character, the caressing seduction of her voice, her beauty that was neither astonishing nor unequalled but derived an inimitable force from her wit, and her fascinating manner which was absolutely irresistible—she made use of all her charms. She realized that a man of Antony's nature could not be kept waiting too long in love; but she led him to dream of the incomparable pleasures that were still to come. Her political ambition was banking upon the craving of this Herculean sensualist, who was only too keen to display his prowess in the alcove: and as a counterpart to love, there rose all round them the tangible show of Cleopatra's immense and inexhaustible wealth. From her arms Antony would, she hoped, jump to battle, supported by the unlimited wealth of Egypt that would flow from her treasury for the purpose of avenging the injustice done to herself and her son.

She astounded Antony, however, with a request of the

most terrible cruelty: that her sister Arsinoë, who, fleeing from her vengeance after Caesar's death, had taken refuge in the temple of Diana at Ephesus, should be put to death together with the High Priest Megabyzus who had taken the Egyptian Princess under his protection. Arsinoë was, no doubt, an ambitious and audacious woman, who had never ceased to agitate for her own rights to the throne of Egypt, and in that very moment was intriguing with the Lord Chamberlain of Alexandria, and also the Viceroy of Cyprus, Serapion, was in the conspiracy, as he had shown when he had placed his small fleet at the disposal of Cassius in the war against Antony.

The request was not to Antony's taste, who still had in his memory the happy days he had spent at Ephesus. Nevertheless, he gave at last his consent to the execution of Arsinoë, who was killed on the steps of the altar in the temple of Artemis. The High Priest Megabyzus was rescued and eventually graced as a special favour to the people of Ephesus who threatened revolt. The Viceroy, as disloyal both to his Queen and to Rome, was executed without regret.

Soon afterwards Cleopatra ended her visit to Tarsus. Antony had promised that before the winter came he would join the Queen in Egypt—to fall into every excess of puerile amusements and offer to the shrine of love and luxury the greatest of sacrifices, Time.([1])

V

ANTONY arrived in Alexandria before the winter.

The people of Alexandria awaited the arrival of the Roman Triumvir with mixed feelings. Was he coming as a new ruler on behalf of Rome or merely as a new lover

---

[1] Plutarch.

for the Queen? Then it was announced that the visitor would disembark unpretentiously, simply as a friend returning the courtesy visit of the Queen; and the Alexandrians decided to give him a warm welcome.

Cleopatra, however, meant to invest the reception with the greatest splendour. The display she had shown at Tarsus was to remain insignificant in comparison with the gorgeousness she had planned to show Antony in Alexandria. Everything was calculated to impress Mark Antony with her unequalled wealth and power. Decorators had been called to the Palace from Greece and the cities of the East, and prizes had been offered to those who would invent the finest decorations and the newest entertainments.

The streets of Alexandria, decorated with welcoming arches and carpets and flags, were to appear, almost by contrast, in their natural grandeur. The ceremonial reception was to start at the Palace doors.

Cleopatra received Antony on the first step of the Palace, surrounded by her mitred Priests swinging censers. Behind the Queen stood her Ministers and her Court in their richest array. As Antony approached, the Queen cast toward him a gilded laurel branch and came down the steps alone to greet him. On bended knee Mark Antony saluted her, at first with the Roman salute, then with outstretched arms in Oriental adoration. His richly chased breastplate and the flowing scarlet mantle of a Roman Commander enhanced his handsome features. They ascended the steps into the Palace in courtly attitude, Antony holding with two fingers the hand of the Queen on his right.

The visit had been planned on both sides with a deep

political purpose. For Antony, this visit was to bear three fruits: firstly, an offensive and defensive alliance with the Queen, so that he could count on her treasury, her army and most of all on her fleet; secondly, the invasion of the land of the Parthians, possibly in the spring of the following year, so that the glory of this victory achieved with the Queen's help would stand for Antony as one of the greatest in the history of Rome; and thirdly, to enable Antony to sweep the effete and unsoldierly Octavian from Rome and proclaim himself the undisputed ruler of the Roman world. Afterwards he would give reality to Caesar's great plan: he would make himself King, marry the beautiful and powerful Queen Cleopatra and found a dynasty: and, by the Gods, he was young and strong enough to leave after him his own Heir. As for Caesarion —there was plenty of time to think of Caesar's child, and love can smooth all paths.

Antony's relations with Octavian were already strained. Octavian's behaviour at Philippi had disgusted the gallant and valiant Antony; the Triumvirate was utterly compromised and reduced to a Diarchy; the people of Rome would not hesitate to choose between a victorious and triumphant Mark Antony and the feeble nephew and adoptive son of Caesar. Filled with these hopes Antony had, before his departure for Alexandria, disposed in what he considered a wise way of his affairs in the Eastern Provinces: with the Senate's approval, he had left the provisional command of the troops in Syria to Decidius Saxa, one of his best Generals, an old soldier brought up under Caesar, and Saxa was to keep him informed of the movements of the Parthians and begin to prepare a campaign. Antony knew that the King of the Parthians, Orodes, had secured the services of a renegade Roman

General, Quintus Labienus, who had fought with the forces of Cassius and Brutus, and Labienus was now busy reorganizing the Parthian army for an attack on the neighbouring Roman Provinces. A war was therefore inevitable; hence Antony's impatience to make a military alliance with Cleopatra.

On the very day of his departure from Tarsus, the couriers had brought him news that in Rome the situation was entering an acute phase and his brother Lucius Antonius and his own wife Fulvia were making ready to launch a full-scale attack on Octavian. This news was both perplexing and upsetting, for Fulvia had no business to meddle in politics and start a quarrel which might soon develop into another civil war; but on the other hand, even if he should give up this journey to Egypt—so attractive and so full of promise—and return to Rome, he knew that his present position would not permit a successful campaign against Octavian and might end catastrophically. Antony was not a great statesman nor an astute diplomat; he decided, therefore, to remain outside the present trouble in Rome and let the Senate and the people think that he was deeply absorbed in the Eastern affairs, and in the meantime seek the far reaching advantages that Cleopatra's friendship seemed to offer.

As for Cleopatra, the Queen's objectives were unaltered: her ambition, her dream, the future of her son Caesarion. That the stay of Antony in Egypt and their life together in Alexandria might have any other effect and another result upon her heart did not cross her vivid imagination. The Gods alone could alter the course.

From the confidential letters and reports of the Captain Quintus Dellius, A.D.C. to Mark Antony in Alexandria, to the Lady Fulvia in Rome.

" It is quite clear that the Queen is out to conquer Antony. Every seduction is displayed, and his inclination to be a playboy is exploited to the full. At the Palace the revels go on day and night, and this city of Alexandria offers every incentive to laxity in morals.

" Antony has taken to go about in Greek dress, wearing white Attic shoes, and the Queen acts the part of a Bacchante. What is strange is that she never leaves his side day or night; she sits up until dawn to interminable banquets, and in the daytime she rides with him to the hunt, goes fishing with him, goes camel-riding along the edge of the desert, never tiring or wearying, always ready for anything. In this respect, she is certainly a most remarkable woman, for in the morning, while he sleeps out his wine, she works with her Ministers and looks after the education of her young son.

" The banquets at the Palace are beyond everything one can see in our Rome. They are real Oriental orgies. One evening, while waiting for the Royal pair to return, I went to the kitchens, and seeing eight boars ready on the spits I asked the chef whether there was an exceptional large company for dinner. ' Oh, no,' he replied, ' only that we never know at what time the Roman Triumvir is ready to eat, and as the meat has to be served to the right point, it is necessary to keep cooking one animal at a time so as to have them always ready to the minute.' And as regards the menus we are served, it would leave our Lentulus Niger speechless. We have five or six courses of fish, oysters, mussels, sea-hogs with asparagus; then we have capons, pies and patties of fish and venison, many kinds of sea fruits and lobsters and polypuses cooked in spicy sauces, and partridges, cutlets of deer and gazelles, pheasants inside sweet crusts, big game, piglets stuffed with beccassins and quails, ducks and turkeys and pea- cocks roasted and served with all their wonderful feathers, woodcocks in all kinds of sauces, tunny fish of Calchedony, sturgeons of Rhodes, lampreys, and patisserie of many kinds that I had never tasted before, and wonderful fruit from the East.

" The dinners go on interminably, till one is really tired, until they end in a *commissatio* presided by an *Arbiter bibendi*, who acts as a Master of Pleasures, one of which consists in mixing various wines into a huge bowl. We lie on the couches crowned with roses; the slaves pour upon our hair cinnamon oil, and now and then rare per- fumes are sprayed into the room and over the guests, mixing with the wines in the cups with the most intoxicating effect. The banquets are enlivened by shows, musical turns and displays of dancing by young women lightly in veils. I must say that the services at the tables are superb: besides the plates and cups of gold en- crusted with precious stones, we are served with a kind of light pottery, almost white, which the Queen calls her Kerama, of exquisite workmanship.

" Antony is certainly in his ideal milieu, and enjoys himself challenging the savants, that the Queen invites to ennoble the conversation, to a show of resistance to the wines. The other night, when Antony was praising her cellar, the Queen told him that Egypt can really be considered the country of good wines, since it was the Egyptian colony of Byblos that was the first great wine centre of antiquity, and the Goddess Osiris took the re- sponsibility for wine from the Asiatic Gods, and wine was sacred in Egypt and the vines were grown, in ancient times, in temple precincts only and the great vineyards and vintages still bear religious names. ' I will take you,' she told Antony, ' to Memphis, where you will be able to order a bottle of Blest-be-Horne-the-first-of-Heaven . . . ' ' By heavens', replied our Antony, ' I shall have to take over Byblos as a personal appannage! Does our adjective bibulous come from Byblos? '

" Yesterday we went fishing on Lake Mareotis, and Antony, to play a joke on the company, had arranged for a diver to attach a fish to his line as soon as his hook went under water. On the afternoon the Queen, who had seen through the game, had a salt fish from Pontus fixed on Antony's hook. The company roared with laughter, and the Queen told him : ' Leave your fishing line, O General, to the meek sovereigns of Pharos and Canopus. You must play with cities and kingdoms! '

" I think, however, that these attempts to awaken a longing for heroic deeds are entirely wasted upon Antony. For our life is nothing but a continuous revel and waste of time."

" The Queen has had an idea, and has formed a Club of the Inimitables. Is it an attempt to give some dignity to our debauch? The Society has, like everything here, a Greek name, *Amime Tobioi,* literally the Insurpassable Revellers, and it is a club of wealthy Alexandrian gentlemen who are giving parties in turn and each must outdo the others in luxury and original entertainments. I hear that fortunes are lavished on these feasts, for there is much competition between the bloods of this wealthy city, and many of them hope, by pleasing our Mark Antony, to gain favour with their lovely Queen. Antony is surely a success at these parties, as I have heard it said that they had never met another man who could talk as enormously as he can eat and drink. And when he is up to it—don't we know it!—his conversation knows no bounds. One night he spoke of his wives, and described the beauties of his first wife Antonia, and told of how he had stolen your Ladyship from his friend Clodius long before he married you, and then he went on and on, drinking pitcher after pitcher of Cyprus wine, and saying that he was happy in Egypt as he had never been in his life and what they were doing in Rome it mattered nothing to him."

"The Society of Inimitables must have run short of amusements, for the Queen and Antony have now re-coursed to a new game, which consists in dressing themselves as servants, with a mask over their faces and going out at night through the poorer district of the city and hammering upon the doors and awaking the peaceful citizens, and at times rough quarrels are the result.

"They have taken to visit in such disguise the Rhakotis, which is the most disreputable district of the city, filled with lewd houses and fetid taverns that are the favourite haunts of sailors. Sure it is, my Lady Fulvia, that this city of Alexandria is a most licentious place. Along the quay every evening at sunset the courtesans take their stands and await for clients. There are, in this city, courtesans of all kinds and from all countries, and for all tastes and purses. Some are well-known, some even famous; and these dress in gay and light silks, a material for dresses that our ladies in Rome do not know as yet; and they wear sandals of gilt leather. There are others who are quite poor and miserable, and stand on the quay barefooted. All these courtesans, I must say, are beautiful and attractive, and all go, at sunset, to the wall that is called the Keramik because it is beautifully tiled with plaques of enamelled pottery of the most lovely colours and designs. It is, this wall, one of the sights of Alexandria; but no less a sight is to see the courtesans take their stand along this gorgeous wall. Each one has her regular pit, and, sometimes, when they get there they find a message chalked on the wall: ' Phrines—Timon son of Tyresias—two gold sovereigns.' It means that the gentleman called Timon son of some rich merchant Tyresias, will pay Phrines two gold sovereigns if she will wait for him. And the girl will stand there, and the passers by will all read that she has secured a good client for the night.

" It is by now clear to everybody that my Lord Antony is deeply in love with the Queen. Does he really love her or is it merely infatuation? And does the Queen love him? Sure it is that she permits him exhibitions of his passion for her that do away with every sign of modesty and self-respect. He does not hide his continuous desire of her: he seizes her and enjoys her at the most unexpected moments, barely screened by a curtain from the eyes of servants and slaves. Only the other night he took her suddenly away from the supper-room, lifting her in his mighty arms from their couch of ivory and gold, and after a short while they returned to their table, smiling. It was really shocking."

" A most disgusting episode has just been reported to me, for I was not invited to this new treat. There is, on the outskirts of Alexandria, a most extraordinary place, which is called the temple of Aphrodite-Astarté, but is in reality nothing else than a place of the most shocking depravity. The garden is quite beautiful, full of flowers and shaded groves, and it looks, at first sight, a marvellous little forest along the shore of the blue sea, traversed by delightful brooks of clear water and lakes designed two centuries ago by an ancestor of Queen Cleopatra. This garden is now a city in itself, dedicated to Love. All around it runs a circular terrace, which encloses it like a ring, some forty feet high and eighty stadia long. In this compound, that is called the city of Aphrodite, are fifteen hundred little houses in which live a like number of Priestesses of the Goddess of Love. These women come from all parts of the world; I am told that there are women of seventy different races and countries. The most beautiful come from the kingdoms of Asia; every year the ships bring to Alexandria no less than one hundred fresh beauties for the temple of Aphrodite and the services in the sacred garden. There are young girls from Persia, Judea, Phrygia, Ecbatana, Babylonia; some come from the lands along the Ganges in India, and these are dark of skin, with large brown eyes that have a dreamy look; and the Persians and Armenians have exquisite profiles, and breasts as round as pomegranates of ivory, and those who are from Africa have a skin the colour of earth after the rain, and they wear big golden rings through their noses, and they have hair short and crisp just touching their square shoulders. And there are others who come from countries utterly unkown to me, and speak languages that no one understands, I am told, except that their rites of love are not much dissimilar than all other women's. There are girls with eyes that seem cut obliquely, and these have hair black as jet and smooth like polished ebony. And there are women from the North, fair of hair and white and pink of flesh, with robust limbs and broad white breasts; and there are women from Sarmatia who wear their hair in triple long tresses; and women from Scythia who look like animals; and gigantic German women whose hair is almost white; and there are women from Spain with silken breasts and heavy dark heads. And all these fifteen hundred women live each in one of the little houses that fill this amazing garden of love, and the houses are all alike; with two rooms, one open to the onlookers, where the women sit all dressed up and adorned, upon a kind of high platform during the hours when the men from the city visit the garden; and the other room is for the lovers when they want to retire, for one brief visit or for the night. Upon the door of each little house—a door of red copper, that is a metal dedicated to Aphrodite—there hangs a phallus for door-hammer, which beats upon an organ of the female sex, and under this strange door-hammer is engraved the name of the occupant of the house.

" In the little peristyle of the house there is a pleasant little court of marble with an oval basin that may serve as bath, and on the end wall is the altar, of pink granite. Each woman devotes her life to the temple, and gives to the temple half her earnings: the rest she may keep for her needs and her ornaments. They are not slaves, they are not public prostitutes; they are Nuns dedicated to Aphrodite-Astarté. When they grow old, they must leave their little houses and find a quiet corner in the garden and set up their private altar on a flat stone; and they are visited sometimes by the poorer men, or they do the housework for the younger and more fortunate ones. Even their children of female sex, if they happen to become mothers, belong to the temple: the Hierophante dedicates them on the first day of their life, deflowering them with a little golden knife, as Aphrodite does not like virginity. Then, when they grow up, they enter the Didascalion, the College of Aphrodite, a grand building behind the temple, and for seven years they are trained in the theory and practice of all the arts of love: the way to look at men, the way to embrace, the swaying of the body, the complication of caresses, the secrets of erotic refinements and kisses. Each pupil, at the end of her training, chooses her day of first experience, for the desire is an order from the Goddess, which each girl must obey and not repress; and afterwards she is granted one of the little houses along the terrace.

" The temple of Aphrodite, the Great Goddess, is the most venerated in this city of Alexandria. It is a colossal edifice more than three hundred feet long, built high above the gardens, upon a platform reached by seventeen huge steps. Its doors are of solid gold, and are guarded by twelve hermaphrodite hierodules, symbols of the two instruments of love and of the twelve hours of the night. The entry to the temple is turned towards North-west, in the direction of Paphos; and the rays of the sun never penetrate the sanctuary of the Goddess of nocturnal love. The eighty-six columns of the temple front are of purple marble to half-way up, while the upper part is snowy white, like a woman's body disengaging itself in its whiteness from a reddish gown.

" Along the epistyle and the metope runs a frieze of erotic and fabulous ornamentations: Centauresses mounted by stallions, goats raped by Satyrs, Naiads covered by stags, Bacchantes loved by tigers, and lionesses caught by mythical griffins. It is an exaltation of the sexual urge, the symbol of the procreating sources: Leda guiding with her hand the amorous swan; Sirene and Glaucos dying in the very fulfilment of love; Pan the Eternal seizing a wild Amadryade; and above all rises

158

16. Coin of Mark Antony.

Aphrodite, Mother of Love.

"Each year a great competition takes place, in the presence of all the fifteen hundred women of the temple, and the competitors endeavour to surpass one another in erotic imagination, for the twelve prizes entitle the winners to enter the Cotytteion. This is a most mysterious monument, of triangular shape, the base of which was time ago the temple of Goddess Cotytto, in whose name there were accomplished the most terrible debaucheries, things that I am fain to repeat, and that I know only by hearsay. On the other two sides of the triangle are eighteen little houses, in which live thirty-six of these prize-winners, who are so greatly sought after by connoiseurs that they do not accept in payment less than one mina of gold. Once a month, at full moon, they meet in the inner garden of this special temple, drunken with aphrodisiac potions, their waist encircled by the ritual phallus. The eldest must drink a lethal dose of an amorous philtre, and the knowledge that she is going to die urges her to try without fear or shame the most dangerous voluptuousness; she becomes the centre of a terrible orgy, and amidst the howling of pleasure and pain, dances and tears, surrounded and pressed by the other thirty-five naked and raving companions, in a spasm of luxury and an agony of demoniac love, she dies. It is said that these thirty-six women of Cotytto cannot live longer than three years, so fast are they consumed by their sapience of love.

"I am loth to say, my Lady Fulvia, that the day before yesterday, the Queen and my Lord Antony went, unmasked, to watch the festival of the Cotytteion in the Garden of Aphrodite-Astarté."

159

VI

Was Cleopatra really in love with Antony? We shall never know for certain; one can only surmise. Her years of nubile existence, interrupted only by the brief interlude with Caesar—the early marriage of her little brother one can discount as an " official " act—had given her a fierce reserve. Those long years, however, had left in her life a sentimental emptiness which needed to be filled. And because the contrast between Caesar and Antony was intellectually so great, Cleopatra felt a strong inclination and love for this young man who was both a savage and a vainglorious playboy, and who gave her with abundance the physical satisfaction that her nature demanded.

Caesar had fascinated her; notwithstanding her wilfulness, her unflinching ambition, Cleopatra had been spellbound before his incomparable mind and power. But with Antony it was different. Cleopatra had not reckoned with the hot blood of prime manhood.

Antony had a personal charm that outweighed all his shortcomings. He possessed in a rare degree those gifts that win the affection of a woman.

But why, one is brought to ask, did Cleopatra bring Antony down to the level of sensual debauchery? This question, if documentarily answered, could disclose the fascinating mystery of Cleopatra's nature and soul. The true soul of a woman is ruled by her sex; only exceptionally it is controlled by her mind. The struggle between Cleopatra's nature and her mind must have been hard and continuous. In her blood was the degeneracy of fourteen generations of dissolute Ptolemy Kings, and the environment of her very life, the custom and morals of the times and of her city and people allowed for excesses which appear shocking in the present day.

On the other hand—and this is perhaps the answer to the psychological problem of Cleopatra—it may be that the Queen realized that the surest and easiest way to bring Antony to accede to her aims and ambitions was by reaching him through the ways he liked best and most; and any woman knows that the best place to wheedle a man is in bed. Even for a great Queen.

Antony was by now completely infatuated. He liked to play the part of Prince Consort to the Queen of Egypt; and the life of a Satrap at the sumptuous Bruchion suited him to perfection.

Life went on as usual. It was like living in a paradise where two demi-gods could make the world revolve at their whim. The most unexpected follies could spring out, like the scarlet or eburnean flowers that bloomed on the tropical trees in the Royal gardens. One night, the Queen made a wager that she would, next evening, give a banquet that would cost ten thousand minas—an enormous sum, almost one hundred thousand pounds of our day. "What is the wager?" asked Antony. "A Kingdom." Antony looked at the Queen, in her star-covered dress, and laughingly he suggested Phoenicia: "The Phoenician cities of Tyre, Sidon and Berytus will be ideal for you; they will weave their silks and dye them in exquisite colours and send them to you in their carved chests of Lebanon-cedar!"

Yet, it was a mad offer. They touched their fingertips to seal the pact, and the Court echoed with polite and cynical cheers.

The following night, Cleopatra and Antony were

carried into the banqueting hall on their ivory and silken couches and put down at the Royal table which stood above the others, supported by gilded Sphinxes. The guests stood expectantly around the tables laden with golden bowls and platters. From the great silver tripods rose the smoke of the perfumed oil burning in the lamps. At the end of the hall, which was encircled by arcades of alabaster, was a great Sphinx of porphyry, and the mythical image had the features of the Queen, crowned with the Egyptian diadem.

The banquet was splendid, but seemed somewhat dull. Nothing grandiose was happening; no exceptional display or performance. " This dinner," said Antony at last, " is not worth ten thousand minas." " You have not won yet," answered Cleopatra. And she called her cup-bearer, and signalled him to refill the gold cup, that was a marvel of workmanship and was supposed to have been executed in Athens in the splendid days of Pericles. Then she lifted the cup and turning to Antony she said: " Now watch, when I have drunk this my wager will be won."

At this, the Queen unfastened one of her famous pear-shaped earrings of pearls and dropped it negligently into the cup; the wine seemed to foam a little and bubble: the Queen drank it swiftly and then turned the cup downwards. The huge pearl had vanished.

The cup had been filled with a special vinegar into which a pearl dissolved entirely. A cry of surprise and regret went up; but quickly the Queen made ready to sacrifice in the same way her second pearl. " Spare your jewels," cried Antony seizing her wrist. " By the Gods, you have indeed won the wager! Phoenicia is yours."

The cup-bearer wiped the cup with a soft cloth, and refilled it with wine of Chios. The banquet went on.

162

But a name that Antony never mentioned, not even in his cups, was Caesar.

All sentimental factors apart, the situation of Antony was definitely better than that of the Queen. His stay in Alexandria had given he Triumvir the opportunity of remaining outside the political squabbles in Rome. His presence in Italy would have complicated things in his disfavour; on the other hand, by his stay in Alexandria he had secured the support of the financial resources of Egypt and of its armed forces. More than anything else, he had laid the foundation for a final marriage with the Queen whenever such move might appear suitable for the creation of that monarchy which death had denied Caesar. Furthermore, Antony was free, at any time, to re-enter the normal life of Rome, with his hands more or less clean, and no one in Rome would consider him the lesser for having sought his pleasure with Cleopatra in view of the tremendous advantages that such a love affair implied: no politician in Rome would discount the potential benefits of an alliance with the powerful Queen of Egypt or berate Mark Antony for having assumed the position of great protector of the Alexandrian Court.

For Cleopatra, the position was far less advantageous. She had engaged in her alliance with Antony her personal prestige and the vast resources of her kingdom; yet in return she had received nothing but promises given in the alcove. And the situation was that without Antony's help every hope of a Roman-Egyptian Throne for herself and her son Caesarion seemed to dissolve in thin air: worse still, nothing could prevent the passing of her kingdom to the Roman Empire. Two men were holding the future of the Roman World in the balance: Antony and

Octavian, and the second was the uncompromising enemy of the young Caesarion and an adversary of Mark Antony. There was a way open to Cleopatra, and it was to make an alliance with the Parthians: the growing commercial relations of Egypt with India, joined with the influence of the Parthians with Northern India, could be the centre of a formidable League of all the Eastern States hostile to Rome—Egypt, Ethiopia, Arabia, Persia, India, Scythia, Parthia, Armenia, Syria and maybe also Asia Minor. It would certainly have constituted a League capable of crushing the Roman Republic or pushing it back to Italy and the West. But however attractive such an idea might appear, and however feasible might have been its extension to the North-African countries which were more than restive under the Roman rule, its realization was full of complexities, while the Alliance with Antony offered easier and more tangible results.

And there was one fact, psychological rather than political, but nevertheless of the highest importance in the situation: and it was that with every passing month Cleopatra felt still more deeply attached to Antony, indeed, she was with child by him. However grieved, resentful or even suspicious she might feel of this man who seemed careless, fickle and as imponderable as a playboy, she felt that she had now fatally placed the defence of her cause on the father of her future child, and there was no retreat from it.

But Mark Antony had left a wife in Rome, and this wife was determined not to surrender Antony to Cleopatra. Moreover, she meant to force the issue, whatever the means, whatever the costs. For Fulvia was no less passionate in love than her third husband Antony, and she possessed infinitely more determination than he. She knew only too well that Antony was faithless and by nature greedy for new women; and she knew equally well of Cleopatra's charms. There was only one means, Fulvia thought, of wrenching Antony from Cleopatra's arms, and it was civil war between Antony and Octavian; and thus she resolved upon this course.

Her letters to Antony in Alexandria began to create strident interruptions in the Egyptian idyll. By forged mandates Fulvia interfered in the distribution of the land allotted to the Legions; she seized eighteen cities of the Empire with troops loyal to Antony, and distributed to them the land, inciting the Legions belonging to Octavian to revolt. Then, with a theatrical gesture, she fled from Rome with Antony's brother Lucius, accompanied by many Knights and Senators, and occupied the fortress of Preneste. The unsoldierly Octavian had no alternative but to start on the pursuit of this new Antony-Fulvia's Party, and succeeded in encircling the forces of Lucius in Perugia.

Soon dispatches arrived in Alexandria telling the results of Fulvia's madness: Lucius in Perugia had surrendered, Octavian had cleverly spared him, but in revenge had burned the city, and on the anniversary of Caesar's death had four hundred Senators and Knights executed in front of Caesar's temple in Rome as a salutary lesson not to disobey Caesar's will, who had appointed the mild Octavian as his rightful successor! At the same time, Octavian sent messengers to Alexandria to make it clear to Antony that he considered that only Fulvia was responsible for this war. Indeed, Fulvia fled from Italy with three thousand cavalry, taking ship from Brindisi for Athens; Antony's mother was with her, and the two women put themselves under the protection of both Antony's and Octavian's enemy, Sextus Pompey! And to make the drama more complete, the new civil war in Rome prompted the Parthians to make fresh inroads into the bordering Roman Provinces that were under Antony's control, and the revolt was fast spreading, for the Syrian Princes made an alliance with the Parthians and the Parthians were penetrating Syria from the Euphrates.

Mark Antony awoke, somewhat with difficulty, from an amorous slumber and bout of intoxication.([1]) He told Cleopatra that he must depart immediately. The situation, indeed his personal position, brooked no delay. His forces in the East had no chance of resisting the Parthian invaders; and his other Legions in Italy and in Macedonia, even if still loyal, were certainly busy in their quarters. He must end abruptly his most pleasant stay in Alexandria.

The last straw was the arrival of a personal messenger from Fulvia now in Athens: she had selected as messenger an old comrade-in-arms of Antony's, Aenobarbus, of the ancient family, one of the bravest Generals, who in all campaigns had always rendered valuable aid to his Chief. When this soldier of the old school arrived at the Bruchion and was conducted in the perfumed apartment of Antony, and found his Commander arrayed in a silken robe, with a scimitar in his girdle and a turban on his head adorned with a large emerald, the old soldier clasped his hands upon his battered cuirass, and overcome by surprise he cried out: "Mark Antony!"

When the day of departure was near, Cleopatra took

---

[1] Plutarch—*Life of Mark Antony.*

Antony to consult her personal astrologer, Sisogenus. The astrologer lived in a high tower, that was reached by three hundred and sixty-five steps, as many as the number of the nights in which the stars in Heaven revealed their horoscopes.

The magician was draped in a yellow gown with a conical hat upon his head. The Queen asked: " What fate awaits the Triumvir when he will land on Roman territory once more? "

The astrologer traced some signs upon the fine sand of the terrace at the very top of the tower; then, with his lean body bent back and his palms outstretched, he gazed into the sky. Then he seized his wand and pointed to the planet under which Antony was born:

" Clear and brilliant it is approaching its zenith! " But suddenly the star grew dim; it drew near another star; but a moment later the second star seemed to fade away and the first shone again in all its splendour. " The second star " said the magician, " is Octavian's star. For a moment it will seem to make Antony's star pale. But then it will fade away."

Antony was no less impressed than Cleopatra by what they had seen in the Heavens with their very eyes. They descended the steps of the tower in great elation. Antony told Cleopatra that the previous night he had seen himself in a dream, walking in a field of flowers: all at once he had felt an obstacle, almost a barrier across his path, then he had walked all covered with sweat, as though he had just escaped from some peril. His dream tallied with the vision of the star.

Nevertheless, when the day of parting came, Cleopatra felt that an element of tragedy was entering her life. It was the beginning of March, and she was three months gone with child. Antony requested her to abstain from taking any initiative of military help until such moment as he would be in a position to send her directions as to the best ways of helping their common cause. She was, therefore, forced to an indefinite period of inaction and profound anxiety. And she must wait the birth of her child in solitude, like a mistress abandoned by her lover. And her child, born of a Goddess, would have no recognised father. And yet she must be the Queen, in a loathsome loneliness; and no astrologer could tell her that four long years would pass before she would again meet Mark Antony.

BOOK FOUR

CLEOPATRA AND ROME

BOOK LORE

I

IF words could be like the retarded images of a slow-motion picture on the screen, we could see with our mind's eye the pathetic desolation of Cleopatra during those years of loneliness.

Alone, amidst the unceasing pomp and ritual of her Court and Kingdom; deserted by lover and fate; bereft of hope; awaiting the birth of her bastard child; day after day asking of the Sphinx what would befall Egypt and her Queen.

The ancient historians have brutally brushed aside the Queen's harrowing disillusion. History is a cruel Recorder, and those who eventually emerge as Victors are always far more generously treated than those who succumb as victims: for the loser there is only scorn, impatience, or the pitiless criticism of the errors that might have been avoided.

We thus know that Cleopatra followed eagerly the events after Antony's departure from Alexandria in the spring of the year 40. She had placed near him spies and observers; there was even a soothsayer whom she had sent with him. She had hoped that Antony would soon send his lieutenant to escort her to him; instead, she had to be content with the news and reports that her messengers transmitted; and news and information were invariably alarming.

Thus she learned that at the end of June Antony had

arrived in Athens where the terrible Fulvia was waiting for him.

Antony was in a black mood. He had by now realized that his Egyptian holiday had cost him Italy, where Octavian was now sole master, and also had cost him the East. Syria and Phoenicia had fallen to the Parthians, and there was no chance of recovering those Provinces with the troops still available. His wife's action had cut him off from Italy, and the advancing armies of the Parthians might, at any time, expel him from his own Provinces.

The meeting with Fulvia in Athens was stormy. She contemptuously told Antony to look at himself in a mirror: haggard, pale, dissipated; and anyhow, what did he imagine he would get out of that woman Cleopatra, while the fate of the world was decided in Rome? This rating Antony could not stand, for he looked more Herculean than ever, and his beard was crisp and his face sun-burnt; and anyway, who had given Fulvia mandate to shatter the alliance with Octavian?

As the political trouble caused by Fulvia outweighed by far the marital sins of her philandering husband, Antony was bitterly hostile to his wife. Was it this, or was it that the conduct of a military campaign proved too much even for the terrible Fulvia? She retired to Sicyone, some sixty miles west of Athens, and declaring that she did not feel interested in life any more, she fell ill and in a few days was dead, while Antony, having joined forces with Sextus Pompey, the last surviving son of the Great Pompey, was ravaging the shores of Italy and announced that he would soon avenge Perugia.

But suddenly, Octavian, heir and successor of that Julius Caesar whom Pompey the Great and all his sons had opposed for years, sent a message to Sextus that he wished to marry his niece Scribonia—and Sextus agreed. Although Scribonia was older than Octavian and twice widowed and even pregnant from her last husband, Octavian made the Senate repeal the Law which permitted no widow to re-marry till the expiration of ten months after the decease of her husband, and having divorced his own wife, who was Fulvia's daughter by a previous marriage, quickly married the Pompeian girl, amid great festivities and the laughter of all Rome who coined the joke that only the wives of the demi-gods can have children in three months. And Antony, hearing of this marriage and on learning of his wife's death, promptly threw all the responsibility of the new civil war upon the late Fulvia, and without delay made peace with Octavian.

The two rivals met at Brindisi and signed a Treaty from which Rome could expect some years of peace. Once again the legacy of Caesar was divided between the Triumvirs: to the effete Lepidus was assigned Northern Africa; Antony took all the Provinces from Albania to the East, that is Greece, Macedonia, Bithynia, Asia, Syria and Cyrenaica; but Octavian retained for himself Italy and the West: and this was the fatal error of Mark Antony—for how could a Roman commit for the second time the folly of forfeiting Rome? Even if Antony was already contemplating the division of the Empire into Eastern and Western, it was nevertheless a folly, a fatal folly in his career.

For the first time since Philippi, Antony had the opportunity of seeing at close range Octavian, and the self-appointed descendant of Hercules and Dionysos made the mistake of taking a poor view of his colleague and rival, judging only his poor physique.

173

For Octavian, although no longer the inexperienced and slightly conceited youth of the days when he had hastily returned from his studies in Apollonia to claim from Antony his heritage of Caesar, was an unprepossessing young man of medium height, unattractive in appearance and mien. He was not ugly of features, but had a sallow complexion, with a spotted skin, and very bad teeth. Only his eyes were beautiful and extraordinarily brilliant, of which Octavian was inordinately proud. His brown hair, naturally curled, never seemed properly combed. He suffered from colds, which made him sniff and sneeze continually, and he always wore as many as four tunics, under which he wore a shirt and a chest protector of thick flannel, and his legs were wrapped in puttees of soft material, an unheard of thing in Rome, where young men were proud of showing their muscular calves. In summer Octavian avoided the sun, and wore a wide-brimmed hat, another absurd eccentricity in Rome where men went bareheaded, caressing with a little finger their beautifully oiled and curled hair.

What Antony did not see was that under the negligent and slightly ridiculous garments of Octavian (and people said that all his garments were home-made!) there was hidden a most clever and capable young statesman: a man who had no ardour or impulsiveness, and entirely lacked magnetism, but who was studious, persevering, astute and calculating. A man who possessed precisely all the qualities that were lacking in Mark Antony.

Indeed, immediately after the Treaty of Brindisi, Octavian suggested two very clever things. The first was to eliminate Sextus Pompey by making a Treaty with him. It is said that when the terms were settled and it was agreed that Pompey should keep Sicily and Sardinia on condition hat he kept the seas clear of pirates and sent a certain quantity of corn to Rome, Pompey invited Octavian and Antony on board his admiral-galley of six oars " that is ", he said " the only patrimonial mansion that is left to a Pompey ", which was a snub for Antony who was then in possession of Sextus' paternal house in Rome. During the entertainment, amidst the general raillery against Antony and Cleopatra, Menas the pirate, who was the Captain of Sextus' ship, whispered in his ear that if he would permit him to cut the cable that anchored the galley to the shore and carry off his two guests, he would not only be master of Sicily and Sardinia but the sole master of the Roman Empire. But Sextus answered: " You should have done it without consulting me; now it would be a breach of hospitality."

The second thing that Octavian did was to offer as wife to Antony his half-sister Octavia. Octavia was daughter of Octavian's father's first wife Ancaria; Octavian's mother was Attia. Octavian had always felt a great affection towards his half-sister Octavia, who was a woman of exceptional merit. She had already been married to Caius Marcellus, who had recently died. Octavia was a lady of domestic virtues and also of kind and noble understanding. Although quite familiar with Antony's past, she felt drawn towards the tyrant that Antony was to be in her life, for good women are often fond of bad men.

II

CLEOPATRA learnt the news of Antony's remarriage when she was daily expecting the birth of her child—Antony's child. She was seized with a fit of savage wrath. To think that she had gone out of her way to seduce him!

To think that she had sunk to the lowest depth of licentiousness to please him!

Now she suspected Antony of having come to Alexandria solely with the intention of despoiling her of her riches. Thwarted, she had been, foiled and tricked by his false promise of love! She had given him everything and now her hopes of obtaining a kingdom for her son, from this unintelligent, unimaginative soldier—were lost.

Her ladies-in-waiting were frightened by her fury; the devoted Charmian took the Queen to her couch, where she lay prostrate, while her doctors and surgeons watched for a sudden child-birth.

In the night Cleopatra gave birth to twins, a boy and a girl. The boy was called Alexander Helios and the daughter Selene; one was dedicated to the Sun, the other to the Moon.

For three long years Cleopatra ruled alone in Alexandria, steeling herself against adversities, educating her beloved first born Caesarion, and endeavouring to forget.

The ships plied their trade from Alexandria to Ostia, carrying to Rome the corn of the Nile valley and bringing back Spanish silver or timber from the northern Alps. Many things which had been neglected during the months of infatuation and useless pining for the unfaithful lover, now claimed her attention. She ordered that all buildings, yards and ships in need of repair be set in order. Every day her Ministers had to report, and were astounded to find how conversant the Queen was with the problems of State. She reorganized the army after the model of the Legions that Antony had left in Egypt; she made important additions to the fleet and improved the ancient and excellent administration of Egypt. She also improved the conditions of her people; extended the system of irrigation with the fertilizing floods from the Nile; and drove off the Nabathaean tribes who threatened her Arabian frontier. Following the example of her ancestors, she promoted the erection of great buildings and the restoration of the old ones, going from city to city with her architects and artists to see that the old temples of Edfu, Hermonthis and Coptis were kept in good order. The temple at Denvera, which she enlarged, still shows her portrait on its tablets. She restored the famous Library of Alexandria that had suffered in the fire at the time of Caesar, and sent her agents to Rome and Greece and elsewhere to collect valuable and interesting books and copies of the old ones which had been lost in the fire.

She attended personally to the education of Caesarion, chose his tutors with the utmost care and often assisted with the lessons. Personally she taught the boy to rule. Caesarion was now a lad of ten, almost as tall as his mother, still retaining the striking resemblance to his great father that, when he was with his mother in Rome, had made people say as a joke "that poor child looks ridiculously like Caesar . . . " Caesarion had a fine, princely bearing; he spoke with a pleasant voice and with sound thoughts, and his mother, herself a rare linguist, had seen that the boy, besides Egyptian and Greek, that were the languages of his Court and people, should learn to master Latin: Julius Caesar, she was fond of telling the boy, used to speak the tersest of language and his oratory could be more effective and certainly far more witty than the pompous rhetorics of Cicero. (Ah, the cunning lawyer, that she had vainly tried to assuage!)

Cleopatra instilled into her son the sense of tradition

and that flame of ambition without which no true great-ness is possible. He must respect and honour his forbears and ancestors, even if some of them, indeed many of them, had great faults and committed dark misdeeds: it is the right of Kings to seek fulfilment of their kingly plans by all the means that appear to be advantageous although other people may suffer or be wiped out in the execution of the kingly duty. And Kings—she taught her son—are the executors of the Gods, but he, Caesarion, was descended also from Venus the Genetrix through the great Caesar whom the Gods had destined to unite the Empire of Rome with the Empire of Egypt and jointly rule with his mother and pass that incomparable Empire to his very son Caesarion. The murderers' daggers had halted that destiny; but its fulfilment would soon return through the alliance with Caesar's good friend, the Triumvir Mark Antony.

She instructed the boy in the complex hierarchy of Throne, Religion and Court. The conception of King-ship and State was still the one bequeathed by the ancient Pharaohs: the whole machinery of the State was set in motion by the will of the King alone; the taxes were paid to fill his treasury, wars were undertaken for his renown, and great buildings were erected in his honour. All the property of the country was his by right, and if he allowed any of his people to share it, it was only as a loan, which the King could reclaim at any moment. His subjects be-longed to him, and he could dispose of them and their lives at his will.

The dignity of a King—she taught her son—went back to prehistoric ages. The King's insignia belonged to a time when the Egyptians wore nothing but the girdle of the negro and when it was considered a distinction that the King should complete this girdle with a piece of skin or matting in front, and adorn it behind with a lion's tail. As in the olden days of the Pharaohs, his title was still " King of Upper Egypt and King of Lower Egypt ", and in the same way, the titles of his servants were still the Superintendents of the Two Houses of Silver, or the Two Storehouses, for each kingdom had its own granary and its own treasury—but this was only fiction, for the union of the two kingdoms was now complete under the Ptolemys.

He would one day be called " Rê, the Son of Rê, the Speaker of Truth, Caesarion " ; and on his accession he would take three other titles : " Horus " and " Lord of the diadem of the vulture and the snake " and " the golden Horus ", to testify to his divine nature, for Horus was the youthful, victorious Sun-God, and the two dia-dems were the crowns of the Gods. One difference only existed between the King and the Gods : while Amon, Rê, Osiris and Horus were called " the great Gods ", the King was only " the good God ".

He would, in due time, shave off his hair and his beard, and replace them, for official ceremonies, with artificial ones, and his beard, which he would fasten under his chin, was longer than any worn by his subjects. And upon his head he would place the uraeus, the symbol of royalty, the brightly-coloured snake which seemed to rear upon the brow of the King threatening all his enemies. And on festive occasions he would wear his crown, either the white crown of Upper Egypt, that was a curious conical cap, or the scarcely less quaint red crown of Lower Egypt with its high narrow back and the gold wire ornament bent obliquely forward upon his brow. Some-times he would wear both crowns, " the double crown ",

179

the white one inside the red, the gold wire stretching forward from the white. In his hands he would carry the crook and the flail, and the sickle-shaped sword, called the Chopesh.

He would appear, at times, in the costume of a God; and on such occasions he would bind his girdle round the narrow and tight-fitting garment in which the people imagined their divinities to be dressed, or he would wear a diadem made of horns and feathers, and carry the divine sceptre.

He must learn the rituals, and become familiar with the super-imposition of the Greek theology on the old Egyptian cults, so that Isis was also Aphrodite, and Jupiter was Amon, and Pluto was Serapis. He would have to enquire daily of the High Priest as to the health of the Divine Bull, and take a personal interest in the inventories of the temple treasuries, which, in a sense, were part of her kingdom's Treasury. And he would keep in close touch with the Chief of Police, who would report daily the smallest disturbances in the market, but also had under his control the Secret Service.

His Palace was not only the Great House of the son of the Gods, but also the seat of government, the very heart and mind of the country. The Great House, therefore, contained the Great Hall of Pillars which was used for the meetings of the Council, and the House of Adoration, that was the Throne Room. Only the King's sons, his nearest friends and the Governor of the Palace were allowed to bear the title of Privy Councillors of the House of Adoration or Gentlemen of the King's Chamber. And the officials raised to the rank of Fan-bearers would also be called Nearest Friends.

He would, in due course, marry his only legal wife and

Queen, his sister " the daughter of the God ", who would be " She who sees the Gods Horus and Set, the most pleasant, the highly praised, the Consort of the God, the Great Consort of the King ". But he shall have his harem, whose inmates, " the secluded ", under the supervision of the Chief Eunuch, would attend to the pleasures of the King.

Caesarion took his lessons with his tutors, or listened to the long talks from his beautiful and intelligent mother, or he would assist at the morning's reports of Ministers and high officials or special messengers: the Chief Administrator of the Nile, explaining to the Queen by way of maps and models which canals needed silting or widening or why in such or such a district the crops had been poor or what taxes might be used to improve conditions. Or he would hear the report of the Royal Bank or the Royal Shipyards and how the dividends were calculated, so that all that was done in Alexandria and Egypt brought gold to the Queen's Treasury.

He would assist at the audiences of Ambassadors from distant countries, paying homage to his mother; or some Roman emissary coming to discuss a new contract for supplies of wheat for Rome (or merely to catch a glimpse of the famous Queen).

He would, at sunset, drive in a broad white chariot with his mother, he in scarlet dress and high white boots, his mother in a purple gown with golden ribbons and carrying a little parasol, while the Macedonian Guard surrounding the Royal carriage rode at the sides carrying long spears and wearing broad hats of white felt. Perhaps the carriage would halt at the Museum, and the Queen would send for the Chief Librarian and enquire if the new poems of Vergil had already arrived. They would drive through the Tetrapylon, the Fourfold Gate, and proceed slowly through the poorer district of the City, and endure the evil smells, so that the crowds could see the young Prince and he could look for the many things of which the Ministers never spoke. Cleopatra had learned in those two years in Rome that the people love to see their rulers at close range, albeit above the level of the street, in an ornate litter or in a gilded chariot. And together they went to see how the building of the great Caesarium progressed: it was Cleopatra's memorial to Caesar, and it was destined to house—as the excavated ruins have shown—the finest collection of Greek art.

III

IN the meantime Mark Antony was amusing himself in Athens and playing as usual the demi-God.

In September of the year 39 Octavia had a daughter: it was the posthumous child of her former husband; but Antony, in a fit of generosity, gave the child the name of Antonia. The child was destined to be the grandmother of the Emperor Nero.

Soon after, Antony took up his quarters in Athens. The main reason was that Antony was finding it impossible to live in Rome with Octavian. He had spent a whole year in Rome, and to please Octavian and urged by the gentle and good Octavia, whose sole concern was keeping the peace between her husband and her brother, Antony had undertaken to act as Priest to the now deified Julius Caesar. But the two men never trusted each other. Their interests, and even more so, their characters and manner of life were too opposed. The Treaty of Brindisi had been sealed with the kiss of friendship and deposited with the Vestal Virgins, custodians of all documents, but relations between the two men were very strained. The Egyptian soothsayer that Cleopatra had placed near Antony and had gained his confidence, extolled Antony's good fortune but told him that Octavian was the cloud in his sky, and continuously urged Antony to keep as far away from Octavian as possible: "The Genius of your life is afraid of Octavian's Genius; when your Genius is alone it stands erect and fearless; when Octavian's Genius approaches it is dejected and depressed."[1]

It was so, for Antony found that Octavian's presence had the effect of arousing his jealousy and anger in countless incidents. Even when they played at games he found that it was always Octavian's dice, Octavian's cocks, and Octavian's quails that won. And the young man had a superior and sneering air that was infuriating!

In Athens Mark Antony adopted completely the Greek ways of life. He dressed in Greek fashions, adding to it certain oriental touches that he had found becoming in Alexandria; and having thus discarded the Roman toga, all preoccupation of Rome's affairs seemed to drop from his easy-going mind. Octavia was a good-looking woman and a docile wife, and she did not seem to object to the harem proclivities of her rather exuberant consort. It was at this time that Antony confided to a friend, who duly recorded the words, that he could not entrust his whole line of descendants solely to a single woman: "Hercules, my ancestor, left, like me, his blood in many places, in order to found everywhere new dynasties."

The Greeks had preserved a pleasant memory of Antony's previous visits; they admired his physique, his military valour and his capacity to enjoy life. Antony also had the good sense to respect their traditions and

---

[1] Plutarch.

to share them. In turn the cunning Athenians lavished on him titles and honours. A chorus of dancing girls offered him the Thyrsus of Bacchus and crowned him with vine-leaves, and appointed themselves as his regular escort. The flattery reached the absurdity of offering this new Bacchus the hand of the virgin Athena who stood before the Parthenon, with golden helmet and the spear of the Olympian Games: Antony, always ready for a new masquerade, pretended to take the offer seriously, and answered that he would accept the marriage provided the bride would bring him a dowry of a million drachmas. The sycophantic Athenians thought their adulation a bit too costly, but nevertheless they carried on the game. Only the High Priest, charged with supplying the money from the temple's treasury, told Antony-Bacchus: " Zeus himself did not demand so much to become the lover of your Mother Semele! "

But Antony had his good points. He assumed the cloak, the slippers and the rods of the Gymnasiarch. One day at the Games he stepped between two wrestlers, and lifting one of the athletes into the air with one hand, held him there struggling, to the delight of the public. He dismissed the Guards at the gates of his Residence and replaced them with the coryphees of Bacchus. He gave an athletic festival, and above the theatre he built a " bower of Bacchus ", like a suspended stage, where he and his friends lay drinking on beds of bracken. He was robed in purple, with golden sandals; and Octavia, poor girl, had to award the prizes to the winning athletes.

The military affairs, too, were now going quite well. The oracles that Antony had consulted had promised him a Triumph for the spring: Antony, full of hopes, watched the budding branches of the sacred laurel and drank with faith at the fountain of Clepsydra. Then he rejoined his troops that were awaiting him in Epirus, under the command of General Ventidius, and with a brilliant campaign defeated Pacoras, son of the King of Parthia, who had made incursions into Syria. The great victory of Cyrrhestica made ample amends in Rome for the terrible defeat suffered years before by Crassus. The Parthians had now been thrice conquered and confined within the bounds of Media and Mesopotamia. This success meant all the more because Octavian was then fighting his own battles on the shores of Sicily. And the victory over the Parthians made Antony think that the conquest of Persia would now be purely a military march.

These were golden days for Antony; hours when he thought that the kingdoms of the world would come his way. It is true that at Samosata he was less successful than his own General Ventidius, for King Antiochus of the Commagenes had agreed with Ventidius to raise his siege of Samosata and pay a war indemnity of one thousand talents of gold and submit himself to Rome; but when Antony belatedly consented to the terms, conditions in Samosata were so bad that Antony was reduced to the necessity of accepting an indemnity of only three hundred talents.

Yet, when Antony returned to Athens from Syria, he was filled with the exultation of victory, and his hopes seemed at the highest. His wife Octavia went to Ephesus to meet him, accompanied by Aenobarbus who had come from Rome to deplore the dissensions between Antony and Octavian and predicted dire consequences. In fact, when the new year came, the Triumvirate was not renewed. Octavia urged Antony to send the fleet that he still kept in harbour, to help her brother in Sicily: surely, she said, Antony himself may one day have need of army reinforcements for his Asiatic campaigns, and Octavian had many Legions available in Italy. But Octavia's sensible appeals made little impression on Antony. He knew that a rupture with Octavian was inevitable.

Nevertheless, in April Antony sailed for Italy, and being refused the Port of Brindisi, appeared at Tarentum with three hundred ships. Octavian remained at some distance, and sent messengers to enquire whether Antony was bringing peace or war? They both waited two months in Tarentum. It was a close trial of strength. Were they both afraid of risking war, or was each trying to consolidate his own position? Did Octavian become more stubborn because Agrippa—his future Prime Minister and wise counsellor—had built him a new fleet?

At long last the two rivals agreed to negotiate. Octavia had accompanied her husband; and she was now with child for the third time. She went to meet her brother, and in conference with him and with Agrippa and Maecenas she appealed to Octavian to consider the peculiarity of her situation: " The eyes of all are upon me, the wife of Mark Antony and the sister of Octavian Caesar; and should these two chiefs of the Empire involve Rome in a civil war, whatever the result might be, it would be most unhappy for me."(1) But her most urgent argument was that if Antony broke with Octavian and therefore with Rome, he would turn more resolutely than ever to the East and go back to Cleopatra. Did Octavia have some secret knowledge of Cleopatra's intrigues?

Octavian replied at first that it was too late; for in

---

1 Plutarch.

three months his fleet would be on the high seas. Nonetheless the negotiations went on; Agrippa, Maecenas, Aenobarbus and Pollion discussed and dissected, and at last a new agreement was reached and duly signed at Tarentum: the Triumvirate—which was now a Diarchy —was renewed for five years. Thus the peace was saved amidst general rejoicing. Octavian, to please his sister, let Antony give the first banquet. As on the previous occasion, the political agreement was cemented by fresh family ties: the little daughter of Octavian by his first wife Scribonia, a child not yet two years old, was betrothed to Antyllus, Antony's eldest son by Fulvia. It was a little complicated, for now, at the age of twenty-six, Octavian was betrothing his daughter to the brother of the child to whom he himself had once been engaged.

Immediately after the settlement Antony left Italy, taking Octavia and his children with him to Corfu. Once more his ambitions were roused. He was, he felt, the real successor of Caesar. It was he, Mark Antony, who still carried with him Caesar's papers, with their symbolic virtue! He would march to the conquest of Persia and he would so enlarge the Empire that the Senate and the people of Rome would have no choice but to acclaim him their real leader. Or—he might conquer the East and rule as the glorious and gorgeous Emperor of his Asiatic Empire!

It was said by Plutarch that, at this vital stage in his life, Antony's passion for Cleopatra, which had seemed to fade away in three years of separation and of important affairs supported by the counsel of a gentle and devoted wife, broke out again.

One reads in an ancient description of Cleopatra that

the beautiful and fascinating Queen had a charm that bound all men to her. Like that butterfly which is arrayed in maroon velvet with a collar of white fur and wings that are marked with eyes like spots of black surrounded by such exquisite variegated colours that have gained it the name of peacock-butterfly, generates almost as soon as it is born an odorous effluvium that attracts the males who hasten from the limits of the horizon only to die after mating with such a beautiful female—thus Cleopatra emanated an effluvium which had the magic power of stirring desire in all men.

Did the magic fragrance arise again in the memory of Antony evoking desires that were all the stronger because of the memories of those unforgettable Alexandrian nights? Love and ambition are the only great motives in men, but love is the greater impulse.

Moreover, Antony was by now convinced that to start a campaign against Persia he must have money, and although the coinage with which the troops were paid was already greatly debased, his army had not been paid for months.

For his Persian campaigns he needed gold, an immense sum of gold; and gold existed in plenty in the Treasure of Cleopatra of Egypt. Cleopatra's untold riches, that Antony knew so well, were the key to Persia; and Antony would be the key to Cleopatra's heart and Treasury.

For once Antony took a quick decision; broke up his camp in Greece; at Corfu he parted company with his wife Octavia and sent her back to Italy. They never met again. Antony departed for the East, set up quarters in Antiochia, and despatched an envoy to Cleopatra—no longer the mellifuous Dellius but the authoritative Fonteius Capito, who was to convey to the Queen an in-

vitation to meet him in Antiochia for the purpose of negotiating a Treaty of Alliance.

It was the first message Cleopatra had received for nearly four years.

IV

THE last year had been, for Cleopatra, a year of long despair. Her sleep was fitful and the state of her health began to give cause for concern. Her physician Olympus was powerless to aid her. Olympus was a clever man, of commanding manner and appearance; he tried his remedies upon slaves, but could not help the Queen who passed from attacks of fever to spells of prostration. The Court called in from Rome the celebrated Asclepiades, who had cured Cicero of a similar melancholy after the death of Tullia; but the mere mention of Cicero's name was enough to increase the crises in Cleopatra. She suffered from headaches and body pains. The gynecologists of Egypt were famous all over the world, and the papyri supply abundant information as the talents of the specialists in women's illnesses. Physicians and surgeons held consultations at the Queen's bedside, but could not suggest an effective cure. The *Book of the Cure for Sickness* and the *Embra,* written in ancient characters, were consulted; they were the most famous books of medicine, the first written by Thoth and Himopton who, before their ascension to the Heavens, had placed their treatise in a temple for the benefit of the sick; the second had been shut, from the times of the Second Dynasty, in a box at the feet of Anubis in the temple of Ousophais. The Egyptian physicians were almost a priestly class, called *sousnos* or correctors; they vowed themselves to chastity, under pain of death; practised vigorous hygiene as a kind of antiseptic, and shaved their heads and bodies every day. They were also very modest in their fees, for they contented themselves with weighing the hair that had grown during the period of the patient's sickness and charging the small weight in gold, and giving part of it to the temple in which they had received their instruction. But they knew only two cures: application of poultices and infusion of herbs. The first were made of lizard's blood mixed with mother's milk, the excrements of a child and the venom of a toad; the infusions were made of liana, saffron, the blood of Osiris and the eye of Set.[1] When Cleopatra refused to try this somewhat empyrical treatment, Asclepiades and Olympus concurred that it might be better to resort to the method that went under the title of " The Art and Mysteries of the Physician who knows the ways of the Heart ", and they were probably right.

At the end, when the Queen seemed to feel a little better, for she had heard that Antony had sent his wife back and was set to commence a war of conquest in the East, her devoted Lady Charmian suggested that the Queen should go and visit one of the ancient and famous sanctuaries. " Do you think so, my faithful Charmian? And maybe you are right, for to kiss the basalt foot of the Gods never does harm and it may bring some good." And the Queen boarded her dahabiah, escorted by the Royal Flotilla, and with purple sails and silver oars she went up the Nile to the temple of Amon-Re at Thebes. She saw again the banks of the mighty River, flanked by the Libyan Plain and by the Arabian Plain, the mountains and the country she had shown to Caesar, so many, it seemed, so many years ago. At the top of the mast, the

---

[1] See the Eber Papyrus.

pilot sat in his lookout cage that was fashioned like a lotus flower. The overseer beat time for the oarsmen clapping his hands.

At length the boat reached Thebes the city of the hundred gates, with Karnak the city of Amon and Luxor on the left, and on the right Ta-Tebnit and Kurna with the colossi of Amon. Thebes was no longer the city of which Homer had sung " the buildings so full of riches ", and ever since Cambyses had despoiled the temple and killed the bull Apis, it was merely a holy city in a state of decadence.

The Queen was received by the Priests, clothed in white, with leopard skins over their left shoulders. The Priests offered incense in the hypostyle hall with its hundred and thirty-four great columns, saying: " I come into Thy presence, O Great One after I have purified myself." They then stepped in front of the shrine and the High Priest opened the seal of clay: " The clay is broken and the seal loosed that this door may be opened and all that is evil in me I throw on the ground." Then he burned incense to the sacred snake, guardian of the God, greeting it by all its names ; and approached the 'great seat' where the statue of the God stood : " Peace to the God, peace to the God, the living soul, conquering his enemies. Thy soul is with me, Thine image is near me ; the Queen brought to Thee Thy statue. I am pure." Then the toilet of the God commenced : the High Priest took off the old rouge from the God's face and divested the statue of its clothes and dressed the God in the robe called the Nems, saying : " Come, white dress ! Come, white eye of Horus, which proceeds from the town of Nechbet. The Gods adorn themselves with Thee in Thy name Adornment." Then the Priest rouged the God's face, presented him with the insignia, the sceptre, the staff of rule, the whip, the bracelets and the anklets and the two feathers which he placed on his head, and a collarette and an armlet made of two red, two green and two white bands. Then he closed again the door saying four times " Come Phah, Thou who hast freed the eye of Horus from his enemies—let no evil man or evil woman enter this Temple. Phah closes the door and Thoth makes it fast, closed and fastened with the bolt ". And he threw himself on his face, kissed the ground and offered incense.

In the heavy heat that floated up to the ceiling the words of the Priests and the soft song of the acolytes diffused a languor full of all the secret yearning of the soul.

Cleopatra followed the ritual, her mind meandering back, to the day when she had visited this temple with Caesar—and life seemed so full of promise—and considered how sad it was now to be one of those creatures whom the Gods condemn to go about without their hearts, which have been seized by the scarab. She thought of the innocent virgins whom the lasciviousness of the Priests immolated under the pretext of initiation. Today she felt uneasy, because Amon had failed to put into her heart the peace for her crumbled ambitions; and she did not really believe in Amon. But when she came out of the temple she looked at the blue sky—the sky so beloved by all Egyptians that they considered its colour sacred. And Cleopatra felt even more uneasy. Was not the blue sky the visible presence of Amon, the blue God? But soon the blue sky turned green, because the sun was setting into the Nile; and the green sky was like Osiris. And so she travelled, on her way back, to Abydos, and went to pray to Osiris the God who was represented with a green mask, the colour of the last ray of the sun as it disappeared into the Nile.

"For there was the hawk that was Horus; and the goose that was Seb and Amon-Re before he took human form, and there was the crocodile that was Sebak, and the bull that was Apis, and the hippopotamus that was Ririt, and the pair of lions Shu and Tefunt, and the vulture and the asp that were the Goddesses of the South and of the North, and Troth with his thin neck and long ibis bill, and Khnum with a ram's head, and Sechet with a lioness's head, and Bast with the cat's head with piercing eyes and erect ears—but Osiris, the son of Seb and Nut, emblem of celestial space, the beloved victim who in the Heavens was the judge of souls, Osiris wore a green mask and his face was lengthened by a pointed beard and a tall white mitre, and his body was draped in a long garment and his hands crossed upon the chest clasped an ox driver's whip and a shepherd's crook."

For Osiris of the Green Mask was the God of Divine Justice who judged all men solely on their merits.

Cleopatra returned to her Palace in Alexandria much comforted by her visit to the shrine of Osiris. And not long afterwards Fonteius Capito arrived with the invitation.

Fonteius Capito had no need to recourse to the diplomacy of Dellius the elegant pimp. He found Cleopatra quite ready to accept the invitation. She was no longer playing with her destiny. The days of gay caprices were over. Maybe she still loved Antony, but in a different way. Now Antony was asking for a revival of her favours, enveloped into a political Treaty. She would agree, for it suited her purpose and it answered her secret prayers. Antony was now all-powerful in the East, and quite certainly he would conquer Persia and maybe obscure the odious figure of Octavian in Rome. She would conclude a compact with Antony. But this time it must be a pact that will bind him to her. If Antony wished to revive their old intercourse and affection, he must declare himself openly the enemy of Octavian and, with her help, start resolutely for the conquest of the unlimited East and be the successor of Caesar. She would go to Antioch and meet again Antony as a friend—his warmest friend—and an ally. But—Capito must understand this quite clearly for his Lord—the Queen will bring her terms.

And the first will be that Antony marries her.

V

ANTIOCH was a splendid city; indeed, it was called Antioch the Magnificent, the Queen of the East. It rivalled Alexandria in splendour and wealth. The city, on the Syrian coast, was set on the River Orontes, not far from the sea, at the foot of the Amanus chain of mountains, actually built on the slopes of Mount Silpins. It contained splendid buildings and monuments, and the fortifications surrounding the city were seventy feet high, flanked by one hundred and thirty towers, of which fifty are still standing. Antioch was famous for her grove of laurels and cypresses, in the midst of which rose the statue of Diana. It was also famous for the retreat of Daphne, loved by Apollo, and changed into a laurel so that she might escape the importune God. The people were a mixture of Syrians, Jews, Persians, Greeks and Romans. Many worshipped the Phoenician Goddess Astarte, the men were fond of the Persian God Mithras. It was also

194

a city famous for its voluptuous pleasures.

But the Cleopatra that Antony saw arriving in Antioch was not seeking pleasures. She did not arrive again in the ship of Aphrodite. Antony did not see before him the girlish mistress of four years ago. Cleopatra was still beautiful, possibly more beautiful. But she was now a mature woman of thirty-two; her bosom was more full, pressing against the silk of her *chiton;* her face was more resplendent, but with a more determined mouth.

And she held the impetuous Antony at arms' length for two nights. On the third day, in Antony's quarters in the Citadel, took place the Conference for the Treaty. Antony attended with his Chief of staff, Domitius Aenobarbus; the Queen was escorted by her First Secretary of State.

For the occasion Cleopatra had chosen a dress that would both contrast and blend with the Commander's scarlet mantle that Antony would be wearing. She wore a silver robe, with high heeled shoes, that made her look taller, and the lights of the room glittered on her jewels, that she had chosen with the greatest care, and in her diadem shone the finest diamond of the world.

The Conference was to the point. There was little discussion, for Cleopatra acted as though she was dictating the terms. Upon the table the Queen's pages spread a map of the East, prepared by the Court Chartographers; and the Queen pointed with her peacock fan to the lands that she was naming. Antony followed her movements with fascinated eyes, and felt that she was more beautiful and desirable than ever.

The terms of the Treaty were:

1. Queen Cleopatra shall place all the resources of

Egypt, financial and military, at the disposal of the Triumvir Mark Antony who may use them for his needs.

2. In return, the contracting parties shall celebrate a legal marriage, according to the Egyptian ritual. (This would enable Antony to evade the necessity of appealing in Rome to the text of Julius Caesar's special Law enabling him to marry, on political ground, more than one wife and in the particular case, the Queen Cleopatra: he would dispense with informing the Senate of his marriage, considering himself, in virtue of the Royal marriage, no longer bound by the Ancient Laws of Rome.)

3. Mark Antony will not assume the title of King of Egypt but that of Autokrator or Absolute Governor of all the East. (Autokrator was the Greek equivalent of the Latin Imperator, that Caesar had made hereditary for his family, but it was equally used to describe the Commanders in Chief of the Roman armies. Antony considered that Imperator was not sufficiently distinctive, while Autokrator implied the quality of an all-powerful ruler and at the same time it did not conflict with the title of Cleopatra who was by birthright the sole Queen and sovereign of Egypt and all its domains.)

4. Mark Antony shall recognise Caesarion, son of Cleopatra and Julius Caesar, as the legitimate Heir to the Egyptian Throne, his own two children receiving from the Queen some minor kingdoms.

5. The Treaty shall place under the sovereignty of Egypt and the domain of Queen Cleopatra and of

her descendants the following outer territories: Sinai, Arabia, including the citadel of Petra, the oriental coast of the Dead Sea, part of the valley of the Jordan including the city of Jericho; a section of the Judean districts of Samaria and Galilee; the Phoenician coast, excepting the Free Cities of Tyre and Sidon; the Lebanon with the northern coast of Syria; part of Cilicia, including the city of Tarsus; the island of Cyprus and a section of the island of Crete.

Antony accepted all these terms. The Treaty was signed at once, in three texts, Latin, Greek and Egyptian, the Greek text to be considered as binding.

It was enormous, it was amazing. It was the triumph of Cleopatra, for it restored the Egyptian power as it existed at the zenith of the Pharaohs fourteen centuries before.

The kingdom of Judea, over which reigned Herod, became an enclave within the Egyptian territories; but the exclusion of this important region from the Egyptian sphere of influence was balanced by the grant of the Cilician regions over which not even the Pharaohs had ever ruled.

What made Antony accept these terms? Without doubt, in that particular moment, he attached the highest importance to the friendship of Egypt: in the fight with Octavian for supremacy he realized that only a great conquest in Asia—Persia or the Indies—would give him a popular triumph in Rome; and the Egyptian Treasury alone could enable him to carry the Persian or Indian campaigns. We may, therefore, discount the sentimental factors from the bargain.

As for Cleopatra, the Queen and the Enchantress

joined in making her a triumphant negotiator. It was a
stroke of diplomatic genius to open the Treaty with the
complete and total surrender of the fabulous wealth and
riches of Egypt; after such a gift she could truly ask
almost anything. Disappointed and deluded by Juliu
Caesar, outraged and abandoned by Mark Antony, Cleo
patra had presented herself at Antioch with an audaciou
calm, and had asked for the realization of all her dynasti
ambitions.

With that Treaty, most of the coast of the Eastern end
of the Mediterranean came under Egyptian rule. The
position of Egypt was thus completely altered: for a long
time Rome had been all-powerful in Egypt, although she
had never formally annexed it. Now Egypt was acquiring
territories such as Cilicia, Cyprus, Crete, section of Syria
which had been definitely established as Roman Province
—and Egypt was receiving them as a gift, at the hand of
the Roman Triumvir who had been entrusted with the
rule of those territories. To what purpose had the war
of Sulla, Crassus and Pompey been fought if an Egyptian
Empire was suddenly springing up where Rome had al
ready raised her standards?

When the Treaty of Antioch became known in Rome
Octavian, the Senate, and the people, all were startled
It was astounding. It was intolerable. In his report to
the Senate Mark Antony said that " the greatness of Rome
was not in what she took but in what she gave ".(1)

VI

THREE days later the marriage of Mark Antony and Cleo
patra was celebrated in the Great Hall of the Palace of
Antioch.

---

1 Plutarch.

The Hall was decorated with lotus flowers, and was filled with the personal staffs of Mark Antony and the high officers of the Egyptian Court who had travelled with the Queen.

The Queen and the Triumvir took their place upon a dais. The Queen wore a long gown of gold tissue, that made her figure look even more slim and supple. A stomacher of magnificent gems encased her breasts. Upon her head was the double diadem of Upper and Lower Egypt, encircled by the sacred uraeus.

Cleopatra had chosen not to be seated upon a throne, so that Antony, who was not receiving the title of King of Egypt, should not have a lesser seat. She was, therefore, seated upon a square taboret of ivory inlaid with ebony, in an exquisite marquetry symbolizing the union of the two Empires, while Antony sat upon another taboret of gilt wood set off with red and blue and covered by a purple cushion studded with gold stars.

The Queen rose, took up a fan and tenderly fanned her Consort. Then, with the ancient golden spatula which through the centuries was used to anoint the Kings of Egypt, she anointed Mark Antony on the head and the hands and mouth—the head that thinks of great deeds, the hands that accomplish them and the mouth that utters wise words. After this, the Egyptian Ministers and the High Priest advanced, and prostrating themselves before their Queen and her King-Consort, they kissed the ground and their feet. The High Priest placed a crown upon the brows of the Sovereigns, and the scribes drew up the papyrus enscribed with the hieroglyphics that would fix for ever the names of the wedded pair and declare the twins Alexander Helios and Cleopatra Selene legitimate as a result of the marriage.

The ceremony being thus completed, the Queen and her King-Consort, tenderly clasping each other, walked down the hall and took their places upon their couches at the dinner table for the wedding banquet. Their table was a solid slab of lapislazuli, a stone very rare in those days, for it came from the mountains of the yet unknown lands beyond the Scythia, whose native people traded occasionally with the Armenians and Persians. The table-top—a wonder to the eye with its clouds of whitish veins running lightly across a ground of rich and variegated blue specked with gold—was supported by sphinxes of gold and adorned with candelabras of gold, specimens of Greek art, and the plates and goblets and cups surpassed in richness and exquisiteness anything that Antony had seen during his stay at the Palace in Alexandria. For the use of the Royal Pair a great novelty was provided, two pronged forks with delicate handles, made out of branches of rosy coral, which had come from China, and rendered it possible for the diners to avoid picking the food with their fingers.

The other guests took their places at the tables around the hall. The black servants, wearing silver waistcoats and golden loin-cloths, and their wrists and ankles tinkling with bracelets of pure silver, advanced in solemn lines, bearing the dishes aloft. Other slaves in white dress with scarlet bands served the rare wines.

The banquet proceeded with great ceremony enlivened by singing and dancing girls, some quite naked, playing the five-string lyre, or quaint guitars. A musician of great skill played upon the Royal Harp, which had thirty-two strings and the frame of which bore the effigy of Queen Nefertiti.

On the occasion of the marriage Cleopatra had a

special issue of coins minted, showing the two heads of herself and Mark Antony, each surmounted by their respective titles of Queen and Autokrator. She also initiated a new style of dating the years of her reign: a coin minted six years later shows indeed the two heads with this inscripton: " During the reign of Cleopatra, in the year twenty-first, which is also the sixth of the Goddess." As Cleopatra had ascended the throne in the year 51, the date of the 21st year corresponds to a period after the summer of the year 31, coinciding with the end of the sixth year after the marriage of Antioch in the year 37.

VII

THE winter passed calmly at Antioch. Antony, now sure of the financial resources necessary for a war, proceeded with alacrity to prepare his Persian campaign which, in his expectations, was to alter completely the existing situation in Asia.

Never before had Rome raised such an army in the East. Antony's army numbered one hundred thousand men, of whom sixty thousand were Italian legionaries, men well proven in wars. All Asia trembled before this army, including the Bactrians who inhabited the country east of the Parthians. Even the people of India were terror-stricken.

All the nations of the East watched with suspense the spectacle of the Roman Triumvir, now Consort of the Queen of Egypt, setting out to subdue the people who had been the bitterest foes of Rome. The news that Queen Cleopatra would accompany Mark Antony as far as the Euphrates, gave rise to great excitement and comment. For, the great question was, to whom would the new conquests accrue—to Rome or to Egypt? Would the

marriage really accomplish the fusion of the two Mediterranean Empires, of Rome and Alexandria?

The wise rulers of the ancient East forecast that never
would Rome agree to divide her imperium with Egypt.
The result of a victorious conquest by Antony could only
be a fatal one for Cleopatra: either she would be deserted
and deceived once again, or it would provoke another civil
war in Rome.

In March of the following year, 36, Antony departed
for the war. Cleopatra escorted him as far as Zeugma,
a town on the Euphrates, some one hundred and fifty
miles from Antioch, near the Armenian frontier. She expressed desire to accompany him throughout the war, for
she had preserved, from her early years, a taste for the
energy and courage of the field; and probably her
presence and her brilliant mind might have avoided many
of the disastrous incidents of that campaign. But at
Zeugma Cleopatra found that she was again with child,
and decided to return to Egypt and there await the birth
of her new son and the return of her triumphant Consort.

Before taking leave of Antony she tried to induce
him to dethrone King Herod and complete her new
domains with the territories of Judea; but Antony advised
her not to meddle in the affairs of Herod, and it was
sound advice.

Cleopatra returned by the valley of the Oronte, and by
the Lebanon route she reached Damascus. From there
she went to Jericho, where King Herod had gone to meet
her. Herod the Great was a charming and clever
sovereign, and he knew quite well that Cleopatra had
tried to drive him from his throne. Purposely Herod had
chosen Jericho as the place of their meeting, for the place

was enchanting, surrounded by palms and plants producing the fragrant balm of Gilead which is mentioned in
the Bible, and was much appreciated in all the East as a
perfume and for its medicinal qualities. And there were
the plants from which was extracted the henna, which
the Jewish ladies used to give an auburn sheen to their
black hair; and there was also grown the camphor and
the myrabolan or zukkûm. It was a " divine region ";([1])
and it was also the key town of the whole of Judea.

Cleopatra and Herod came to an understanding over
the Judean territory that Antony had included in his
donations to the Crown of Egypt; then, at Herod's invitation, Cleopatra continued her voyage across Herod's kingdom, visiting Jerusalem and Gaza.

But as soon as the Queen advanced into the Judean
territory, Herod conceived a plan to have her murdered.
It was certainly very imprudent of Cleopatra to cross the
territory of the King whom she had deprived of part of
his lands. Had Cleopatra forgotten that Antigonus, who
had the impudence to usurp Herod's throne for a while,
had paid for his temerity by being publicly executed in
Antioch? Or did she want to humiliate the proud Jewish
King by visiting that part of territory which she had taken
from him?

As for Herod, he saw in Cleopatra a dangerous enemy,
and felt that Antony's policy, prompted by Cleopatra,
constituted the greatest menace to himself and to the
entire East. Would not Antony himself be grateful to
Herod for delivering him and Rome from the ambitious
and difficult Queen of Egypt? King Herod was well-
known for his amorous tendencies; but at that time he
was madly in love with his wife Mariamne—a woman

[1] Josephus.

who fired his senses as no other woman could, and to whom Herod became so sensually attached that, when Mariamne died, he had her body embalmed in honey and kept the corpse in his own apartment for his macabre pleasure.

However, Herod's councillors advised the King to desist from his plans of assassinating Queen Cleopatra: they represented to him that Mark Antony, whose Persian campaign depended upon the Egyptian Treasury, might find most disconcerting the death of the Queen at such a time. Moreover, Queen Cleopatra occupied a position of supreme dignity, and such a dark deed on the part of the King of Judea would appear most condemnable in the eyes of the world, not to speak of the Egyptians themselves.[1]

Herod gave up the idea of murdering Cleopatra; and for the sum of two hundred talents of gold a year Cleopatra agreed to grant Herod a lease of the provinces that Antony had taken away from him and given her. Then he gallantly escorted the Queen as far as the Egyptian frontier, and before taking leave gave her some magnificent presents.

Cleopatra returned to Alexandria, and in her Palace at the Bruchion she awaited with full confidence the good news of the Persian campaign.

In the meantime she prepared herself for the birth of her fourth child. From Jericho she had brought back many cuttings of balsam trees, and as an excellent Queen, had them planted at Heliopolis.

VIII

THE Persian campaign was disastrous. Antony's first

[1] Josephus.

error was to commence the war too early in the spring, before the weather was settled. The second error was in his too precipitate and disorderly tactics.

From Zeugma, after the departure of Cleopatra, Antony went to the plateau of Herzerum to review his great army. This was composed of sixty thousand infantry troops, and ten thousand cavalry, who, though chiefly Gauls and Spaniards, were reckoned as Romans belonging to the ordinary Legions of Rome. The allied troops amounted to thirty thousand men, including thirteen thousand cavalry and infantry supplied by Artavasdes, King of Armenia and other troops placed at Antony's disposal by the King of Pontus, Polemon. There was a considerable number of mechanised units, with war engines, catapults and battering rams of heavy type.

But Antony should have wintered in Armenia, where his troops, tired of the long journey across Europe, could have properly rested, and then, with settled weather he could have conquered Media before the Parthian troops were drawn out of their garrisons. Instead, in his impatience, he put his troops on the march too soon; and leaving Armenia on the left, he passed through the Province of Atropatene, and laid waste the country. In his haste he left behind him two Legions and the allied contingents with the siege engines: onagers, carroballistas, catapults, scorpions and a ram eighty feet long; and this artillery followed in a cumbersome train of three hundred carts. Had any damage happened to these engines, it would have been impossible to repair them in those regions, where no timber of sufficient length and strength for the purpose could be found. This army-train was entrusted to Oppius Statianus.

In the meantime Antony, who had followed a more

205

direct route, laid siege to the large city of Phraata, the residence of the wives and children of the King of Media. Here he discovered his error in leaving the war engines behind; for want of which he was obliged to throw up a mount against the city walls, which involved great time and labour.

King Phraates came up with a large army, and learning that Antony was without his war engines, he sent a large detachment to intercept them: this party fell upon Statianus, who was slain on the spot with ten thousand of his men; many others were taken prisoner, and the machines were seized and destroyed.

After this serious blow, the King of Armenia, Artavasdes, although he had been the pretext for the war, pretended to be panic stricken and withdrew his troops: six thousand horse and seven thousand infantrymen.

Antony, who seemed most anxious to bring the war to a close, went on with the siege of Phraata; but the Parthians, filled with boldness by their success, came up against the Romans, and adopted their habitual tactics of harassing the enemy incessantly: always present, always elusive, drawing the enemy out with feint retreats and causing them heavy losses by discharging their bows while fleeing away, or charging in small sorties with their catafract armour or men covered with coats of mail which completely covered horse and rider and rendered them invulnerable.

Antony, who knew that inaction would cause despair and timidity, led out ten Legions, three Praetorian Cohorts heavy armed and his whole cavalry, purportedly for foraging. He believed that this was the only method of drawing the enemy after him and bring them to a battle. After one day's progress he observed the enemy in motion; hereupon he put up in his camp the signal for battle, but, at the same time he struck his tents as if his intention was not to fight but to retire. The Parthians were struck with astonishment at the order of the Roman army, when they observed them pass at regular intervals without confusion and brandishing their pikes in silence.

At a signal, the Roman cavalry and infantry suddenly fell upon the Parthians with loud shouts. The Parthians stood the attack with firmness, although they were too close to bring into use their powerful bows. Then they took to flight: and Antony, believing himself victorious, hurried after them; but when his infantry had followed the enemy some fifty furlongs and the cavalry at least one hundred and fifty, Antony found that he had not slain more than eighty of the enemy and that only thirty Parthians were taken prisoner, while his side had sustained much heavier losses.

Next day Antony returned to the camp before Phraata. Great was his astonishment when in their march his army met some straggling troops of the enemy who they had put to flight the day before, and then larger detachments and at last the whole Parthian army, which appeared quite fresh and indeed fell upon the Romans like a storm. Two Legions sustained heavy losses, and it was with great difficulty that the Romans reached their camp.

The Median garrison, in the absence of Antony had made a sally, and the Romans had fled. On his return Antony, greatly annoyed by this act of cowardice, ordered the severe punishment that was the discipline of the Roman army, the decimation: the defaulters were divided into tens, and in each group one was put to death; those who escaped the fatal count had their rations served in barley instead of wheat.

The war became ever more difficult. By September Antony had the dread of famine facing him, for he could not forage without a terrible slaughter of his men. Nor was King Phraates better placed, for knowing the temper of the Parthians he was apprehensive that as soon as the autumnal equinox was passed and the winter set in, he might be deserted by his own army which would not endure the open field.

The King of the Parthians, therefore, recoursed to a stratagem. He ordered those of his officers who could speak Latin not to offer much opposition to the Romans when they met them out foraging, but to permit them to carry off provisions. He commanded his men to approach the Romans in friendly fashion, to compliment them on their valour, to express a high opinion of the Roman army. They were also instructed, whenever the opportunity arose, to blame Antony's obstinacy, which exposed the men to the severity of a winter campaign, while King Phraates wanted nothing better than peace.

The news that the enemy desired peace quickly spread through Antony's army, who received it with joy. Antony himself was disturbed, and to make sure that the rumours reported were in accord with King Phraates' views, he sent some of his staff to the King to request the return of the Roman standards and the prisoners that still remained in Parthian hands since the defeat of Crassus: by that demand Antony hoped to save his face. But King Phraates replied that the return of the standards and prisoners could not be considered: Antony, however, was at liberty to retreat in safety, if he preferred to do so.

To retreat was indeed the only thing Antony could do. After a few days he began his march back. It was the end of October. On this occasion, Antony did not dare to address his troops. But so strong was his soldiers' affection for him that, understanding their Commander's dismay, they showed him greater respect and obedience.

The retreat of Mark Antony from Media was one of the greatest catastrophes of military history, comparable to Napoleon's retreat from Moscow. Antony had decided to return by the road by which he had come, that was a plain and open country. But a native, who professed himself well acquainted with the practices of the Parthians and had proved his faith to the Romans when the train of war engines was lost, now advised Antony to take the mountain road on his right and not expose his heavily armed troops in open country to the attacks of the Parthian bowmen. If Antony, the man said, would trust him, he would guide him by a way that was shorter and better furnished with necessaries. It is surprising that Antony did not order the Median man to be executed at once as a suspicious spy. Instead, Antony remained perplexed, both suspicious of the Parthians and anxious to shorten his journey. When the Median was asked what pledge of his loyalty he would give, the man replied that they could chain him till, under his guidance, the Roman army would be safe in Armenia.

In this condition he led the Romans peaceably along for two days. On the third, Antony was no longer expecting trouble from the Parthians and the army marched along the bank of a river in little order. Suddenly the Median guide noted that the embankment had been recently demolished and the road was flooded—evidently the work of the Parthians, designed to retard Antony in his march. The guide expressed the view that the Parthians could not be far off—and, anyway, how had they known that Antony would take that road?

Almost at once the Parthians came upon the retreating army. Antony's archers repulsed a first attack and a second one was beaten off by the Gauls who charged furiously. Antony ordered both wings and the rear to be covered by such troops as were armed with missive weapons, and the army marched along in close formation. The cavalry had orders to repel attacks, but not pursue the enemy to any great distance. On the fifth day, Flavius Gallus, an officer of great courage and valour, asked Antony to give him a number of light-armed men from the rear and a few cavalry and with these he would attempt some daring exploits. In several attacks Gallus repulsed the enemy; but instead of rejoining the main body of the retreating army, he obstinately continued the fight. He refused to obey the summons to withdraw; then, quarrelling with his own Quaestor Titus, he persisted in the combat against the Parthians till he was surrounded. In his distress he sent for assistance and at this juncture Canidius, one of Antony's favourite officers, committed a capital error. Instead of leading the whole army against the Parthians, he sent out one detachment after another, and thus by degrees he lost in this action no fewer than three thousand men killed and five thousand were brought back wounded to the camp. Amongst the dead was the brave Gallus who had four arrows shot through his body. Antony visited all the wounded, and consoled them with real grief and affection, while the wounded soldiers, pressing their General's hand, entreated him not to worry about their sufferings: " While our General is safe, all is well." Their love and respect for their Commander was wonderful: not a man, from the first officer to the humblest soldier, but would have preferred the favour of Antony to his own life and safety.

But the success filled the Parthians with such contempt for the Romans that they spent the night by their camp in the hope of seizing the baggage, while many of Antony's troops deserted. At daybreak a larger number of Parthians came up, nearly forty thousand cavalry men, for the Parthian King had sent over his own bodyguard, so confident was he of absolute victory: the King of the Parthians never took part personally in any battle.

The situation for Antony was now desperate. He decided to address his troops and called for a black robe. But his friends advised him to desist from this, as a mourning apparel would have discouraged the troops. Antony put on the red cloak and spoke in his usual effective manner. Those who had been victorious he praised, those who had fled he reproached. The valiant ones encouraged him with every sign; the cowards asked to be subjected to any punishment he would think fit. Upon this Antony raised his hands to Heaven and prayed to the Gods: "That if his happier fortune was to be followed by future evils, it might affect only himself, but his army be safe and victorious."

The following day the army marched out in better order; and when the Parthians attacked again they found their calculations upset. The harassing continued for several days, until the Romans came upon a steep hill, halted and formed a hollow square. Placing in the centre those who were exhausted or only lightly armed, the men knelt on one knee and covered themselves with their large bucklers. The second rank did the same, so that the continuity of shields, making a kind of bronze roof, appeared like the steps of a fortress, and formed the safest defence against the Parthian arrows. The Parthians, on seeing the Romans on their knees, thought they were

211

asking for mercy, and came close with their spears. But the Romans leaped up with loud shouts and cut to pieces all those who came first to the attack and put the rest to flight.

This method of attack and defence was repeated every day; nevertheless the Roman army made little progress in their march. Moreover, the men were much distressed for want of provisions; they could not forage without fighting; the corn they could get was but little, and even for that little they had no means of grinding it for all equipments had been abandoned as all the beasts of burden were dead or employed in carrying the sick and wounded. Those who sought for roots and herbs to cook found a new tragedy: any man who ate those herbs or roots immediately lost his memory and his senses; and the madness pushed them to turn inanely the stones they met as if they were upon some important task. Soon the camp was full of men bending to the ground and pushing about big stones, till at last they were carried off in a fit of bilious vomiting. In this desolation, Antony found again his qualities of a great Commander. He comforted the men, he sat by the side of the suffering; at times he was unable to restrain his tears of pity. But often he was heard to exclaim: "Oh, the retreat of the ten thousand!"—meaning that the famous retreat told by Xenophon in his *Anabasis* had been far harder than his own. One night when the situation was more critical than ever, Antony sent for his personal officer and made him swear that should a general massacre occur the officer would put his own sword through him, cut off his head and throw it away, so that Mark Antony should neither be captured nor recognised after death.

Then the Parthians, when they found that they could

not break through the Roman ranks, became less warlike.
They told the Romans that they would leave a few Medes
only to protect some of their remotest villages. Antony
nursed fresh hopes, and thought once more of taking the
easier road through the plain. While he was about to put
this plan into execution, a man rode to the camp in the
dress of a Parthian. The man, who was named
Mithridates, asked to be permitted to speak with someone
who understood the Syrian or the Parthian language. A
certain Alexander of Antioch was sent to speak with the
man; and this Mithridates told him that under the hills
that could be seen in the distance the whole Parthian army
was lying in ambush, "for at the foot of the mountains
there is a spacious plain, and there they expect to meet
you. In the mountain road you have thirst and toil to
contend with; but should Antony take the plain he must
expect the fate of Crassus". After he had given this
information the man departed. Antony called a council,
and asked the view of the Median guide, who agreed with
the directions of the Parthian. Antony, therefore,
ordered each man to take water along with him, and
took the mountain road by night. As there was an in-
sufficient number of vessels, many men carried the water
in their helmets, others in bladders.

The Parthians pursued Antony during the night.
About sunrise they came up with the rear, weary as it was
with toil and watching. Being at once obliged to fight
and continue the march, the men's thirst became un-
endurable. At last the front came to a river, the water of
which looked cool and clear; when the men eagerly threw
themselves to drink, they found that the water was salty
and acrid and it caused great pains in the stomach and
bowels. The Median guide had informed them of this;

but the men had disregarded his advice, and had drunk eagerly of the stream. Antony ran amongst the ranks, entreating them to forbear a little longer, and sounding a retreat gave the signal for pitching the tents, so that the troops might at least have the comfort of shade.

While they were fixing the tents, the man Mithridates came up again, and urged the army to hasten across the next river, as the Parthians did not propose to carry their pursuit beyond it. Antony loaded the man with gold, and at once left the camp.

That night there was mutiny in the ranks. Those who were known to possess gold or silver were slain and plundered, and the money that Antony carried for the army pay was stolen. Antony's personal baggage, with the rich bowls and tables, was also stolen and the objects broken up and the pieces divided amongst the plunderers.

With the daylight the Parthians harassed them again. A hard fight took place, but at long last the army reached the river and enjoyed its water. In sight of the river the Parthians unstrung their bows, and bade their enemies to pass over in peace. Within six days Antony's army reached the river Araxes, which divided Media from Armenia. A fear of another ambuscade ran through the survivors; but they passed over in safety. The retreat had lasted twenty-seven days.

When they set foot in Armenia, they kissed the earth in gratitude and relief, and embraced each other with a pleasure that could only be expressed in tears.

Antony, on reviewing the remnant of his army, found that he had lost twenty thousand men of infantry and four thousand cavalry, more than half of whom had not died in battle but of sickness.

This is the narration of the fatal Persian Campaign of
Mark Antony, as told by Plutarch.

The journey across Armenia to reach the headquarters
in Syria was most disastrous. Eight thousand men died of
starvation and maladies. At long last the remaining
troops took quarters in a fort between Berytus and Sidon,
called the White Hair or White Village. There Antony
sent for Cleopatra.

The disaster of the campaign, upon which he had
founded such high hopes, left him in a state of shame and
insufferance. Waiting for his Queen to arrive, and at the
same time unhappy at the idea of her contemptuous re-
proaches, he sought solace in the wine pots. Every day
he drank himself into oblivion. His nerves gave way.
At times he suddenly left the table and ran to the sea-
shore, and scanning the horizon with his two hands to his
brow he looked in the distance for the purple sails of the
Royal ship that would bring Cleopatra to him. For good
or for evil, Antony now longed for Cleopatra—like a man
lost in a desert thirsts for water.

IX

At last Cleopatra arrived, on her royal galley, the
Antoniad, followed by a fleet of cargo-boats bringing
uniforms, footwear, cloaks and weapons for the tattered
army of Mark Antony. She also brought sacks of gold
and silver to pay the troops. She insisted on being present
at the paying, so that the Legionaries should be in no
doubt that the money they were receiving came from the
inexhaustible Treasury of the Queen of Egypt, wife of the
Triumvir.

No sooner had Antony recovered a little that he felt

he needed to redeem himself after his shameful Persian campaign, and he spoke of marching forthwith into Armenia, to avenge himself on King Artavasdes who had let him down by withdrawing his contribution of troops.

Cleopatra was adamant. She had never been enthusiastic about a Persian war and she told Antony in plain words that all attempts Rome had made to conquer the Parthians had ended in inevitable disaster. To persist in the idea of conquering a country that was so vast and disposed of unlimited resources, was a useless waste of men and money. She had financed the campaign because it had been part of Caesar's original plan, and maybe a victory would have helped Antony in Rome. But now, she had no intention of repeating the experiment; it would be senseless. The only thing to do was to concentrate on the fight against Octavian and bring it to a speedy conclusion.

While Cleopatra was insisting that Antony must return with her to Alexandria, Antony received news that his wife Octavia had arrived in Athens with help for him. Cleopatra made him write at once ordering Octavia to remain in Athens. But two weeks later a messenger arrived from Octavia, the noble Niger.

The good Octavia wrote that Antony's order to stay in Athens humiliated her, for what should she do with the help she had brought in person from Italy? She had clothes for the troops. She had beasts of burden, she had money and gifts for officers and men. She even had with her two thousand picked men, fully equipped for Antony's army.

It was almost a comic situation: the two wives of Mark Antony, each bringing him help and money—the Roman one, however, urging him to restart his campaign and avenge what all the world knew was a military catastrophe; the Egyptian one, instead, prompting him to give up foolish ideas of impossible glory and return with her to the more pleasant and sensible task of recuperating and getting ready for the real project. Thus his two wives had come sailing for the same and yet opposite purpose, across the Mediterranean from opposite directions, and each was determined on one thing—to save for herself that husband, who was certainly not a paragon of marital fidelity and who as a Conqueror was beginning to look somewhat doubtful. The one offered him a royal throne, and the other appealed to him in the solemn and sacred name of his Fatherland. Indeed, Octavia's cargo was heavy with a load of traditions and duties, the world of Rome, the Forum and the Capitol. Cleopatra's cargo was laden with the appeal that few men can resist—the call of an incomparable mistress.

Cleopatra stood at an advantage, for Octavia spoke through a messenger, and Cleopatra was there in person. And there developed the most dramatic battle of the two women for the possession of Mark Antony.

Cleopatra realized that behind the generous and magnanimous efforts and help of the straightforward and loyal Octavia was hidden the scheming hand of the crafty Octavian, who knew only too well that to offer Antony the means of re-starting the crazy Persian campaign was to push him irretrievably into a second and possibly greater defeat and destroy him for ever in the eyes of the Roman people.

She recoursed, therefore, to every feminine ruse to make him give way. She feigned to be dying of love for him; she starved herself to look ill and consumed by grief;

when he was entering her room she fixed upon him her eyes full of adoration, and when he went out she sighed in languor and ready to faint. She looked at him with eyes full of tears which she wiped surreptitiously, turning her head away as if to hide her sorrow.([1]) At the same time Cleopatra's entourage brought all kind of pressures to persuade Antony that he was heartless towards the Queen. "Octavia," they urged "is your wife in Rome, but Cleopatra too is your real and Royal spouse, Queen of nations and yet content to pass for your mistress, and if you desert her she will surely die."

Antony's most intimate friend and counsellor was Manutius Plancus; and the clever fellow allowed himself to be laden with generous gifts from the Queen and in return he advocated her cause.

So it came that Antony sent to Octavia in Athens a message ordering her to return to Rome and keep to her house as a dutiful wife. She could, if she wanted, send him the troops she had brought and the supplies and the ships, which anyhow, were ships due to him by her brother for the fleet he had lent him at Taranto.

Niger said *Vale* to the Triumvir, bowed to the Queen, and departed on his mission. And Cleopatra, blooming once again under the sun of love, wasted no more time and took Mark Antony back to Egypt.

Alexandria was somewhat changed. There was no longer the "Inimitables Club" nor the Bacchic atmosphere of that forgotten winter. Nor was Antony the same. He was now approaching fifty, and his huge frame was becoming bloated; certainly he did not have the spare figure and the imperious face of Julius Caesar.

---

[1] Plutarch.

19. Octavia, wife of Mark Antony, sister of Augustus.

He still loved the banquets, and appointed as Master of Ceremonies his friend Manutius Plancus. That Consular personage became the organizer of Antony's revels, and one night during dinner Plancus masqueraded as the sea-god Glaucus. He was painted blue from head to toe and wore a crown of seaweeds on his head with a long fish-tail behind. It was not funny, it was merely gross. Yet it was the kind of fun that Antony liked. Cleopatra no longer found it amusing.

She tried to interest Antony in the government of her Empire; and suggested to him that he should reorganize the Egyptian army on the Roman model. To make him keep up a more kingly mode of life, she asked Antony about his plans for the conquest of Armenia. In any case, Cleopatra thought, this should be a short and easy campaign, and it would give Antony an opportunity of obliterating from his record the stigma of the Persian War.

It so happened that an important person arrived in Alexandria, the King of Pontus who, having been prisoner of the King of Media since the first Parthian war, was now sent to the Queen of Egypt with the message that the kingdoms of Media and Parthia had broken their alliance, and were now at war. The King of Media was asking for Antony's intervention.

This message excited Antony who saw in the offer an opportunity to beat, this time, the redoubtable Parthians. But Cleopatra knew only too well the duplicity of those Oriental Kings, and begged Antony not to embark again upon a risky campaign. Indeed, she made Antony ask King Artavesdes of Armenia, who had deserted him after the Persian defeat, to join him at once in Alexandria, to discuss the new situation. But Artavesdes felt no inclina-

tion to place himself in the hands of the Roman Triumvi
he had betrayed.

In the spring of 34 Antony departed for Syria, in
tending to subdue Armenia and Media. Cleopatra wen
with him.

It was not extraordinary on the part of the Queen to
go to Syria with Antony, as it was deemed more expedient
now that Egypt had a vast Oriental Empire, that in the
summer the seat of the government should move to Syria
and all the Court went with the Queen and her Consort
Already the ancient Pharaohs, at the time of the Egyptian
Empire, used to rule, in the summer months, from Syria
Cleopatra was now bent on resurrecting all the tradition
of ancient Egypt.

From his Syrian headquarters Antony summoned again
King Artavesdes, but the Armenian King disobeyed the
injunction. At this, Antony opened hostilities.

It was a lightning campaign; indeed, it was no more
than a campaign of plunder and sack. King Artavesde
was taken prisoner, and Antony proclaimed Armenia a
Roman Province. To ingratiate himself with the
Legionaries, he let the troops sack and pillage; in the
town of Acisilenes they plundered the ancient temple o
Anaïtis and broke the statue of the goddess, that was o
fine gold, and divided the pieces among themselves.

When Antony was back in Syria, Cleopatra advised
him to open negotiations with the King of Media. As a re
sult, their little son Alexander-Helios was married to the
child-Princess Iotapa, daughter of the King of Media
who, having no heir of his own, designated the infan
couple as his joint successors.

After this military success, Cleopatra took Antony bacl

to Alexandria, and gave him a Triumph. For the first time in history a Roman General was celebrating his Triumph outside Rome. It was an act of blatant defiance, enough to shock Rome and the Roman people: for by this Cloepatra was proclaiming Alexandria as equal to Rome. It was a proclamation that there was now an Eastern Empire whose capital was Alexandria and Cleopatra its Queen and Empress.

X

THE Triumphal procession started at sunrise from the Royal Palace; it followed the Quay as far as the temple of Neptune God of the Seas; from there it traversed the Forum; across the beautiful gardens entered the road of Canopus, and proceeded along the mausoleum of Alexander the Great and the tombs of the Ptolemy Kings. The Porticos of the Gymnasium and the Tribunals were crowded with people. The Roman Legions opened the processions; then came Antony's chariot copied from the chariot used by Julius Caesar in his quadruple Triumph. Behind the Victor's chariot marched in chains the Armenian King with his wife and children; but Cleopatra had decided that a King who was also a poet should have chains of gold. Then came the Armenian prisoners, the vassal Princes wearing their crowns; Egyptian troops carried the trophies and figurations of the conquered cities, and others held aloft long and curved Persian scimitars.

The procession turned along the Road of Serapis and reached the high and stupendous Serapeum. There Cleopatra awaited her triumphant Consort, surrounded by her Court, her Ministers and the Priests and Priestesses of Serapis.

221

Antony alighted from his chariot, and amidst the applause of the crowd and the clangour of hundreds of sistrums and cymbals, mounted the steps of the temple and offered to Serapis the ritual sacrifice as in Rome he would have done to Jupiter in the Capitol. Then he led his prisoners and captives to the Queen.

Cleopatra was seated on a golden throne, upon a platform supported by silver columns, beneath a canopy of red and azure.

The poor King of Armenia, out of breath with the long march and covered with dust, resolutely declined to bend his knees before the Queen and did no more than to salute the Queen by her mortal name. According to the Roman usage, after a Triumph the royal prisoners should have been put to death, and most certainly Artavesdes, who had now committed the further crime of having publicly offended the Queen.

But Cleopatra looked at him, and touched by his dignity, turned to Antony for approval and spared the King and his family.

After the Triumph, the whole people of Alexandria were treated to a banquet in the gardens and parks.

At sunset, the hour that was sacred to the Alexandrians, as the sky took the colour of the placid waters of the Nile, a second ceremony took place in the gardens of the Gymnasium: the solemn proclamation of the living Gods —Cleopatra-Isis and Antony Dionysus—Osiris.

This second procession was no longer warlike. Cleopatra-Isis did not ride in the procession: she was already upon her throne, for she was, and intended to be, the divine reincarnation of Isis. She wore the robe consecrated to Isis, a multi-coloured dress, signifying that

Isis was the Queen of all the worlds. This gown was attached to the Queen's waist by a girdle, and two broad ribbons suported it over her bosom, leaving her painted breasts uncovered. The skirt—as it can be seen in the murals of the temple of Hathor Energetes II in the island of Philae—was very tight, revealing the beautiful lines of the Queen's body. With this tight skirt the Queen could not walk, but could only advance in short steps, which gave a hieratic appearance to her progress.

Her head was covered by a dark-blue peruke, from which rose two straight yellow feathers, while the brow was encircled by a narrow red ribbon, bearing in front the golden uraeus with its darting asp's head, that was the ornament of Isis, while the two feathers were the symbols of the highest sovereignty. The two feathers were held by two red discs like two suns at sunset, from which arose two green ram's horns, emblems of generative ardour. The fingers of her right hand, stained red, held the ansate cross, symbol of divine life, and in the left hand she held the sceptre, which was a rod five feet long topped by a lotus flower.

Antony had not dared to wear the dress of Osiris, nor the dress of the divine Egyptian Kings, as Cleopatra was afraid that this would seem a sacrilege on the part of her Roman King-Consort. He wore an elaborate purple robe fastened on his breast by a clasp of precious stones, and in his belt was a curved sword. On his brow was a diadem and in his hand he held a sceptre.

Cleopatra was on her Throne of solid gold with Antony at her side on a level throne; and at her feet were four smaller thrones, with her four children—Caesarion, the twins Alexander-Helios and Cleopatra-Selene and the infant Philadelphus. Caesarion, now a tall youth of fourteen, wore the Macedonian cloak. The five year old Alexander was in Armenian costume—a tunic with sleeves and baggy trousers of Persian cut, while his twin sister was in white silks, and each wore a small diadem. The child Philadelphus, barely two years old, was in Macedonian dress with a chlamys and high white boots. Each Prince was surrounded by a bodyguard in the national costumes of the lands upon which they would reign one day.

Before the assembly and the crowd, Antony solemnly proclaimed Cleopatra Queen of Kings, Sovereign of Egypt, of Cyprus, of Coelesyria and Africa, and of all the territories he had granted her in the Treaty of Antiochia.

Then, he proclaimed Caesarion, son of Julius Caesar, co-Regent with his mother and heir to her Crown, and gave him the formidable title of King of Kings: (1) and taking from a cushion the three centuries old crown of the successors of Alexander the Conqueror, he placed it upon the boy's head. Caesarion still looked astoundingly like his father, and Mark Antony's feelings, in accomplishing the act and proclamation that Cleopatra had demanded, left him more than perturbed.

To his own child Alexander-Helios Antony gave the Kingdom of the newly conquered Armenia, thus repeating his facile game of giving away the territories he had conquered in the name of Rome, adding to it the Kingdom of Media, that would ensue at the death of the present King, and the Kingdom of Parthia " which he would soon conquer for his son ". To the twin sister Cleopatra-Selene he gave Cyrenaica and Libya, and the tiny Philadelphus was proclaimed King of Phoenicia, Cilicia and Northern Syria.

---

[1] Dio Cassius.

To commemorate the event new coins were issued, bearing the inscription in Latin *Cleopatrae Reginae Regum Filiorum Regum.*

That same day a temple in honour of Antony-Dionysus was commenced.

XI

CLEOPATRA'S statecraft had proved supreme. It excelled, indeed, that of any ruler of her period, for Cleopatra had blended the subtleties of Oriental tradition with the determination of the West, and had improved upon it with the instinctive genius of a woman.

Her kingdom was now a model of peace, order and prosperity. The fact that we do not know the name of any of her Ministers stands to prove that none of them had need to be an innovator. All Cleopatra's policies were her own. In a world in which Rome was yet torn by internal strife and civil wars, while striving to subjugate all the nations, Egypt stood as a mighty rival and was immensely more prosperous. The fear that for three generations had made the Ptolemy Kings beg and buy from Rome their right to survive had now disappeared: Cleopatra was as powerful as Rome. Indeed, she stood as the arbiter of the fate of Rome through Mark Antony. Moreover, to have made Antony proclaim Caesarion " son of Caesar ", was to make Octavian a usurper. And this was sweet revenge for Cleopatra, who had never forgotten the unpleasant face of the vapid young man in the Transtiberine Villa.

She was, she felt, the real founder of the new Egyptian Empire. Alexandria was now the Capital of a great Eastern Empire which embraced the whole of the former realm of Alexander the Great except Greece, Macedonia and Thrace: but these countries were, after all, part of Antony's sphere of power. From the Egyptian stand-point, the Empire included now all the ancient kingdoms of the Pharaohs and the Seleucides. The assignation of territories to her young children was an astute subterfuge, for while it was not a too flagrant challenge to Rome, it put the actual rule into her hands. The appointment of the little Alexander as King of the regions between the Euphrates and the Indus constituted a menace and a warning to the Parthians; and even more significant was the assignation of the area between the Euphrates and the Hellespont to the infant King of Syria, for it con-veyed a very definite message to Rome: the Roman Provinces in Asia Minor were now part of the Egyptian Empire.

Cleopatra put the position quite clearly to Antony. Alexandria, she told him, was infinitely better suited than Rome as the seat of government of a world Empire. First of all because of her geographical situation. From Alex-andria one could reach Antioch in a journey of six hun-dred miles and Tarsus in eight hundred, while Rome was at a distance three times greater. It was much easier to reach Athens and Southern Greece from Alexandria by way of Crete than it was from Rome by way of Brindisi. Ephesus and the other cities of Asia Minor could be reached from Alexandria by sea or overland in a much quicker time than from Rome by sea, the route overland being out of the question. Also nearer Alexandria than Rome were all the other important islands and lands of the Mediterranean basin, Rhodes, Crete, Lycia, Galatia, Bithynia, Pamphylia, Cappadocia, Pontus, Armenia and Commagenia. Rome was situated much too far away from the Eastern territories she was striving to rule; she was too far also from her Western territories: too far from the yet unexplored Germany, too far from the Gaul that Caesar had conquered, too far from Spain. And the West was as yet too uncivilized; a long time must pass ere the West could attain the importance and wealth of the Eastern countries now included in Cleopatra's Empire. Lastly, Alexandria and Egypt possessed a civilization, a culture, an importance and resources that Rome was obliged to seek in other countries and nations.

She enunciated to Antony the sources of military power; she displayed under his eyes all the data that the maps could reveal, and all that could be expressed in words and pictures. All this she told Antony: the time had come to stand against Octavian. She did not say against Rome. But she added: " For me! "

But was Mark Antony equal to such a task? Antony —a man that neither history nor the poets have been able to portray. What was he this famous lover of Cleopatra? A misguided warrior, or merely a bombastic buffoon for whom the bed and the winepot had more attraction than glory?

The catharsis of Cleopatra's tragedy commenced the day that the realization of her dream was achieved. Now that her Royal Consort was at her side she felt once more lonely, and she tasted the desolate anguish of the woman who whilst in the arms of the man she has chosen for better or for worse sees in her mind the face of the man that she would have followed to the end of the earth: and for Cleopatra the name of that man was Caesar.

Life at the Palace of Alexandria pleased Antony immensely. It was a magnificent setting in which to play

the Oriental satrap. The Palace had been considerably
enlarged and rebuilt in recent years. The walls were of
the finest marbles; the lofty columns were of porphyry,
a stone that was found only in Egypt and was called the
stone of Kings for it was purple like their robes and
mantles. The ceilings were of sculptured woods,
gilt and coloured, or exquisitely inlaid in fantastic
marquetry. The beams were covered in gold leaf. Some
rooms had floorings of agate and onyx; others were of
rosy alabaster. The doors were encrusted with tortoiseshell with the panels relieved in jasper, cornelian or other
hard stones. The furniture was of ebony inlaid or mixed
with ivory; some occasional-tables were entirely made of
ivory exquisitely carved. The trade with the Indies had
filled the Palace with the rarest and most magnificent
textiles; the curtains had the warm hues of the cloth
dipped in Syrian dyes; the couches were covered with
brocades glittering with gold threads; others had the
unique red of the cochineal.

In this Palace Antony played, with the enjoyment of a
child, his rôle of semi-divine Autokrator of the East. He
was surrounded by slaves, male and female, of great
beauty; his bodyguards were Ethiopian stalwarts whose
bodies shone like bronze and huge Germans with white
skin and flaxen hair.

The affairs of State and problems of government bored
him. One day he was presiding over a Court of Justice
when he saw the Queen's carriage passing: without a
word of explanation he rose from his chair and running
out in the street jumped into the carriage and returned
with the Queen to the Palace.

He had himself appointed Superintendent of the
Games, and organized all kinds of sports and amusements.

His great joy was to be applauded as Bacchus. For the Dionysian Feast he organized, with the assistance of his Master of Ceremonies Plancus, a great procession in which bibulous actors and mimes dressed as Sileni poured out wine to the crowd from their wineskins. Antony himself appeared in a coach in his favourite rôle, in a gold-embroidered cloak of purple, with a crown of ivy on his curls, the thyrsus in his right hand.

But the crisis in the relations between Antony and Octavian had reached its breaking point. Everything the two men did seemed to make the gulf wider and wider between them and their hostility increased.

Octavian was now absolute master of Rome and Italy, Illyria, Gaul, Spain and two African Provinces. He had a colossal army of forty Legions, which was more than he required. After his victory over Sextus Pompey he was acclaimed throughout Italy by the people, the aristocracy and the Senate. His popularity was immense. Social conditions in Rome were still deplorable and funds were lacking; but Octavian had given the people peace, and peace is the most welcome of gifts. The political " purges " had now come to an end; there was a growing feeling of confidence that a stable state of affairs would soon be restored. Octavian had re-married, and in Livia he had found the shrewdest of counsellors; Livia taught him that clemency properly displayed is the wisest policy. At twenty-seven Octavian, heir and adoptive son of Julius Caesar, and surrounded by wise Ministers, was paving his way to be proclaimed Augustus. And he wanted to be rid of Mark Antony no less than Antony and Cleopatra wanted to be rid of him.

Antony had missed the opportunity of making himself

a national hero. Had he conquered Persia his reputation would have been as great as Caesar's. But his fate was decided at Phraata, and now all hope of eclipsing his rival was gone. In his reports to the Senate about the Persian campaign Antony had represented himself as the hero who had survived terrible misfortunes, but the people of Rome had read a different meaning into the official jargon and regarded him as a Commander who could thank his stars for having survived a disgraceful retreat. The easy victory over Armenia had not impressed Rome. The thanksgiving festivals for the victories of the ever absent Mark Antony were no more sincere than the sacrifices offered by Octavian to ask protection of the Gods for his colleague and brother-in-law. And the Triumph celebrated at Alexandria had been the end of Antony's career.

A campaign of lies, half-truths and rumours was commenced by both Octavian and Antony against each other. When Octavia had returned from Athens, Octavian had looked upon the high-handed treatment she had received as a personal affront to himself, and therefore ordered his sister to leave the house of her husband and live alone. But good Octavia refused to leave her husband's house, and entreated her brother that it would be infamous and disastrous for Rome if Antony and Octavian should involve again the people in a civil war, one for the love of a woman—" that woman! "—and the other out of jealousy. She continued to live in her husband's house, taking care of her children. Friends of Antony who came to Rome to transact business or to solicit honours she entertained and sponsored. Yet, even her kind conduct did harm to Antony, for his injurious treatment of this good wife excited general indignation.

Antony's proclamation of Cleopatra as Queen of the territories which had been conquered by the Legions of Rome was denounced by Octavian in the Senate. Antony retaliated through his deputies: he charged Octavian with wresting Sicily out of the hands of Sextus Pompey and not dividing it with him. He charged Octavian with not having returned the ships he had borrowed and he accused Octavian of having reduced Lepidus, the third Triumvir, to the condition of a private man by taking away his army and his Province. Lastly, he accused Octavian of having distributed all the lands in Italy among his own soldiers and left nothing for the soldiers of Antony.

To this, Octavian replied in the Senate that Lepidus was relieved of his high duties because of his inability to sustain them. That which he had acquired by war he was ready to divide with Antony, but at the same time he expected a share of Armenia and Egypt. He said that Antony's soldiers had no right to lands in Italy because Media and Armenia, which they had bravely added to the Roman Empire, had been allotted to them by the Roman Senate.

Then the polemic took a more personal turn. Octavian publicly reproached Antony for living with a mistress and dishonouring his rightful wife. Antony wrote a letter to Octavian in which he let his pen become scurrilous: "What has changed your attitude towards me? Is it because I sleep with a Queen? But she is my wife. And have I just begun or have done so for nine years? And besides, have you, Octavian, only Drusilla([1]) for bed-companion? I hope this letter will find you well, so well indeed that you will not have displeased Tertulla, or Teren-

---

[1] Livia Drusilla, the last wife of Octavian.

231

tilla, or Rufilla, or Salvia, or Titisenia, or the lot of them together. What, indeed, does it matter where or by whom one's passions are inflamed! " Mounting his accusations, he reproached Octavian of having taken the wife of an ex-Consul, in her husband's presence, from the dining room to his own room and brought her back to the table with red cheeks and disordered hair. And he accused him " of making use of his friends to procure him mistresses, in which pursuit they would strip mothers of families and young girls to inspect them as they would the slaves sold by Toranius ",(1) and upbraided him for the " feast of the Twelve Divinities " which Octavian had held secretly, and at which he was dressed as Apollo.

The final break between Antony and Octavian was now inevitable.

XII

THREE bitter truths faced Cleopatra at the peak of her glory: the first was that her chief enemy and danger was, as it had always been, still Rome.

The second was that she could fight that enemy only through Mark Antony, and this meant setting Antony again his Fatherland. The third was that Antony was not a great man.

This third truth was the most disappointing. The disappointment was not only sentimental, indeed, perhaps it was not sentimental at all. Cleopatra had ceased to love Antony with the ardent love she had given to her Dionysian lover. Maybe she had never loved Antony at all in a sentimental sense; certainly not as she had loved Caesar. Ah, the memories of those distant days with Caesar, so enrapturing, exciting and uplifting!

---

1 Suetonius, in his *Life of Octavian Caesar Augustus,* LXXI, says that " having at first had a taste for young men, he developed particular fondness for virgin girls, whom Livia sought everywhere for him ".

She had turned to Antony as a political expediency, and she had liked him well enough, for he could be enjoyable, and moreover he loved her very passionately, and a woman always feels an attachment to a man who is infatuated with her. But she had seduced him as a man may seduce a woman, and that was the drama of the whole situation, for the long process of continuous seduction had revealed the real character of Mark Antony. It had stripped him of all his trappings, it had laid bare a gross man, the Triumvir who was the result of circumstances more than of his own ability and genius, a conqueror that could be satisfied with a little victory, vainglorious, without high and vast ambitions, who loved the revels more than glory—a man who was no Alexander, no Julius Caesar, and certainly not the match of that shy cunning young man who was weaving his web in Rome, Octavian.

It was a sad summing up. But Cleopatra was not daunted. She must now fight on her own—she must be the leader and Antony the instrument. Antony, in her heart and her design, became a puppet arrayed in his breastplate of chased gold and his purple chlamys; now she would be her own Foreign Minister and her own Commander-in-Chief.

It was a decision as audacious as Alexander's expedition to Hindustany, or Caesar's conquest of the West: Cleopatra would wage war for hegemony against Rome.

XIII

In the early months of the year 32, Cleopatra and Antony assembled their forces in Ephesus. The ancient city, built where the River Caystrus flows into the sea, not far from Smyrna and opposite the Isle of Samos, the city that was famous for the white-marble temple of Diana, delicately decorated with gold and cedarwood, became the greatest military base of the Mediterranean world. Cleopatra had brought from Egypt a fleet of two hundred ships of war, ships that were bigger and more heavily armoured than the ships used by Rome or by any other sea-Power; and she had brought a vast army of infantry troops, marines and maintenance corps. From the Egyptian Treasury she had taken a sum of gold that would suffice for a two-years' war. Every day troopships and cargoes arrived from Syria and Armenia. Antony had called to Ephesus the Legions that had been re-equipped after the short Armenian campaign, and the Oriental sovereigns who had entered the alliance promoted by Cleopatra were arriving with their armies: the Kings of Mauritania, Upper Cilicia, Cappadocia, Paphlagonia, Commagenia, Thracia, Galatia, and many other chiefs.

There were soldiers of many races; Gauls tall and powerful, with long hair curled up on top of their heads and drooping moustaches, dressed in their short leather jerkins called saga; Greek stone-throwers, with slender waists girdled by iron belts, on the head a bronze helmet adorned with feathers; Carians carrying amulets against wounds; Lydians who looked like women dressed in long robes and earrings; Egyptian seamen, square shouldered and half naked in their short white waistcoats; and Moors of haughty bearing, holding their tall shields with bare arms tingling with silver bracelets; there were hordes of mercenaries and slaves, some accompanied by strange pets and mascots, some escorted by huge Molossian dogs.

It is doubtful whether these allies had a clear idea of the reasons for the war. As their Commander was Mark

234

Antony, the Triumvir who for years had yielded supreme power over them, it could not be described as his war against Rome; nor would it have been prudent to present it as a fight in support of the Queen of Egypt whose expansionist aims were looked upon with suspicion by many of the Eastern Potentates.

Antony had somewhat clumsily presented it as a universal support to deliver Rome from an autocratic government and to restore the ancient Republic. This declaration had been made more for Roman consumption that for the benefit of his allies, and Antony believed that such a stand would not fail to rally round him a large number of people in Rome, who were strongly suspicious of Octavian's aims and ambitions. Furthermore, Antony —and this was to please Cleopatra—declared that he was fighting for Caesarion, son and legitimate heir of Caesar, and many people still held a belief that the document designating Octavian heir and successor of Caesar was an apocryphal one, the original will having been suppressed by Caesar's widow Calpurnia, out of spite against Cleopatra.

Probably this was the ablest and strongest point of Antony's otherwise untenable situation, for deprived of this, his preparation for war was nothing less and nothing more than a war against his own country. As he had always posed as a protector of the infant son of Julius Caesar and Cleopatra, he could now claim that he was going to oust the usurper Octavian and replace the legitimate heir of the great and beloved Dictator. As for Cleopatra, Caesar's widow and Antony's spouse, she would discard her crown in Rome but would retain it within her own kingdom and the territories assigned to her, as Julius Caesar had suggested in the last year of his life.

Life in camp being somewhat fatiguing and disagreeable, all that medley of petty Oriental Kings and Tetrarchs vied with one another in supplying the Queen with banquets and entertainments to provide distractions. Nothing could please Antony more. To a group of musicians and comedians he gave as a present the entire city of Priene in Ionia—a gift that the recipients found rather inconvenient to take possession of. In the spring he took sail for Samos with some ships, in company with several Kings who found the diversion quite pleasant. Antony had organized a surprise, for he had embarked on two ships many of the actors and dancers, and for three weeks the island of Samos was en fête. As Cleopatra had remained in Ephesus, one could indulge in all kinds of amusements.

In mid-spring about four hundred Roman Senators arrived at Antony's headquarters. They came as sympathizers, to inform Mark Antony of the situation in Rome: more than anything else they wanted to acquaint him of the rumours that were circulating in the city against him, and which could be put about by one source only, Octavian. Octavian had laid certain accusations before the Senate, and had given notice to the members who were for Mark Antony to leave the city. The four hundred had taken ships for Ephesus, leaving in Rome about eight hundred other members of the Senate, some supporting Octavian, while a good many others were in favour of a neutral attitude.

The voices circulating in Rome said that the Queen Cleopatra had a sinister influence upon Antony; that he had shown himself in Alexandria in a golden chariot dressed as the God Osiris; that he was going about in an

236

effeminate Eastern garb, with a golden sceptre in his hand and a curved scimitar in his belt; that in the suburb of Canopus he had played the cymbals in a tavern amidst drunken sailors and vulgar harlots; but what roused the greatest resentment in the Roman people was the voice that said he had given Cleopatra a bodyguard of Roman Praetorians whose shield bore not the traditional symbol of Rome but the initial of her name. This, the people said, was disgracing the honour of the Roman soldiers.

When the four hundred friendly Senators saw at close range the situation and the mode of life at headquarters in Ephesus, they were greatly surprised. More than anything it incensed them to find that, to please Cleopatra, Antony called his tent not with the Roman name Praetorium, but the Royal Tent. Antony himself wore the purple cloak of a Commander with white shoes on his feet and on his head the broad felt hat of a Macedonian! And it was really true that the shields of the Roman body-guards, instead of the eagle and the four great letters that were the symbol and coat-of-arms of Rome—S.P.Q.R.—bore the letters A. and C. artistically entwined!

All this and many more perturbing things displeased the Senators. They saw the active and leading part that the Queen was taking in the preparations of war. It became clear to them that Antony was no longer the defender of the Republican institutions of Rome. One of the Senators, Cnaeus Domitius Aenobarbus, who was an old die-hard, refused to address the Queen by her title and insisted on calling her simply by her name in Roman fashion. One day he took Antony aside and told him plainly that the presence of the Queen in a Roman army was entirely out of place, that it would be grossly misunderstood in Rome, and he advised Antony to send her back to Egypt and to her Court, and let her be represented by Caesarion whose rights were supported by many people, and who was, if nothing else, a man and a son of Caesar.

Antony, whose mind was more than vacillating, saw the reasonableness of the argument, and suggested to Cleopatra that she should return to Alexandria and leave the conduct of the war to him.

From that moment the Royal Tent became a hive of dissensions, quarrels and petty plots. Cleopatra secured the support of one of the most trusted counsellors of Antony, Publius Canidius, to impress Antony with the argument that the Egyptian fleet would fight much more valiantly under the eyes of their Queen, and equally the Egyptian gold would flow more readily if the Ministers in Alexandria felt it was needed for the Queen.

The sugggestion of Aenobarbus was therefore lost. But the Roman Senators split into two factions, some stood by Antony and the Queen, and others favoured a reconciliation between Antony and Octavian for the sole purpose of ridding the world of Cleopatra.

The Queen became highly suspicious. Could she still trust Antony? Now that she had provided a great fleet and financed the war, did he intend to cast her overboard and pursue only his own interests? She knew that even at this eleventh hour Antony had secretly sent word to their arch-enemy Octavian offering to down arms if he would do the same. She had, at first, believed it a political manœuvre; but now she felt doubtful of the honesty of Antony's intentions. She had a strong suspicion that Antony would much prefer to make peace and reach once more an understanding with Octavian to share the Empire—and this, by all the Gods, this making of peace she must prevent at all costs, for the peace of Rome would mean the end of her and of her kingdom!

Cleopatra concentrated, therefore, her attentions on her handsome and valiant spouse Mark Antony—" her Dionysian husband ". The charms that had worked wonders at Tharsus and at Antioch were renewed. Soon Antony was once more the infatuated and lustful lover. Besides, he was now fifty, a dangerous age; the winepot was making him inclined to avoid the trouble of making decisions and lend a lazy ear to the always clear-minded views and advice of Cleopatra. How she came to despise this colossal lover, who after each dispute became unhappy and lachrymose and the more she treated him rudely the more acquiescent and loving he was!

In June, Cleopatra took a drastic step. She asked Antony to divorce Octavia.

The fact was that Cleopatra's agents had come in possession of some letters exchanged between Antony and Octavia. Thus Cleopatra had discovered that all the time he was dying of love for her, Antony had kept a secret correspondence with his Roman wife! He wrote that he was grateful for the devotion she showed to him, and grateful for keeping him informed of all that was going on in Rome, and now he was looking at her as the most desirable of mediators. Octavia wrote that she had looked after the education not only of her children but also of those that Fulvia had borne Antony. She had constantly entertained a set of Antony's friends, and now she was considering herself the only thread of communication between Antony and her brother Octavian.

It was unbelievable! Cleopatra showed Antony the

last intercepted letter, waving frantically before his face the little roll held by an ivory stick with Octavia's seal—a gentle dove carrying a missive in its beak! What kind of man—she asked with furious contempt—what kind of man was he? Did he want her to go to Rome to break with her very hands that precious thread? Antony became lachrymose as usual, and promised to divorce Octavia. Without delay Cleopatra saw to it that messengers were despatched to Rome with orders to Octavia to leave her husband's house, which was the traditional form of divorce, or repudiation as it was called in law.

At the same time Cleopatra made Antony order the army to pass immediately into Greece. It was equivalent to a declaration of war against Octavian.

The news of the repudiation of Octavia alarmed immensely the friendly Senators. It was ridiculous that the war should have as an ostensible reason a divorce: was Antony such an enfeebled man that he was ready to repudiate the most virtuous and exemplary of wives for the graces of she whom the Roman people, rightly or wrongly, still considered nothing else than a betwitching Oriental mistress? And what would the Legionaries think? It was absolutely necessary to silence all rumours and quiet the discontent in the camp.

Promptly Antony delivered a harangue to the Roman Legions, reaffirming his intention of re-establishing the ancient Republic as soon as victory was achieved, and once again he exhibited his magnificent oratorial powers.

Cleopatra's suspicions of Antony's duplicity and her doubts of his lack of determination as a Commander-in-Chief were increased by his conduct when they arrived in Athens. The affirmations of republican aims as the purpose of the war might still be considered a good pretence, although it seemed dangerous to open such a divergence between her autocratic sentiments and the democratic principles of that Rome which she proposed to transform into the second capital of her own Empire.

But Antony's mode of life in Athens seemed to her inexcusable. Worse still, it was purposeless. He made the Athenians recognise him as a divine person, and insisted that divine and royal homage should be paid to the Queen. This the Athenians did with a certain good humour, because Cleopatra was a Macedonian and they considered her as one of their own land. Besides, the Athenians were quick to grasp that this vast military expedition was no concern of theirs, and the war would not ravage either their city or Greece, but would be decided probably in Epirus, just as the two other wars had been decided at Pharsalia and at Philippi. To please Antony they placed Cleopatra's statue on the Acropolis next to the one they had already erected to Antony, and called Cleopatra " daughter of Aphrodite ". To Antony they voted all kinds of honours. Antony strutted like a peacock when these honours were solemnly announced, and pointing to the Queen at his side, with a wide gesture of his hand, he said that he was indeed proud to be the Consort of the Queen of all the Earth.

Soon after, he organized a great Dionysian Festival. He had a platform erected at the very top of the principal theatre, a kind of rustic grotto hung with vine leaves, such as were the grottos consecrated to Dionysus; hundreds of little cymbals and wineskins and other Bacchic emblems were attached to the grotto; and on the Festival day, Mark Antony, dressed as Bacchus and surrounded by his friends in similar costumes, presided from mid-air at a shocking orgy. At night he was transported through the city in a mad procession, and proclaimed son of Dionysus in the Acropolis. The Athenians laughed.

Another time, at a banquet, he shocked all present, Roman Senators, officers of the army and Eastern Potentates, by suddenly kneeling in front of Cleopatra, and washing her feet.

During this period, two of the most influential members of Antony's party left Athens in disgust and returned to Rome. One of them was Manutius Plancus, the same who in Alexandria had acted as Master of Ceremonies and one night had played the sea-God with his body painted green and a false fish-tail tied to his waist. But Plancus had witnessed the will that Antony had made before leaving Rome for Macedonia, and the knowledge of this will was to be a strong ace in the hand of Octavian.

Another was Marcus Silanus, an old Officer of Julius Caesar in Gaul. He brought back to Rome his reliable impression that Antony was utterly debilitated. At the same time Manutius Plancus spread all kinds of absurd stories, the gist of which was that Antony had been driven mad by the magic philtres that the Queen made him drink during their orgies, her aim being the destruction of Rome.

XIV

ROME was expecting a declaration of war at any moment. By the end of the summer things had reached breaking point. The huge army and the great fleet massed on the other side of the Ionian Sea could no longer be ignored. It was no longer a case of rivalry between two Triumvirs; it was plainly a threat of attack by the whole East against Rome. Even if one could discount the petty Oriental

Kings, the presence—and the behaviour—of the Queen of Egypt at Antony's Headquarters put the seal upon the situation.

By the time the nobility had returned to the city from their country villas, Octavian had made up his mind. His slyness and his natural disinclination to war—a kind of physical cowardice in the face of combat—had been prevailed upon by the astute Livia. With her womanly instinct, Livia felt that Antony had gone too far, and that the balance of popular opinion was leaning in Octavian's favour. Livia realized that the surest way to prompt Octavian to action was to embellish her advice with the trimmings of the great and marvellous works and deeds he would be able to do once victory over his enemies and rivals would enable him to announce to the whole world the era of his *Pax Romana*. She advised him to go and see his good friend and counsellor, Maecenas, in his fine villa on the Esquiline Hill. There, while admiring the fine view of the city stretching on the banks of the Tiber and the austere beauty of the Campagna as far as the Sabine Hills, Maecenas listened to the young man recounting the troubles and squabbles in the Senate, and would tell him that all could be adjusted by using prudence and moderation; and he would tell Octavian that in the present political uncertainly it would be wise to do something for the Plebs whose voice always carried great weight in popularity—one could, for instance, repair the Marcia aqueduct to avoid scarcity of water in summer, and open cheap or even free Public Baths, to give the populace the same comfort that the patricians enjoyed in their private sudatoria.

While Octavian was thus relishing the pleasure of playing the wise and just ruler, his Prime Minister and

Great Admiral Marcus Agrippa was feverishly building a fleet.

By the autumn Octavian felt that he had enough trumps in his hand to make a bold decision. The affair of Antony's will, revealed to him by the returned Manutius Plancus who came with a great show of democratic fervour, confirmed, beyond doubt, his opinion of Antony.

So Octavian went to the temple of Vesta, where all the important wills and State documents were kept in the custody of the Vestal Virgins, and asked the Mother Superior, "in the State's name", to surrender Mark Antony's will. No one has recorded whether the Nun protested and Octavian had to call in the Guards to force the vault. It is more than likely that the Reverend Mother Superior submitted to the sacrilegious imposition with good grace, for the sacred house of the Vestal Virgins was in need of some embellishments.

Now that he had the will in his hands Octavian summoned the Senate to a special sitting. Without mincing words he launced his onslaught on Antony. "The long list of Mark Antony's misdoings—he said—was only too well known all over Italy. It was clear that Cleopatra had ruined Antony's mind by the use of the philtres which, whether magic or simply execrable love stimulants, had undermined his character and sapped his will. No Roman in his senses would go about dressed as an Eastern sovereign; no Roman Commander would think of celebrating his Triumph anywhere else but in Rome; no Roman citizen would make himself the paladin of a foreign Queen against Rome."

This was a very clever argument, for in this way Octavian seemed to exculpate, if not actually exonerate,

Antony of the great crime of being ready to march against Rome, and turned all the responsibility onto Cleopatra. By this he avoided hurting and antagonizing Antony's sympathizers in and outside the Senate, whilst he was sure that the animadversion to Cleopatra was a general feeling.

"The war itself"—Octavian added—"was conducted not by Mark Antony, but by a most unusual General Staff composed of an Egyptian eunuch, a lady companion of the Queen named Charmian, and the Queen's hairdresser, an Iranian woman by the name of Iras. These were the latest military advisers of the Triumvir Mark Antony. Only a man fully bewitched by a woman could descend to such a level and forego completely his dignity and his honour. Should the Honourable Senators still feel any hesitation, he had here a document that removed any possible doubt."

Putting his hand in the long fold of his purple-bordered toga just over his chest, that was usually used as a pocket, Octavian took out the fatal will:

"This"—he said—"is Mark Antony's last will and testament, executed by him before he left Rome for the East. Pray the Honourable Senator on my left desist from lifting his hand in an interruption which I can easily guess: far more wicked use was made by Antony and his wife Fulvia of papers forged in the revered name of my father, Julius Caesar, than to stoop to enquire how this vital document has come into my hands."

And Octavian read to the astounded Senators the main passages: Antony referred in his will to Caesarion as Caesar's true and legitimate son and bequeathed large sums to his own children by Cleopatra. Then the will stated that "should he die in Rome, his body should be carried in solemn procession across the Forum, but afterwards conveyed to Cleopatra in Alexandria and buried there ".

It sounded incredible. Octavian, who had studied rhetorics at Apollonia and was well versed in all oratorial effects, made a pause and held the will with his two hands, turned towards the packed benches. No one spoke. There was nothing to be said. That a Triumvir, that Mark Antony, the avenger of the Great Dictator, should want to be buried in a foreign land, in an enemy country, was inconceivable; it was against tradition, against all human and Roman respect. The man must indeed be insane.

Whereupon Octavian, speaking in lowered tone as if he were loth to mouth the words, asked the Senate to declare Mark Antony interdicted for mental causes, and deprived of all public office. Mind—not to declare him an enemy of Rome, but just liable to interdiction; like a naughty young man who in his infatuation for an unworthy woman has lost his senses and has run into mischief.

When the assents to deprive Mark Antony of his offices and abrogate the Consulate for the following year, which had already been conferred upon him jointly with Octavian were given, Octavian formally asked the Senate to declare war upon Cleopatra, Queen of Egypt.

The following day Octavian went to the temple of Bellona which stood in the Campus Martius just outside the Pomerium, and according to the ancient rites, dressed in the vestments of a Fetialis Priest, he threw a golden javelin against the small column that had been used for ages to announce the outbreak of hostilities.

By this Octavian signified to the people that the war was against an enemy outside Rome—a foreign enemy.

XV

WHEN details of this news reached Athens, the Royal Tent was the scene of further and more heated quarrels. The friendly Senators had received a message from Octavian inviting them to return to Rome " where they would be well received "; and many did so. The others exerted further pressure upon Antony to induce him to rid himself of Cleopatra. She herself was fully aware that her presence jeopardized Antony's position, but she no longer trusted Antony, and felt more than sure that should she go he would promptly come to an arrangement with Octavian.

Only war could now decide the issue. She would make Antony wait for Octavian to open hostilities. She knew that the state of war would cause serious repercussions all over Italy in the increased prices of victuals and goods, while Egypt would supply her army with grain and cereals without disturbing conditions in Greece. Indeed, her Treasury was almost inexhaustible, while Octavian would have great difficulty in raising the money to pay his troops. Moreover, with an army of more than one hundred thousand infantry and twelve thousand horsemen assembled in Greece, Cleopatra had left four Legions in Cyrenaica, four in Egypt and three in Syria.

Before the winter season commenced, the whole army was moved to Patras, near the Gulf of Corinth, some two hundred miles from the Italian coast. The fleet of two hundred ships was sent further north, towards the Gulf of Ambracia, which formed a large natural port with an inlet. Advance posts were placed at Corfu, that was only seventy miles from Brindisi, at the tip of Italy.

There the fleet would await events, which could be

reasonably expected not to commence before the end of the winter gales and tempests.

But a first step was soon made by Octavian: a flying squadron, a kind of Commando force under Admiral Marcus Vipsanius Agrippa, arrived one night over the high seas and seized Methone on the southern coast of Greece. It was clear that this swift force was looking for a suitable port where to land Octavian's army.

Thus the stage was set for the great battle that would decide the fate of the world. Should Cleopatra prove victorious, the past two hundred years of Mediterranean history would be obliterated and the East would probably extend its sway as far as the Atlantic; if Octavian won, Rome would become the mistress of the whole Mediterranean and the lands beyond.

The fate of the world was decided in the great naval battle of Actium, outside the small Gulf of Ambracia.

But before the momentous day, winter, spring and summer had to pass in inactivity and further indecision in Antony and Cleopatra's camp. In the course of the winter Antony transported part of his army to the north shore of the channel that was the natural port of Actium, so that he commanded the access to the port. Octavian in the meantime succeeded in passing his troops from Brindisi and Taranto to Corfu, and from there to the mainland of Epirus, gradually coming down towards the Gulf of Ambracia, and building a huge line of fortifications, like a wall descending as far as the Ionian Coast, so as to be able to unload with safety the reinforcements and supplies that he must receive from Italy. But Agrippa was clever enough to place his fleet in a position from which they controlled the entry to the Gulf and thus

Antony's fleet was bottled up in Actium.

In the spring the respective positions of the two forces were these: Octavian was unable to leave his fortified camp because Antony commanded the surrounding points. On the other hand, Octavian controlled the Ionian Sea and kept Antony's fleet bottled in the channel. Antony had laid siege to Octavian's camp, but Octavian rendered impossible a sortie from the port. Each was able to receive supplies, Octavian by sea from Italy, Antony over land from Greece. In such an almost even situation none was eager to make a first move, the only possible solution being an attempt on Antony's part to draw Octavian's force further inland, or to attempt a sortie from Actium with the intent of cutting Octavian's line of supply. During these months the two enemies challenged each other from afar like the heroes of Homer; Antony sent a challenge to Octavian to decide the war in personal combat in full sight of each other's troops. Octavian declined the invitation.

Now and then a detachment of Antony's army passed to the enemy. Secret agents of Octavian acted as a defeatist Fifth Column in the vast and far from compact camp of Antony, and they had an easy game for they spoke on behalf of the common Fatherland.

The omens for Antony were bad. Already when he was in Patras, the thunder had struck the temple of Hercules, his ancestor; in Athens the figure of Bacchus in the southern frieze of the Acropolis, directly above the theatre of Dionysus, was overturned by the wind, and the same storm swept away two statues on which his name was engraved. Now, some strange birds destroyed a nest that the swallows had built in the stern of Cleopatra's flagship, the *Antoniad.*

Many a time Antony stood upon a hill on the northern shore of the inlet and considered his position. In the inlet was his fleet, well in touch with the army inland. The access to the port was well closed by a number of galleys, and it was inaccessible. But if he surveyed, from a point further ahead where the statue of Apollo stood, if he surveyed the enemy's position, not a mile away, he saw the enemy lying in wait, inactive like himself, but in wait. Of the two the better situated was undoubtedly Octavian, who lay in wait and had the freedom of the sea.

The sight of the place was for Antony full of memories. It was in a similar situation and in this same land of Greece that he had fought two other civil wars, the first time as a young officer when Caesar and Pompey had faced each other at Pharsalia, the second time at Philippi when he was the victor over Cassius and Brutus and Octavian had behaved like a coward. Caesar and Pompey had been confronted for weeks before the fight; and so had Octavian and Brutus faced each other for weeks at Philippi and neither had forced the other to fight. As now, a Roman had hesitated before fighting another Roman; and in both instances it had been himself, Mark Antony, who had forced the issue. But he was young then, young and full of ardour under Caesar, young and full of faith in himself at Philippi. Now he was no longer so young, his heart was weaker and he was not so sure of his cause. This was the great point.

Many of his Roman advisers were for a battle on land, to draw the enemy out and fight a great battle. This semed to Antony too, the wisest decision, and on land he knew where he stood. Moreover, he would be at the head of his soldiers, and his soldiers would fight for him like brave men, for they worshipped their great and hand-

some Commander Mark Antony. The fleet was a powerful one, more powerful than any fleet he had ever seen,
but it was an Egyptian fleet, manned by Egyptians, who
did not even understand his tongue, and anyway in their
deepest heart despised and hated him as a Roman.

Cleopatra was all for forcing the blockade and re-
gaining control of the sea. She had not much faith in the
big army, which she had come to consider too mixed, too
heterogeneous, too unwielding. She had full confidence
that a powerful sortie by the two combined fleets, her own
and Antony's, a total of three hundred vessels, would
be able to force the blockade and isolate Octavian's fleet.
Once in the open sea, they would close Octavian in a
pincer and hold him in a blockade without a chance of
supply or escape. Leaving part of the fleet to carry on
the blockade, she and Antony would sail for Italy with
some thirty thousand Legionaries, fall upon Rome, where
no forces nor civil authority remained, for Octavian had
compelled the whole Senate to follow him in camp. One
audacious naval battle and everything would be open to
them.

Thus Cleopatra argued; but Antony was lending a
listening ear to his Roman friends, who, once again, were
urging him to send Cleopatra back to Egypt. Cleopatra
—they said—was the enemy expressly named in
Octavian's declaration of war; Cleopatra—they said—
was the cause of the jealousy in the camp and amongst
their own allies. Cleopatra was a cause of irritation to
the Roman Legionaries; she must retire to Egypt and
await there the result of the war.

It was indeed true that Cleopatra's presence was a
source of many mischiefs. Her tempestuous temper, her
insufferance of petty quarrels, her disdain for small minds,

all concurred to make her enemies. One of the allied Sovereigns, the King of Paphlagonia, passed with his troops to Octavian's camp, taking with him a detailed account of the dissensions in Antony's camp. Domitius Aenobarbus, whose presence gave a high moral prestige to Antony's party, passed to the enemy rather than accept the plan of the Queen of forcing the blockade and trying the issue at sea. Fate, however, prevented him from seeing the end of the conflict, as soon afterwards he died of malarial fever contracted at Actium.

The desertion of Aenobarbus made Antony furious, and he had a frantic dispute with the Queen, whom he peremptorily ordered to leave the army and return to Egypt. Highly offended, Cleopatra announced that she would go forthwith taking her fleet with her. As this did not suit Antony, he fell again to his amorous entreaties, mixing war and love in the same lachrymose plaint. Cleopatra looked at him with contempt, but postponed her departure. Two nights later, while at supper, she asked her cup-bearer to fill her cup with some wine of which all the other guests had partaken, and after drinking a mouthful she tendered the cup to Antony as a sign of re-conciliation. Greatly moved by the gesture, Antony brought the cup to his mouth seeking the very spot that the Queen's lips had touched, when swiftly she dropped in the cup some of the flowers from the garland that was on her head. Antony brought it again to his lips, but Cleopatra seized his arm: " Do not drink, for the flowers are poisoned." Antony let drop the cup in terror, and Cleopatra added with passion: " I could have killed you, as easily as that, any day, any moment, if only I could live without you! "

From this moment Antony accepted her decisions.

Their plan, which they kept secret, was this: at the first opportunity the fleet would make a sortie, the success of which could be considered certain. As soon as the fleet had control of the sea, Antony would prepare the departure of Cleopatra, who would then return to Alexandria in safety, and watch from there the end of the conflict in Greece and in Italy. As a preliminary step Antony would encircle more closely Octavian's camp and place him in the condition of being unable to quit his fortified encampment. Afterwards Antony would embark his picked troops on the ships ready to take to the sea, and attack Octavian's fleet, thus destroying the enemy both by land and sea. After the victory Antony would go to Rome alone, and making himself sole ruler he would send for Cleopatra and celebrate again their nuptial before the Roman people.

XVI

THE whole army was informed that on the 29th of August the fleet would attempt to force the blockade. As a number of vessels were badly armed and manned or in a state of disrepair owing to the long immobilization in port, they were isolated and burnt to avoid being seized and refitted by the enemy. Sixty of the best Egyptian vessels were prepared for the combat: three hundred other smaller units were to act as rearguard. The sixty Egyptian ships were all big units with from three to ten banks of oars, and these were supplied with their full complement of men, in all twenty thousand infantry and two thousand archers. The front-line units were enormous battleships, fully armoured, their prows bristling with long sharp spurs of iron, while their sides were solidly covered with sheets of metal riveted to the wood, against which any ordinary man-of-war would break. Moreover, these Egyptian battleships were armed with long-range catapults, fixed upon high towers: nothing like it had been seen before upon the seas, and they were, in all respects, the forerunners of the modern dreadnoughts.

A heavy tempest, however, raged on the sea for four days. On the first day of September the sea was becalmed. In the evening Antony visited the ships to encourage his men. The scouts reported that Octavian was preparing for battle. He had embarked eight Legions and five cohorts of Praetorians.

On the morning the following day, the second of September, Antony went aboard his flagship. While going aboard, Antony noticed that he was followed by an echineis, the so-called ship-stopper. This was the worst sign of bad omen among seamen, so that Antony decided to go on another ship. When Cleopatra heard of this, she shuddered.

Antony, with Poplicola, was to lead the right wing, Coelius the left and Marcus Octavius with Marcus Justeius would command the centre. Antony was rowed between the ships in a light vessel, approaching each unit and ordering his men to hold their position on account of the weight of their vessels and fight as steadily as if they were on land. He ordered the pilots to stand as firm as if they were at anchor, and to receive the attacks with firmness and by all means to avoid the disadvantage of the straits. Antony and Cleopatra had parted that morning full of bitterness, Antony declaring that the quarrels left him in no fit condition to direct such a great battle.

Early in the morning the ships of Octavian moved up to about three-quarters of a mile from the mouth of the

254

inlet. They were admirable ships, much smaller than the huge battleships of Cleopatra's fleet, but far more manœuvrable and speedy. They disposed themselves in three squadrons, the left wing under the command of Agrippa, the right under Octavian and the centre commanded by Lucius Arruntius.

It was rumoured that when Octavian left his tent to review the fleet, he met a man who was driving an ass, and having asked his name the man answered " My name is Entychus, that means Good Fortune and the name of my ass is Nicon, Victory ".

The battle opened with an advance of the left wing of Antony. Agrippa moved forward to intercept the vessels. The attack was not made with any violence or impetuosity, for the Egyptian ships were too heavy to reach a speed that would make an effective ramming, and those of Octavian did not dare approach, prow to prow, the enemy vessels armed as they were with many long spurs. The engagement, therefore, was like a battle on land, or the storming of a town, for there were generally three or more ships of Octavian's fleet around each of Antony's battleships, assaulting them with pikes, javelins and fire-brands, while Antony's artillery men, from their tall towers, showered weapons of all kinds from their engines. Then Agrippa opened his left wing in an endeavour to surround the enemy, and Poplicola, trying to prevent it, was separated from the main body, which, seeing that its commander was lost, fell into disorder and was attacked with great vigour by Arruntius.

The battle raged four hours. But it was already clear that fortune was with the smaller ships of Octavian. Antony's flagship had a hard fight to prevent being

255

boarded by the enemy. Many of his ships sank, others went up in flames. A terrible feeling of despair seized Antony. Would the army on land hold good in case of a defeat at sea?

The afternoon came. The bronze trumpets shook the roadsteads; the galleys rushed at each other; missiles, arrows and balls of burning resin whistled through the air. The Egyptian mastodons kept hurling showers of iron upon the enemy. Towards sunset a strong northern breeze rose from land, blowing in a direct line from Rome, in the direction of distant Egypt. The sea became oily, with long waves that increased the confusion.

Then, suddenly, with an abrupt lunge the *Antoniad*, Cleopatra's flagship, pushed her way through the units and made for the open sea, followed by the Royal Squadron, in full sails.

Cleopatra was abandoning Antony to his fate. What had made her take such a decision? Was it the sting of the wind that striking her face made her long for her Egypt still secure and unconquered? Was it the impatience to escape at last from this entangled and suffocating web of intrigue and deception and duplicity? Or was it the agonising culmination of her disenchantment from a man who was not the champion of her rights and even less the standard-bearer of her ambitions? She is not ready to share his defeat. Whereas he is soaked with wine and dissipation, Cleopatra is as clear of mind and full of vigour as she has always been. It will not be easy to throw her from the throne.

Almost at the same moment Antony's flagship disengaged itself from the attacking ships, and Antony with unbelieving eyes saw the beautiful *Antoniad* making for the Peloponnesus with a fair wind in its purple sails.

256

At this sight Antony forgot the battle, the war, the great issue of the Empire upon which he was to rule; he thought of nothing else but of his beautiful incomparable mistress running away from him without a word of farewell. His officers and friends saw him pale and stagger, beat the rail like a man demented, calling aloud: " Cleopatra! "

The soul of a man is guided by love. For a woman's love a man will do anything, great deeds or great crimes. There is no virtue and no honour in love; there is only the happiness of possession or the misery of losing the woman one loves. In that moment nothing else counted for Antony but to rejoin Cleopatra. Thus, Mark Antony showed the world that " a lover's soul lives in the body of his mistress ".([1]) Still wrapped in his scarlet cloak, he boarded a five-oared galley, and accompanied only by the Greek rhetorician Aristocrates and by his bodyguard Lucilius, Antony went after Cleopatra's purple sails.

When she saw him coming, she put up a signal in her vessel and Antony went aboard. Neither of them could look the other in the face, and Antony sat down at the head of the ship, where he remained for two days and two nights, refusing all food, and holding his head between his hands.

It was the second day of September in the year 31 B.C., the fourth day before the nones of September, the year 723 of Rome—a day in which took place the most fatal of all romantic episodes of love that history has ever recorded.

---

[1] Plutarch.

BOOK FIVE

CLEOPATRA AND ETERNITY

BOOK III

I

AFTER the flight from Actium all was tragedy and pathos.

Back in her Palace at the Bruchion, Cleopatra was once more ready to defy the world. She tried to cancel from her mind the memory of that pathetic journey across the sea, with Antony sitting in the prow of the ship for two days staring at the waves. On the second night a strange ship had appeared in the darkness. " Who are you that pursues Mark Antony? " he had cried. A voice from the black waters had replied: " I am Eurycles the son of Lachares, and I follow the fortunes of Caesar to avenge my father's death."

The *Antoniad* arrived at Cape Taenarus on the most southerly point of the Peloponnesus, which according to the legend was the entrance to the Nether regions. Here the handmaiden Charmian and Iras brought Cleopatra and Antony together again. But what comfort could they give to each other? What love could they still find in their hearts?

The news reaching Taenarus was that Octavian had captured Antony's fleet; more than five thousand men had perished in the battle. Cleopatra advised Antony to send a message to his lieutenant Canidius to save what he could of his army by leading it into Asia by way of Macedonia. Some of his transport and some of his friends came up to him, and Antony divided one shipload of treasure and gold among his friends, desiring them to

261

provide for their own safety. They refused the treasure and expressed their sorrow in tears. Antony entreated them to accept it, and dismissed them with letters of recommendation to his agent at Corinth whom he ordered to give them refuge till they could be reconciled with Octavian. This agent was Theophilus, the father of Hipparchus, who was well-liked by Antony; but he was the first of his freedmen to pass over to Octavian.

Three days later the two fugitives set sail again, heading for the coast of Libya, and Antony put ashore at Paraetonium, a desolate spot, some hundred and fifty miles west of Alexandria. He retired to a melancholy desert, where he wandered up and down, with only his two attendants, Aristocrates and Lucilius.

Cleopatra returned to Alexandria, endeavouring to make the defeat and the flight look like a strategic move. Her arrival took place at the end of September; and the fleet entered the Great Port with all the flags flying, the bands playing, the *Antoniad* gliding solemnly along the steps of the Palace. It was a transparent make-believe, for in the quick journeying of the summer months the news had travelled fast across the sea, and the sailors told a different tale in the taverns. But Cleopatra was bringing written orders from Antony to the Legions quartered in the city, provided they would obey them. The first thing was to keep the Capital of her kingdom in hand and prevent insurrections.

Then Cleopatra took stock of the situation. Antony was becoming more an embarrassment than an asset, a discredited proscript, always drunk, with a prize upon his head. His presence near the Queen would be a danger not only for Cleopatra personally, but for the safety of the Dynasty. Maybe he would now put an end to his

262

life in the solitude of Paraetonium, in the traditional Roman way, as befitted a defeated General. But Antony did nothing of the sort. He decided to retire to the tiny island of Antirrhodes, and there he affected to live like Timon the misanthrope of Athens. He sent messages to Cleopatra, informing her that the ingratitude of his friends had put him out of humour with mankind. The Queen, although involved in far graver things, humoured him, and built for him on the very tip of the quay a charming villa, which Antony called the Timonium, and there he spent his days reading Plato and discoursing upon his misfortunes and the consolation of high thoughts. He found comfort, he wrote to Cleopatra, in watching across the waters the Royal Palace, and contemplating at night the powerful lantern of the Pharos guiding the ships of other men who could still hope for better days.[1].

Like the rumble of an earthquake the news of Actium had spread dismay over whole of the Hellenic and Asian world. On the spot where his tent had stood before the sea-battle, Octavian had laid some big square plints of hewn stone and upon them had erected the figure-heads of the battleships of the enemy, and on the site of the camp he founded a new city, which he named Nikopolis, the City of Victory. Then he had overtaken Antony's Legions on their way to Macedonia, and made them submit. The Eastern Kings and Princes had fled to their countries, promptly making overtures to the victor.

Cleopatra's sole aim, in this situation, was to save her throne and the independence of Egypt. Her dreams of a

[1] This Timon of Athens had been a strange man, who once told the people of Athens " there is a fig-tree in my yard, on which many worthy citizens have hanged themselves; and as I have determined to cut it down, I give this public notice, so that such as choose to have recourse to this tree for the aforesaid purpose may repair to it before it is cut down ". (Plutarch.)

Roman-Egyptian Empire were gone, there was no hope of preserving any of the territories that Antony had given her by the Treaty of Antioch. Egypt, however, could be defended, preserved and maintained; and she would try to defend it and pass it to her eldest and dearest son, Caesarion.

She firstly turned her mind to diplomacy, the revival of an Eastern Alliance against the new Roman invader. Media was already allied with Egypt through the marriage of the infant Alexander-Helios with the little Princess Iotapa who was living at the Egyptian Court completing her education. Besides Media, the Parthian lands and the Indies were completely outside the control of Rome; Parthia was, quite true, an enemy of Media and was furthermore situated between Media and the vast Indies; but what would happen if the still intact Egyptian fleet could turn the Arabian coast and effect a junction with the Median army in the Persian Gulf? The Indian States could then join the Alliance and force the Parthians to enter the confederation.

To give reality to this plan Cleopatra decided on an operation that was so audacious that twenty centuries had to pass before men attempted it again. She decided to transport her fleet from Alexandria to the Red Sea.

Between the Rea Sea and the Mediteranean there was an isthmus dividing Africa from Asia, which, at its narrowest point, was thirty-five miles wide. It was the northernmost arm of the Red Sea, which corresponds to the modern Suez Canal, and was traversed by that branch of the Nile that from the Delta reached the Mediterranean at Pelusium. Five centuries previously, Darius the First had succeeded in joining the Lakes of Ballah and Timsah, and from these to the Gulf of Suez through the Bitter

Lakes. Along these canals the ships of the Persian conqueror had followed a route not much different than the
present Suez Canal. Three centuries later King Ptolemy
Philadelphus had reopened Darius' Canal, and built at
the southern exit, near the fort of Clysma, a vast system
of locks.

But now, after three hundred years, the largest part of
this canal was once more buried under the sands. To
transport her fleet from Alexandria to the Red Sea, Cleopatra built an army of huge tractors, copied from the
ancient drawings of the carts by which the Pharaohs had
transported the blocks of stone to build the Pyramids.
The work was immense, the labour and costs were
enormous. When her Treasurers submitted that the
Exchequer might not have sufficient funds, Cleopatra
ordered the Temples to give up their treasures and the
wealthiest citizens to contribuite "spontaneously". The
battleships that had escaped at Actium were drawn by
beasts and men across the desert and refloated in the Red
Sea. There they would be safe from Octavian and ready
to sail in due time for the Indies and Southern Persia.

In November Antony arrived in Alexandria, already
tired of his retirement at the Timonium. He was surprised at the activity of Cleopatra. In fact, he had already reconciled himself with his defeat, and confident
of the financial assistance of his "wife" the Queen, he
spoke of writing to Octavian to inform him of his
complete and final retirement from public life. He would
live as a private citizen in some city to be agreed, for
instance, Athens. To Cleopatra he expressed his opinion
of the futility of continuing the fight. It would not be
difficult, in his view, to come to an arrangement with

265

Octavian that would settle matters for some long time and preserve the throne for Cleopatra and her descendants.

But while Cleopatra, in complete disregard and disdain of Antony's views, went on with her diplomatic negotiations, convinced as she was that soon Octavian would invade Egypt from Syria—a delay that was caused only by shortage of cash to meet the cost of the armies—a catastrophe occurred. The Arabs of Petra, who were not on good terms with the Egyptians, descended upon the new basin of Suez and set fire to the ships transported with such labour and costs from across the desert.

Soon afterwards further bad news was received: Canidius came in person to Alexandria to inform Antony that everywhere his troops had fraternized with Octavian's troops. At this news Mark Antony, according to the code of honour, should have killed himself upon his battle sword: again, he did not obey the code.

At the end of the year King Herod of Judea came to Alexandria to discuss the situation with Antony, his former protector and friend. To Cleopatra he limited himself to paying his respects and compliments. She had not forgotten his intention to have her assassinated when she had visited his territories on her return from Antioch! And, indeed, the Jewish King now expounded to Antony a most simple plan. Why did he not do something momentous, kill the Queen, free the Roman world of this stubborn and dangerous woman and then proclaim himself the hero of the day? Antony told Herod that he could not bring himself to kill the woman he still loved. It is surprising that he did not acquaint Cleopatra of such dark suggestions. King Herod did not delay his departure from Alexandria, and soon afterwards he went to pay his homages to Octavian in Rhodes. He told the victor that although he was an old friend of Mark Antony's he felt that now he would place his loyalty elsewhere. King Herod was a Jew and Octavian the son of a moneylender. They understood each other perfectly. Herod saved his crown.

There was a brief lull in the situation. At the beginning of the year 30, Octavian had to return hastily to Italy to quell troubles in the army due to his inability to pay the troops already discharged. But at the end of March he was back in Asia, thinking evermore of the necessity of ending the game with Cleopatra for the urgent purpose of gaining possession of the Egyptian wealth.

Cleopatra saw new hopes in Octavian's pecuniary embarrassments and thought that she could find a new way out of her difficulty, by celebrating the coming of age of her son, Caesarion, and proclaiming him the rightful King of Egypt as Caesar Ptolemy. She could then nominally retire and act merely as her son's First Counsellor. Caesarion was now seventeen, having been born at the beginning of the year 47: taking advantage of the fact that soon after Caesarion's birth the calendar war reformed by adding eighty days to that particular year to rectify the inexactitude calculated by the astronomer Sosigenes, the birthday of the boy fell therefore in the middle of April.

The celebrations were splendid. Cleopatra meant them to convey to the people of Alexandria that now they had a man as Sovereign.[1]

To please Antony, his son Antyllus whom he had of Fulvia, now living with them at Alexandria, was the same

[1] Dio Cassius.

267

day proclaimed of age and, according to Roman usage, he received the *toga virilis*. The feasts lasted several days. The Alexandrians forgot the impending invasion.

The popular feelings rose so much that Antony, who could never be gloomy too long, decided that he would end his days in revels. He would lead again " a feast of laughter and wine " and his boon companions would be called " the companions in Death ", the *Synapotha-noumenoi*. Antony could no longer sing a song of youth, for he was now fifty-two and very portly indeed; but he felt young in heart. And as he was a good deal of a charlatan, he invited his guests to " banquet with Death ", and enjoy the fleeting happiness of passing youth.

In June Octavian arrived in Syria and all the garrisons went over to him. He sent Cornelius Gallus to take the command of the Legions in North Africa. The first post to surrender was Paraetonium, where Antony had meditated upon his defeat. It became clear that Octavian would soon come overland from Syria into Egypt. Cleopatra felt afraid for her son Caesarion, and sent him away for safety. She entrusted the boy to his tutor Rhodon, who took him to Coptos. They went up the Nile, and across the Desert they made for the Port of Berenice. Caesarion was travelling with a considerable suite, taking with him a large sum of money for the plan was to reach Berenice by the end of June, and my mid-July to travel with the trading caravans and reach one of the Hindu-stani Courts. Maybe the young son of the Queen of Egypt would be able to organize that vast alliance of Eastern countries that his mother still had in mind.

Cleopatra remained in her Palace and never for one moment did the idea of taking flight cross her mind. She would stay in Alexandria and defend, to the last, her Capital and her throne. It was noticed that in these days of danger, when the sands were running fast, Cleopatra surrounded herself with the portraits of Julius Caesar. Oft-times her devoted Charmian found her reading the old letters of the great Dictator. What would her life have been if Fate had not armed the murderous hand of Brutus?

She attended day and night to the defence of Alexandria, but she knew only too well that the Egyptians were not a fighting race, and the bankers and merchants of Alexandria would come to an arrangement with the victor, whoever he might be. In those most fateful days of her life, she felt that the Ptolemys had reigned over Egypt but were never masters of their capital in any spiritual sense. Its very wealth, the trade that was the source of its very power prevented Alexandria from having any political faith. Bankers and merchants would accept a new King, whoever he might be, for they knew that the new King would need their money and their support.

In those days Cleopatra tried to negotiate with Octavian. She would not have been a woman if she had not tried. She sent a Greek tutor of the little Princes, by the name of Euphronius; he was to inform Octavian that Queen Cleopatra was ready to surrender on condition that her son Caesarion would be kept on the throne. The ambassador was carrying, as a token of sincerity, the Queen's crown and her sceptre. And Antony sent, by the same messenger, the request of being allowed to retire to private life! How ludicrous, this bourgeois preoccupation of finishing in comfort his span of life, when Cleopatra was nobly sending her Royal insignia with the request that should the victor not return them to her, he should pass them on to her son!

Octavian replied, as the diplomats say, with a *fin de non recevoir:* Antony's request was not even considered, and instead of answering Cleopatra's offer, Octavian sent to the Queen a messenger of his own, who was to deliver to the Queen a secret message. He was prompted by the most friendly sentiments towards the Queen and inclined to leave her Egypt and her sovereignty—on condition that she would get rid of Antony.

As all the ancient historians have written about the true intentions of Octavian, one feels disgusted at the base deception that the future Augustus was trying to perpetrate upon the unhappy Queen. For Octavian's real intentions were to capture Cleopatra alive, together with her son and her children and drag them to Rome to be exhibited in his triumph. And in respect to the ancient traditions, he would have Cleopatra put to death on the Tarpeian Rock at the foot of the Capitol. Dead enemies do not give any more trouble.

Octavian's ambassador to Cleopatra was called Thyrsus. He was a freedman, for the habit of entrusting missions of confidence to former slaves had already started, and it was indeed Octavian who, in later days, expressed the cynical view, recorded by his great-nephew Claudius, that " slavery generates those virtues that free-born men so seldom possess, gratitude and loyalty ".

Thyrsus was an intelligent and tactful man, but Cleopatra could pay back Octavian in his own deceitful coins. She kept the ambassador at Court, entertained him royally, and let him believe that she was quite ready to place herself in Octavian's hands.

But Antony, everyday more foolish and stupidly boastful over his " banquets with Death ", thought it fit to show himself jealous of this ambassador who was so often closeted with the Queen; and one day he had Thyrsus seized by some of his men and severely thrashed, after which he despatched him back to Octavian with a ridiculous letter, in which he said that he had been unable to tolerate the fellow's manners, and if Octavian was annoyed, he could hang Antony's freedman Hipparchus and be quit. The thing was worse than foolish; it was useless and childish, and Cleopatra, although annoyed and offended by such vulgarity, for the sake of peace, behaved towards Antony with great tenderness and celebrated his birthday with such magnificence that many of the guests who went to the feast poor, returned wealthy.

Antony did many other foolish things. On learning that the army of Cornelius Gallus was marching upon Egypt from Cyrenaica, he sailed post-haste for Paraetonium, where he meant to appeal to his old troopers, but as he commenced to harangue the soldiers, Gallus drowned his voice with a fanfare of trumpets and a few mintues later made a sortie and pushed Antony and his escort back to the shore, and set fire to several of Antony's ships. Antony returned to Alexandria and accused Cleopatra of having betrayed him!

A few days later Antony, still full of suspicions and fears, sent again Euphronius to Octavian with a large sum of money and his own son Antyllus to plead for him. Octavian kept the money, but refused to allow the son to plead for his father.

In this confusion of characters and deeds, in July Octavian arrived in Egypt and seized Pelusium.

The last act of the drama had begun.

II

SOME years before, Cleopatra had built, according to the ancient usage of the Egyptian Kings, a mausoleum for her own tomb. It was in the zone of the Royal Necropolis, or Soma, along the Canopus Road, and it was situated quite near the Temple of Isis-Aphrodite, which rose on the sea-shore, a little to the east of the promontory of Lochias.

This mausoleum was a building of great beauty, and also of great size, built of rare marbles and comprising several rooms and chambers. The plan of the building was the traditional one for tombal constructions, a decorated portal of cedarwood gave access to a raised hall adorned with columns, from which one passed to an inner sanctuary, where the sarcophagus of vivid porphyry was ready to receive the embalmed body of the Queen. From the hall a marble staircase led to an upper floor, comprising two rooms, the floor of which was formed by the polished blocks of black granite that composed the ceiling of the hall and sanctuary below. Dormer windows cut into the thick stone gave light and air to the upper chambers, while the hall and the sanctuary proper were in true Egyptian style—lit and aired only by slits cut high up in the walls, close to the ceiling. The thick walls kept the summer heat out of the building, and the sea breeze constantly refreshed the upper rooms. The cries of the seagulls, above the rhythmic sound of the breakers and the distant noise of the city, echoed into the empty rooms like the voice of another and distant world.

In this mausoleum Cleopatra had already transferred, in the last few days, a great part of her treasure, all her jewels, and emeralds, pearls and gold, some beautiful

furniture of ebony and ivory and a large quantity of incense, cinnamon and spices, as well as flax and torches.

She had also spent some time with her doctor, Olympus,
who was well versed in the science of poison, having
studied in Assyria the effects of certain plants such as
henbane and belladonna, which had the power of causing
both death and recovery, according to the strength of the
dose. Several poisons were prepared by Olympus and,
in the presence of the Queen, tried upon prisoners. Some
were quite rapid but caused great pain, one was almost
instantaneous but caused convulsions that left the features
distorted after death; none seemed to give a prompt and
calm death.

At the end of July, Octavian's army arrived outside
Alexandria and set up camp near the Hippodrome. At
the sight of his great enemy under the city walls, Antony
again found his courage, made a brisk sally and routed
Octavian's cavalry. Then he returned to the Palace and
ran to Cleopatra armed as he was, pressed her in his arms
and, full of elation, recommended to her favour an officer
who, he said, had excelled in gallantry during the engagement. Cleopatra presented the officer with a cuirass and
helmet of gold. The same night the man went over to
Octavian.

This last deed of desertion on the part of his officers
made Antony challenge Octavian to a single combat.
Octavian merely answered that " Mark Antony might
think of many other ways to end his life ".[1] This contemptuous reply spurred Antony, who decided to seek
battle. Alas, the folly of grandiosity seized him again; he
made his archers shoot arrows into Octavian's camp, with

---

[1] Plutarch.

273

messages attached promising that every soldier who surrendered to Antony would receive fifteen hundred denarii. But Octavian sounded a parade, informed the troops of Antony's offer, adding that this was a sign of desperate conditions, and promising his men a much richer spoil when they had conquered Alexandria.

Antony determined to attack Octavian by sea and land simultaneously. The night preceding the battle he ordered a great banquet and asked his personal servants to pass the wine round plentifully " that the day following they might belong to another master ". At these words his friends were affected and wept, whereupon Antony exclaimed that his expectations of a glorious victory were at least equal to those of an honourable death. At the dead of night, when the whole city was silent and trembling in trepidation, suddenly a great noise arose, the sound of music was heard and the cries of Bacchanals. It was Antony heading a procession through the city, as far as the gate that led to the enemy's camp.

At dawn, Antony led the infantry out of the city, and placed his troops on a rising ground. While he was taking stock of the enemy's intentions, he saw his entire fleet advance towards the enemy. For a moment he joyfully believed that the fleet would attack, but he saw, instead, the oarsmen lift their oars in sign of truce. Octavian's navy answered in the same way and then the two fleets sailed together into the Great Port. No sooner was this done than the cavalry deserted Antony in the same way and surrendered. Any fight now appeared futile and Antony, abandoning all hopes, returned to the city, and entered the Palace crying maledictions upon Cleopatra " who had betrayed him to the enemy he was fighting only for her sake."

Learning that he was running through the apartments with a sword in his hand, the unhappy Queen escaped from the Palace, and with her two faithful women Charmian and Iras, ran to the mausoleum across the Palace gardens and courts, and closing with their hands the heavy portals and barricading the access with the offering tables and ritual benches the three women ran upstairs and, probably with the intention of calming the mad fit of Antony, Cleopatra told Charmian to ask some people in the street to convey to Antony the message that " the Queen was dead ". It was the typical mischievous message of a woman, in the midst of tragedy to frighten her infuriated lover.

The message reached Antony while he was giving vent to his senseless fury in his rooms. Court officials, servants and guards were leaving the Palace and seeking shelter before the conquering enemy arrived. Believing the news to be true, Antony staged another piece of melodrama: " Mark Antony," he cried, " Why do you wait? What is life to you when it is taken from her, for whom alone you wanted to live? " Having spoken these words he called his attendant Eros, and opening his mailcoat upon his breast, he declaimed once more, " O Cleopatra, I am not distressed that you have died before me, for I shall soon be with you; but I grieve to think that I, who have been so great a soldier, should be inferior in courage to a woman ". And then he addressed his attendant, " My faithful Eros, one day I made you promise that you would kill me whenever you would think it necessary for my honour. The time has come, strike me with my own sword! " Eros looked at him in admiration and pity, and seizing his own sword slew himself and fell at Antony's feet. " This, Eros, was greatly done: your love did not

275

permit you to kill your master, but you have taught him what to do." And seizing his battle-sword with both hands, Antony plunged it into his bowels with an upwards blow, and let himself fall on a couch.

The wound, however, was not fatal, and as the loss of blood stopped, Antony came to himself and entreated those who had eventually come to his room, to put him out of his pain. But they fled, and he remained there in agony, till Cleopatra's secretary, Diomedes, came with a message that the Queen wanted Antony with her in the mausoleum. When Antony heard that she was alive, he regained spirits, and begged Diomedes to have him transported to the monument. In their arms Diomedes and some servants carried the dying Antony as far as the portals of the mausoleum. But now the three women were no longer able to draw back the heavy latches, and could do nothing but lower a cord from an upper window and try to pull Antony up. It was a dispairing scene with the Queen exerting all her strength, straining every nerve and distorting her features in the effort to draw up the body of Antony, while he, thus suspended in the air, stretched pathetically his hands to her.

At last, when the three women had pulled the heavy burden into the room, they laid Antony upon a bed, and Cleopatra wiped the blood from his body and face, and called him tenderly her lord, her emperor, her husband! The funereal place echoed for long with the cries of the desperate Cleopatra, who rent her clothes, beat and wounded her breast in desperation. Her soul was now totally absorbed in Antony's misfortune; the quarrels were forgotten; she even forgot that she had a greater tragedy at her door.

Antony asked for a drink and became calm. He advised

Cleopatra to endeavour to negotiate with Octavian through Proculeius. Then he told her " not to feel sorry for him and his fate but rather to rejoice in the remembrance of their past happiness, since in his life he had been illustrious above all men and the most powerful, and was not inglorious in his death, for he had conquered like a Roman and it was only by a Roman that he was conquered ".[1] These were his last words, and so died the man upon whom an ancient historian was soon to write this epitaph: " He was intelligent, but did many foolish things; he was courageous, but his cowardice caused him to fail in many undertakings; magnanimous and mean, despoiling others and prodigal of his own, often capable of pity and more often of cruelty; once very weak he became very powerful; originally very poor he became very rich, without deriving any profit from these advantages ".[2]

A few minutes after Antony's death, Proculeius arrived at the mausoleum from the street and asked an audience in the name of Octavian.

He knocked at the barricaded portals begging Cleopatra to receive him while the three terrified women tried to converse with the messenger from a window. But Proculeius hammered at the door, his knocks and his arrogant words reverberating through the hall and upper chambers.

This was the most fateful and macabre scene in Cleopatra's life. Here in a tomb, with the bloody corpse of her husband, and the enemy's messenger waiting to take

---

[1] Plutarch.
[2] Dio Cassius.

her prisoner. At last Cleopatra ran downstairs and talked with Proculeius through the heavy door. She told him that she was ready to surrender if Octavian would promise to recognise her son Caesarion as the rightful King of Egypt. Proculeius replied evasively that Octavian would show great clemency to the Queen.

The absurd conversation went on. After a while Proculeius sent an account of it to Octavian, upon which another messenger, Gallus, was sent to confer with Cleopatra. The deceit was then concerted, for whilst Gallus carried on the discussion through the barricaded door, Proculeius sent some of his men to rear a ladder against the wall. He gained entrance through an upper window and with two men ran down the hall. One of the women screamed, " Wretched Queen, you are taken alive! "

Cleopatra turned round, and at the sight of the helmeted figure of Octavian's messenger, she pulled out a dagger from her gown and attempted to stab herself. But Proculeius jumped on her and entreated her not to injure herself and so Octavian, " Do not deprive so humane a prince of the glory of his clemency! " Rough hands fumbled over her body and took the dagger from her, searching for weapons or a hidden poison. The hour of humiliation had come. The door was opened; more soldiers entered and the Queen was escorted upstairs with Charmian and Iras. Later another messenger arrived, Octavian's personal secretary Epaphroditus, who brought orders that the Queen should be treated with the greatest kindness, but must be prevented at all costs from putting an end to her life.

Cleopatra was a prisoner in the tomb with the gruesome horror of Antony's dead body to keep her company.

III

THE same day, towards sunset, Octavian entered Alexandria. It was a most unusual entry for a conqueror; it was an act of hypocrisy, typical of the man who had chosen for himself the mask of a clement and benign ruler, and it was only a ruse.

Octavian entered Alexandria by the Road of Canopus, not on horseback at the head of his Legions, but seated in a carriage, wrapped in his toga, and holding the hand of an Alexandrian philosopher by the name of Arios. His General Staff followed, but they did not look meek. The people of Alexandria, who had dreaded devastations and plunder, were duly impressed by this new type of Roman conqueror who was entering their city conversing affably with a philosopher. Tired after fifty years of dynastic and revolutionary disturbances, the Alexandrians were quite willing to accept another foreign government which promised peace.

Octavian went immediately to the Gymnasium, where a Tribunal had been erected for him. Many leading citizens had already assembled there—politicians, intellectuals and financiers, the three castes that are always on the alert to be on the winning side—and paid Octavian homage. He gave assurances that the city would not be hurt, and told them that, in the first place, it was the city built by Alexander, in the next place, he had always hoped to admire the beauty and magnitude of Alexandria; and lastly, he would spare it for the sake of his friend Arios. At this the philosopher turned to Octavian and in grateful and humble terms begged the conqueror to pardon all the worthy citizens, and tendered a list. Octavian took the roll, and with his pale face, calm and clement, answered without opening it, " They are all pardoned ". The act had been planned with great care.

That same night the people came out of their hiding and staged a great demonstration of homage in front of the Palace.

On the morrow, the conqueror was not so clement: the first to die was Antony's son Antyllus who was beheaded in the temple that Cleopatra had built to Julius Caesar; then was the turn of Canidius who knew too much about the victory at Actium, the Senator Ovinus who had accepted the post of superintendent of the royal factories of Alexandria, Senator Turullius who had cut down the forest sacred to Esculapium at Cos to build ships for Antony, and Cassius Parmensis who, with Turullius, was the last survivor of the conspirators who had murdered Caesar.

Cleopatra's children by Antony, Alexander-Helios and Cleopatra-Selene were spared and held in custody to be shown at Octavian's triumph in Rome. Cleopatra was informed that should she attempt to commit suicide the two children would be instantly killed. And all killings and arrests were for " reason of State ".

Afterwards Octavian paid an official visit to the finest public monuments and buildings; showed great admiration for the University and the Library, promised to continue the independence of which students and scholars had enjoyed under the former Kings, conversed with the learned men of the Serapium, and lastly went to pay homage to the tomb of Alexander the Great. Exactly twenty years before, the great Julius Caesar to whom Octavian owed his present fortune had wept before this coffin, saying " I weep because at my age this man had already conquered the world! " His adopted son and successor did not weep. Octavian showed great interest in the mummy of Alexander and he asked that the crystal coffin be opened. With hands that were always clammy he touched the face of the great conqueror.

Cleopatra was allowed to give honourable burial to Antony, although many Roman officers had begged the privilege for themselves. She interred him with her own hands and performed the funeral rites with great magnificence, burying Mark Antony in the tomb that had been reserved for him in another mausoleum near her own. So was the wish that Antony had expressed in his will fulfilled—the wish that had shocked the Roman people to the point of calling him demented.

Surrounded by her weeping and wailing women, the Queen beat her breast with her hands, calling aloud Antony's name.

But although that breast enclosed the stoutest of hearts, her delicate hands could be as strong as her indomitable will and the grief that shook her at the funeral caused the wounds she had already inflicted to become inflamed. Moreover, the events had shaken her nerves, and on returning to the rooms in her mausoleum, Cleopatra was seized by fever and for several days was delirious. When the fever abated, she refused all food, hoping to die and escape the fate she feared at the hands of Octavian. But Octavian again sent word that should she continue in this determination, he would slay her children at once.

A few days later Octavian paid a visit to Cleopatra. It was August 28th. He came unannounced, " to make ", he said, " a visit of condolence and consolation ".

Cleopatra was, at the moment, resting on her couch. She was now thirty-eight, and the recent tragedies had cancelled, all at once, the marvellous freshness of her face and figure. With her wounded breast, her feverish eyes, her disarrayed hair, she presented a pathetic sight to Octavian. In the hour of their encounter she was no longer the legendary enchantress whom he had seen as a youth in the far away days of the Transtiberine Villa. Only her voice had retained its mysterious seduction.

She jumped from her couch to receive her visitor, and Octavian stood before her with his sly eyes bent to the ground in respectful mien. Did she, in that instant, search the hated sallow face that had inspired her with such aversion in the days of her life with Caesar in Rome?

Octavian escorted her back to her couch, and seated himself a few paces away. She was the first to break the silence, and endeavoured to justify the part she had taken against him. When she found that these apologies fell flat on deaf ears, she recoursed to prayers and entreaties as if she really desired to live and was convinced that he would treat her leniently. With trembling voice she spoke submissively and incoherently, her gown slipping from her shoulders, her bare feet tapping the floor in agitation. She begged Octavian to accept the surrender of herself on condition that he would pass her throne to her son.

She got up from her couch, and from a coffer she took a number of letters of Julius Caesar and a portrait of him, and handed them to Octavian, " They are letters of your great father, O Octavian, and this is his likeness in the days that I was his wife, and you know that he placed upon my head with his hands the crown of Egypt.([1])

---

[1] Dio Cassius.

But Octavian thrust the letters aside. And Cleopatra, rising again from the couch, took from the coffer an inventory of all her jewels and treasures and placed it into his hands.

One of her treasurers, Seleucus, who had come with the visitor, accused her of having suppressed several items from the list. At this Cleopatra jumped in fury from the couch and seizing the man by his hair, struck him on the face. Octavian smiled sourly at this spirited resentment, and tried to pacify her. " O Octavian Caesar," she cried, " how can I tolerate that while you honour me with a visit in my wretched situation, I am affronted by one of my servants? Supposing that I have reserved a few trinkets, they were not meant for my own person in this miserable misfortune, but as little presents that I was reserving for your wife, Livia, and your sister Octavia . . . " The lies pleased Octavian, for they gave him the impression that she really wanted to live. He, therefore, assured her that whatever she had reserved she might dispose of at her pleasure, and she could count on the most honourable treatment. With this final deceit he took his leave.

On the morrow Cleopatra asked permission to visit Antony's tomb. This was granted, and she had herself conveyed to the tomb, and kneeling she addressed the Manes of the dead: " It is not long, O Antony, since these hands have buried thee. Alas, they then were free; but thy Cleopatra is now a prisoner, watched by guards, lest in the transports of her grief she should disfigure this captive body which is reserved to adorn the triumph over thee. These are the last offerings, the last honours that I can pay thee. Nothing could part us while we lived; but in death we are to be divided, and you, a Roman, lie

283

buried in Egypt, and I, the Queen of Egypt, must be put into my grave in Italy. Yet, if the Gods of yours and my country have any power of mercy left, let them not suffer me to be led in chains to our disgrace! Hide me, O Antony, hide me with thee in thy grave, for among my bitter misfortunes nothing has been more terrible than these short days passed away from you! "(1)

She scattered flowers and incense upon the tomb, kissed it and returned to her mausoleum.

When she got there, her faithful women were surprised to hear her order a sumptuous supper and ask them to dress her.

There was in Octavian's train a young patrician, Cornelius Dolabella, who had fallen in love with Cleopatra, and in his endeavour to show her his utmost devotion, he had sent her a letter to inform her that within three days Octavian would return to Syria and she would be sent to Rome.

Charmian and Iras bathed and dressed Cleopatra with loving care. They sweetened her face with creams and spikenard, with antimony they gave the old touch of mystery to her eyes, made her lips and cheeks like burning roses, the wounded breasts, no longer so firm and beautiful, they raised in two delicate cages of filigree gold. Then Cleopatra asked to be dressed with her queenly dress of white silken muslin embroidered with pearls. She chose the jewels for her pectoral and the gleaming buckle of her girdle, and asked Charmian to place the double crown with the uraeus upon her head.

Thus arrayed in all her queenly splendour, Cleopatra sat upon her dining couch and sent to Octavian a tablet

---
[1] Plutarch.

bearing her seal. In it she begged him to permit her body to be buried with Antony.

When Octavian in great alarm arrived at the mausoleum and broke the door of the chamber, he found the Queen lying upon her golden bed, dressed in her royal ornaments. She seemed to be merely asleep, her beautiful face was composed and serene, her countenance showed no sign of suffering.

The handmaiden Iras lay dead on the floor, Charmian, dying and unable to stand, was holding with her loving hands the diadem upon Cleopatra's head. One of Octavian's officers said angrily, " Charmian, was this well done? " " Perfectly well," she said, " and worthy of a descendant of the Kings of Egypt." She had no sooner said this than she fell down dead.([1]) It was on the 30th of August, the year 30 B.C., 724 of Rome.

It is not known with certitude how Cleopatra killed herself. Octavian ordered an immediate inquest and even made use of the psylly in the hope that she might revive. The psylly were a race of men who, according to popular saying, were all males, for there was no woman born in their tribe, and they had the power to suck out the poison of any serpent, and they were not harmed when bitten by a snake. It was even said that they tested their offsprings (born apparently without mothers) by throwing them among serpents as soon as they were born. But no psylly could resuscitate Cleopatra.

It was known that the Queen used to carry poison inside a hollow bodkin that she wore in her hair; others said that a serpent was kept in a water vessel. Then some-

[1] Plutarch,

body remembered that during the morning a peasant had arrived at the mausoleum with a basket, and in answer to the guard's question he had removed the leaves and let them see that the basket was full of figs. The officer of the guard, who had allowed the peasant to enter, remembered that at the sight of the fellow the Queen had exclaimed " Here he is! " and having delivered his basket the peasant had speedily departed. This gave rise to the theory that under the figs was hidden an asp, a small poisonous snake whose bite caused instantaneous death. On examing the body of the Queen two small marks were seen upon her left arm, that might have been caused by the bite of a snake.

When Octavian celebrated his triumph in Rome, behind his chariot came a statue representing Cleopatra dead upon her couch with a golden asp encircled around her left arm, and thus the legend arose that Cleopatra had killed herself with the asp she had procured with the stratagem of the figs.

Octavian gave an order that the Queen should be buried with all honours, and in accordance with her supreme desire she was buried near Mark Antony. As the burial took place immediately, the body of Queen Cleopatra was not embalmed.

The curtain had now descended upon the great drama. Alexandria was quiet and reconciled to her new Roman rulers. Egypt would become a Roman Province; in fact, Octavian had already planned to preserve Egypt as a personal appanage of his descendants. The world would now be at peace and ready for the Augustan Age.

Without delay Octavian ordered that Caesarion be found and put to death. It was most inconvenient to have alive such a striking resemblance to Julius Caesar his father, and anyway, Octavian remarked, " there is no room for two Caesars in this world! "

Soon afterwards he made ready to depart from Egypt. As a last order, he gave instructions that all the statues of Antony and Cleopatra should be overthrown and destroyed. As soon as the order was issued, a wealthy merchant of Alexandria obtained audience of Octavian and begged that the statues of the Queen should be left as a sign of respect for the Egyptian people. Beckoning to some slave he had with him, the wealthy merchant set down ten sacks containing a thousand talents in gold.

The statues of Cleopatra were spared. Yet, not one remains, only the legend that has stirred the hearts of men and the imagination of poets for two thousand years.

HISTORICAL APPENDIX

OCEANUS GERMANICUS

HIBERNIA

BRITANNIA

Mona
Abus Fl.
Metaris Æst.
Aquæ Solis
Londinium

Bolerium Pr.
Damnonium Pr.
Oceanus Britannicus
Vectis
Brivates Portus
Mediolanum
Condivicnum

Oceanus Cantabrius

Tribucum Pr.
orum Sinus
m Pr.

HISPANIA

Durius
Anas
Tagus
Corduba
Hispalis
Gades
Calpe
Herculeum
Abyla M.

Ulterior

GALLIA

Genabum
Liger
Bibracte
Arverni
Nemausus
Arelate
Narbo Martius
Massilia
G. Narbo
Pyrenæi Mª

Saguntum
Tarraco
Barcino

Balares Iª
Balearis minor
Balearis major
Pityusæ Iª

MARE

GERMANICUS

GER

EU

NOR

RAETIA

Helvetii
Gallia Cisalpina
Mediolanum
Placentia
Genua
Luna
Pisæ

Corsica

Sardinia

ROM

Capu

Drepanum
Lilybæum
Selinus
Agrigentum
Cossyra
Sinus Neapolitana
Leptis minor
Thapsus
Panormus
Utica
Hippo Regius
Carthago

AFRICA

Cirta
NUMIDIA

Palus Tritonis

Cercina
Syrtis minor
Meninx I.

MAURITANIA

Subur

ROMAN EMPIRE
in 49 B.C.

■ . . . . . Roman Territory and Provinces
■ . . . . . Allied States

Roman Miles
0   50   100   200   300   400   500

English Miles
0   50   100   200   300   400   500

CHRONOLOGY

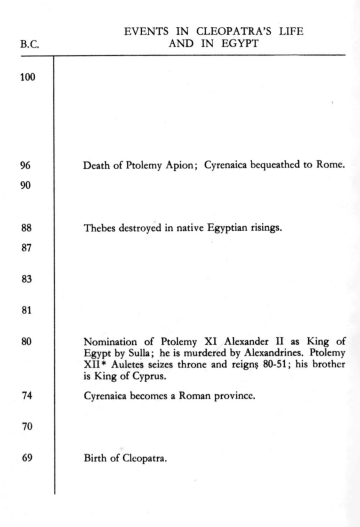

	EVENTS IN CLEOPATRA'S LIFE AND IN EGYPT
B.C.	
100	
96	Death of Ptolemy Apion; Cyrenaica bequeathed to Rome.
90	
88	Thebes destroyed in native Egyptian risings.
87	
83	
81	
80	Nomination of Ptolemy XI Alexander II as King of Egypt by Sulla; he is murdered by Alexandrines. Ptolemy XII* Auletes seizes throne and reigns 80-51; his brother is King of Cyprus.
74	Cyrenaica becomes a Roman province.
70	
69	Birth of Cleopatra.

* Called Ptolemy XIII in the book; most authorities, however, call him Ptolemy XII.

ROME AND THE ROMAN EMPIRE	ARTS, PHILOSOPHY AND SCIENCE
Birth of Julius Caesar.	Period of late Republican art begins in Rome; fashion for Greek art stimulated by the sack of Corinth in 146 B.C. Demand in Rome for copies of all known Greek master-pieces.
Social War: *Lex Julia* offers citizenship to all loyal communities.	
Sulla and Marius in power; massacres in Rome.	
	Sulla brings text of Aristotle's works to Rome.
Sulla is dictator; he reforms the Republican Constitution.	
Slave rising led by Spartacus (73-71) is crushed by Crassus.	
Pompey and Crassus impose themselves as Consuls.	Birth of Virgil.

B.C.	
68	
66	
65	Failure of Crassus' and Caesar's plan to annex Egypt.
64-63	
61	
60	
59	Adopting Caesar's proposal, the Senate recognizes Ptolemy XII Auletes as King of Egypt.
58	Cyprus becomes a Roman province after suicide of Ptolemy Auletes' brother.
57	Ptolemy Auletes driven from Alexandria.
55	Ptolemy Auletes restored by Gabinius, Governor of Syria, and Mark Antony, his cavalry commander.
54	

ROME AND THE ROMAN EMPIRE	ARTS, PHILOSOPHY AND SCIENCE
Cicero is elected Consul.	Beginning of Cicero's correspondence.
Pompey is given extraordinary powers in the war against Mithridates. First Catiline conspiracy.	
	Birth of Horace, lyric poet and satirist.
End of Seleucid Empire; Syria becomes a Roman province. Five Catiline conspirators executed in Rome. Caesar elected *Pontifex Maximus*.	Birth of Strabo, Greek geographer and historian. Cicero: *In Catilinam*.
Pompey returns to Rome; a great triumph is held.	
First Triumvirate formed by Caesar, Pompey and Crassus.	
Caesar is Consul. Pompey marries Caesar's daughter, Julia.	Birth of Titus Livius, Roman historian.
Caesar campaigns in Gaul.	
Flight of Auletes to Rome reopens Egyptian question.	
Caesar's command in Gaul is renewed for five years.	Pompey dedicates first stone theatre in Rome. Death of Epicurean poet, Lucretius, author of *De Rerum Natura*.
Death of Julia, wife of Pompey and daughter of Caesar. Defeat and death of Crassus.	Death of Poet Catullus, b. 87. Use of stone arches to build bridges and aqueducts is now standard Roman practice.

B.C.	
51	Death of Ptolemy Auletes; accession of Cleopatra VII and her brother Ptolemy XIII.
49	Civil War: Ptolemy XIII versus Cleopatra.
48	Ptolemy XIII drives Cleopatra out of Alexandria. Pompey lands in Egypt and is assassinated. Caesar arrives in Egypt and first meets Cleopatra.
48-47	Caesar's Alexandrian War: Ptolemy XIII defeated and drowned in the Nile. Caesar installs Ptolemy XIV and Cleopatra as rulers.
47	Birth of Ptolemy Caesar (Caesarion).
46	Cleopatra goes to Rome where she stays until 44.
45	
44	Cleopatra returns to Egypt. Death of Ptolemy XIV; Ptolemy XV, Caesar is co-ruler with Cleopatra.
43	

ROME AND THE ROMAN EMPIRE	ARTS, PHILOSOPHY AND SCIENCE
Caesar completes conquest of Gaul.	Cicero: *De Republica.* Caesar: *Commentarii de Bello Gallico.*
Caesar organizes Gaul and crosses the Rubicon. Civil war follows. Caesar is proclaimed dictator.	Sosigenes, Greek astronomer, working in Alexandria; later collaborated with Caesar over Julian calendar.
Battle of Pharsalia: Pompey is defeated and escapes to Egypt.	
Mark Antony is *Magister Equitum* to Caesar. Caesar's return to Rome in September, 47.	
Caesar's victory at Thapsus in Africa followed by suicide of Cato. Caesar made dictator for ten years.	Cicero: *Tusculanae Disputationes.* The first year of the Julian Calendar.
After his final victory at Munda, Caesar is made dictator for life and his person sacrosanct.	Caesar: *Commentaries on the Civil War.*
Assassination of Caesar on the Ides of March. Civil War. Lepidus is elected Pontifex Maximus.	Cicero: *Philippic Orations* against Mark Antony.
Battle of Mutina. Antony is outlawed by Senate. Octavian adopts Caesar's name and is elected Consul in August. November: formation of the Second Triumvirate, Antony, Octavian and Lepidus. Ruthless proscriptions.	Birth of Ovid, author of *Metamorphoses.* Halley's comet. Death of Marcus Tullius Cicero.

EVENTS IN CLEOPATRA'S LIFE
AND IN EGYPT

B.C.	
42	
41	Meeting of Antony and Cleopatra at Tarsus on the River Cydnus; they spend the winter together at Alexandria.
40	Cleopatra gives birth to twins, Alexander Helios and Cleopatra Selene.
39	
38	
37	Antony returns to Cleopatra after two winters spent in Athens with Octavia. Treaty of Antioch extends Ptolemaic Empire. Marriage of Antony and Cleopatra by Egyptian rites.
36	Birth of Ptolemy Philadelphus, son of Antony and Cleopatra. Antony's expedition against the Parthians unsuccessful.
35	

ROME AND THE ROMAN EMPIRE	ARTS, PHILOSOPHY AND SCIENCE
Battle of Philippi: Brutus and Cassius defeated by Antony and Octavian.	
Parthians invade eastern Roman provinces. Perusine War: Octavian versus Fulvia and L. Antonius, wife and brother of Mark Antony.	" Second Style " of wall painting at Pompeii and Herculaneum reaches its height in mid-first century with architectural and landscape vistas painted on the walls.
Brundisium: division of Roman world between Octavian in the West and Antony in the East. Antony marries Octavia, sister of Octavian, after death of Fulvia.	
Concordat of Misenum with Sextus Pompey who continues, however, intermittently to attack the Triumvirs until 35 B.C.	Virgil at work on the Bucolics, published in 37 under patronage of Maecenas.
Parthians finally defeated by Ventidius, Antony's lieutenant.	
Treaty of Tarentum between Antony and Octavian. The Triumvirate is renewed until 31st December, 32 B.C.	Greek die-engravers design Roman coins throughout the first century – a running commentary on Rome's martial and administrative achievements.
Sextus Pompey finally defeated at Naulochus. Octavian deposes Lepidus from the Triumvirate.	
Octavian starts series of successful campaigns in Pannonia and Dalmatia. Death of Sextus Pompey.	

34	Antony campaigns in Armenia; capture of King Artavades. Triumph celebrated at Alexandria. Proclamation of the Empire of the East.
33	Propaganda war between Antony and Octavian is intensified; vicious attacks made on Cleopatra.
32	Antony and Cleopatra winter at Ephesus. Both Consuls flee Rome to join Antony. Divorce of Antony and Octavia.
31	September: Battle of Actium; Antony and Cleopatra flee to Egypt.
30	August: invasion and conquest of Egypt by Octavian. Antony commits suicide. Meeting between Octavian and Cleopatra. Cleopatra commits suicide and Egypt is incorporated into the Roman Empire.
29	August: Octavian returns to Rome. A triple triumph is celebrated.
27	Octavian is called Augustus. Act of settlement divides provinces into senatorial and imperial; Egypt is directly under Augustus.

ROME AND THE ROMAN EMPIRE	ARTS, PHILOSOPHY AND SCIENCE
	Death of Sallust, author of *Bellum Catilinae* and *Bellum Jugurthinum*.
Octavian publishes Antony's will and declares war on Cleopatra.	Domitius Ahenobarbus brings back Greek sculptures of Scopas to Rome.
	Start of production of Greek style pottery at Arretium (Arezzo) – until 30 A.D. Virgil completes the *Georgics*, and starts working on the *Aeneid*.
Closing of the temple of Janus in Rome signifies that the Empire is at peace.	Death of Cornelius Nepos, Roman historian.
The line of Julio-Claudian Emperors begins with Augustus Caesar; lasted until 69 A.D.	Death of M.T. Varro, Roman scholar and antiquarian. Period of Augustan art (31-14 A.D.) coincides with "Third Style" found at Pompeii and Herculaneum, the latter ending with the earthquake of 63 A.D.

GENEALOGY OF THE PTOLEMIES

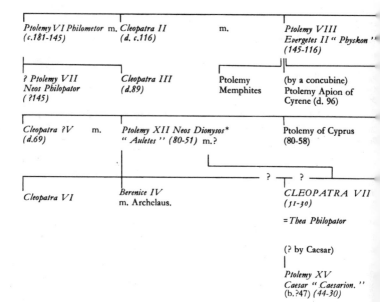

Eurydice   m.

Note on Dating.

All dates are B.C. unless otherwise indicated.
Dates given in brackets are of the
reigns of the Ptolemies unless otherwise indicated.

Ptolemy Keraunos

Ptolemy VI Philometor m. *Cleopatra II*   m.   *Ptolemy VIII*
(c.181-145)   *(d. c.116)*   *Evergetes II " Physkon "*
                                               (145-116)

? Ptolemy VII   *Cleopatra III*   Ptolemy   (by a concubine)
Neos Philopator   *(d.89)*   Memphites   Ptolemy Apion of
(?145)   Cyrene (d. 96)

Cleopatra ?V   m.   *Ptolemy XII Neos Dionysos**   Ptolemy of Cyprus
(d.69)   *" Auletes " (80-51)* m.?   (80-58)

                                                     ? — ?

Cleopatra VI   *Berenice IV*   *CLEOPATRA VII*
                m. Archelaus.   *(51-30)*

                                                     = *Thea Philopator*

                                                     (? by Caesar)

                                                     Ptolemy XV
                                                     Caesar " Caesarion. "
                                                     (b.?47) *(44-30)*

* *Ptolemy XIII in the text ; most authorities call him Ptolemy XII.*

Ptolemy Lagos m. Arsinoë
(second cousin of
Philip II of Macedon)

Ptolemy I Soter   m.   Berenice
(305-283)

m.   Arsinoë II   Ptolemy II Philadelphus
                                                    (283-246) m. Arsinoë

                                                    Ptolemy III Evergetes
                                                    (246-221) m. Berenice

                                                    Ptolemy IV Philopator
                                                    (221-203) m. Arsinoë III

                                                    Ptolemy V Epiphanes
                                                    (203-c.181) m. Cleopatra I

Cleopatra III
(d.89)

Ptolemy IX Soter II   Ptolemy X
" Lathyros " (116-107)   Alexander I
y (88-80).   (107-88)

Cleopatra   m.   Ptolemy XI
Berenice III   Alexander II
                               (murdered 80)

Arsinoë IV (b.66)   Ptolemy XIII (51-47)   Ptolemy XIV (47-44)

Antony

Alexander Helios   Cleopatra Selene   Ptolemy Philadelphus
b.40)   m. Juba II of Mauretania   (b.36)

                          Ptolemy of Mauretania   Drusilla
                          (d.40 A.D.)   m. Antonius Felix

GENEALOGY OF THE JULII

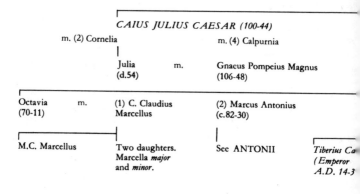

CAIUS JULIUS CAESAR (100-44)

m. (2) Cornelia   m. (4) Calpurnia

Julia   m.   Gnaeus Pompeius Magnus
(d.54)   (106-48)

Octavia   m.   (1) C. Claudius   (2) Marcus Antonius
(70-11)   Marcellus   (c.82-30)

M.C. Marcellus   Two daughters.   See ANTONII   Tiberius Ca
                    Marcella *major*   (Emperor
                    and *minor*.   A.D. 14-3

GENEALOGY OF THE ANTONII

M. Antonius Creticus (Praetor 74)

C. Antonius   L. Antonius   MARCUS ANTONIUS
(Praetor 44)   (Consul 41)   (c.82-30)
                                         (Consul 44; Triumvir 43)

m. (1) Fadia.   m. (2) Antonia   m. (3) Fulvia
                   (divorced 47)   (d.40)

                   Antonia   M. Antonius   Julius Ant
                   m. Pythodorus   "Antyllus"   m. Marcell
                   of Tralles   (45-30)   *major*

Caius Julius Caesar
(Praetor) m. Aurelia

Julia
m. M. Atius Balbus

Atia (d.43)
m. Caius Octavius
(Practor 61)

(3) Livia Drusilla   m.   *AUGUSTUS (Octavian)*   m.   (1) Clodia
m. T. Claudius Nero   *(63 B.C. – 14 A.D.)*   (2) Scribonia

Drusus Claudius   Julia   m.   (1) M.C. Marcellus
Nero   (2) M. Vipsanius
m. Antonia *minor*   Agrippa

See ANTONII

Vipsania Agrippina
m. Germanicus

See ANTONII

M. Antonius
(Consul 99 B.C.)

C. Antonius
(Consul 63)

Antonia m.
M. Antonius

---

m. (4) Octavia (70-11)   m. (5) *Cleopatra*
(divorced 32)   *(c.69-30)*

Antonia *major*   Antonia *minor*   See PTOLEMIES
m. L. Domitius   m. Drusus
Ahenobarbus   Claudius Nero

Gnaeus Domitius   Germanicus   *Claudius*
Ahenobarbus   m. Vipsania   *(Emperor*
m. Julia Agrippina   Agrippina   *A.D. 41-54)*

Nero   *Gaius " Caligula ''*   Julia Agrippina
(Emperor   *(Emperor*
A.D. 54-68)   *A.D. 37-41)*

THE ORIGINS OF EGYPTIAN CIVILIZATION, RELIGION, AND LANGUAGE

Egyptian civilization was already about three thousand years old in Cleopatra's time, and despite some infusion of Greek ideas and customs after Alexander the Great's conquest of Egypt, the old way of doing things was still very much alive. Cleopatra herself, as inheritor of the pharaohs, carried on much of the age-old tradition of this ancient kingdom.

The beginning of the historical period in Egypt is generally dated at about 2900 B.C. when the semi-mythical Menes, founder of the First Dynasty, brought all of Egypt under his rule. Before Menes the Delta (Lower Egypt) and the Valley (Upper Egypt, stretching from the Delta to the first Nile cataract at Aswan) formed two distinct kingdoms.

Nevertheless the roots of Egyptian civilization go back a great deal further than this. The presence of Paleolithic, or " Old Stone Age " man in Egypt is attested by the discovery of a succession of " industries, " or methods of making stone tools, in the terraces of the Nile Valley. The far more highly developed Neolithic, or " New Stone Age " culture is marked in Egypt, as it was elsewhere in the Middle East, by the adoption of primitive agriculture, the domestication of animals, the making of pottery and of polished (instead of chipped) stone tools, and the beginnings of sophisticated building methods. By about 4000 B.C. there is already evidence of the cultivation of wheat and barley, and the domestication of cattle, sheep, goats and pigs.

The advent of fully developed civilization in the Middle East is usually marked by the adoption first of copper, then of bronze (usually an alloy of copper and tin) for the making of tools and weapons, and the invention of irrigation, which made possible a far more intensive agriculture in the fertile river bottoms. During the fourth millennium B.C., under combined African and Asiatic influences, the important Predynastic culture developed in Egypt. In this late Neoli-

306

thic period the basic economic, social and political institutions of ancient Egypt began to take shape. With the invention of writing at the beginning of the historical period Egyptian civilization had fallen into a pattern which, in general terms, it was to hold almost to the time of Cleopatra.

Although the language of ancient Egypt is related to that of the Semites and Berbers, the Egyptians as a people are ascribed to the Mediterranean race and are a mixture of several stocks whose anthropological characteristics have scarcely changed to the present day. Egyptian hieroglyphics —a method of writing with conventionalized pictures, used chiefly to represent meanings that often seem arbitrary and are seldom obvious—had already been perfected at the beginning of the historical period; and indeed the use and understanding of the system progressively degenerated throughout dynastic times. By the period of the Middle Kingdom hieroglyphic writing began to be supplanted by the hieratic form, a cursive script, which in turn was replaced in the sixth century B.C. by the demotic, an even simpler cursive script, which was so conventionalized that its hieroglyphic origin could scarcely be discerned. Thus by the New Kingdom the hieroglyphics of ancient Egypt were not well understood; by 500 B.C. their use for any purpose had become a rarity.

Predynastic Egyptian religion is not clearly understood. Certainly in the earliest period each town had its own deity; Ptah, for instance, was worshipped at Memphis, Atum at Heliopolis, Amon at Thebes, Osiris at Busiris, and most of these gods were conceived of as animals. Horus was the god of the kings of Lower Egypt and simultaneously, as the hawk, first the god of the heaven, then of the sun. The original god of the kings of Upper Egypt was Set, but later Horus became the royal god of both kingdoms. Eventually, however, the solar religion prevailed in Egypt, originating at Heliopolis where the priests of Atum-Re elaborated the first Egyptian theology and made the worship of Re (whose symbols are obelisks) the state religion. This did not occur until Dynasty V, after which Re became identified with many

307

local gods.   Coexistent with this solar-oriented cult is the myth of Osiris, who was killed by his brother Set and restored to life by his son Horus, or in later versions, by his wife Isis.   He then became the king of the underworld and later, according to the *Book of the Dead* (c. 550 B.C.), the judge of the deceased.   It thus appears that the Osiris faith and the solar faith existed side by side, and that two gods of the dead were officially accepted.   Osiris and Re together had become the guardians of the king and his people.

CHRONOLOGY OF EGYPTIAN HISTORY

Manetho, an Egyptian priest (c. 280 B.C.), wrote a history of Egypt in Greek, of which fragments have been preserved by Josephus and others.   He grouped the kings of Egypt from Menes to Artaxerxes III (343 B.C.) into thirty dynasties, and although his chronology is far from accurate his dynastic arrangement is still used.   For the period after 2000 B.C. a fairly accurate chronology can be constructed from ancient sources, such as the Palermo stone and the Turin papyrus, from astronomical data, and by the use of " dead reckoning ".   All earlier dates are uncertain.

c. 2900–2700 B.C. *Dynasties I-II.*   Capital: Thinis.   The two kingdoms of Upper and Lower Egypt were first united by Menes and his successors.

2700–2200   *OLD   KINGDOM.*   Dynasties III-VI. Capital: Memphis.   Zoser (Djoser), the founder of Dynasty III (2700-2650), built the step pyramid of Sakkara.   Snefru (Dynasty IV, 2650-2500) built the pyramid of Medum and developed navigation.   The three colossal pyramids at Gizeh were erected by Snefru's successors, Cheops, Chephren and Mycerinus.   Dynasty V (2500-2350) marked the culmination of

2700–2200 cont. Egyptian culture—in art, architecture, technology and speculative thought.

2200–2100 *Dynasties VII-X.* This is an intermediate period of feudalism and political upheaval, in which the centralized state and the power of the Pharaohs disintegrated; contemporary literature shows a search for ethical values.

2100–1788 *MIDDLE KINGDOM.* Dynasty XI (2100-2000), capital: Thebes, and Dynasty XII (2000-1788), capital at Lisht (near Memphis) or in the Fayum. The XIth Theban dynasty reunited Egypt politically; the XIIth dynastic age is that of classical Egyptian literature. Architecture and the plastic arts also flourished. The zenith of the Middle Kingdom was reached c. 2000 B.C.: Amenemhet I (2000-1970) curbed the power of the provincial barons and began wars of territorial expansion; Sesostris III (1887-1849) conquered Nubia and campaigned in Palestine; Amenemhet III (1849-1801) reorganized mining operations in Sinai, carried out hydraulic works for irrigation in the Fayum, and built there the group of palaces known as the *Labyrinth*.

1788–1580 This second intermediate period was one of rule by usurpers and shadowy vassal rulers (Dynasties XIII-XIV) and finally by foreign invaders, the Hyksos Kings (Dynasties XV-XVI, 1680-1580, capital: Avaris in the Delta). The Hyksos (" Rulers of Countries ") were a mixed horde of semi-nomadic Semites and Hurrians from Palestine, Syria and farther north, who

1788–1580 cont.   introduced the horse, the chariot and many new weapons into Egypt.

The XVIIth Theban dynasty under Kings Sekenenre and Kamose began the war against the Hyksos.

1580–1090   *NEW KINGDOM.* The Imperial era in Egyptian history. Dynasties XVIII-XX. *Dynasty XVIII.* Capital: Thebes (1580-1350):

Amosis (Ahmose) expelled the Hyksos and reestablished royal authority over Nubia and the feudal provinces. Amenophis I (Amenhotep) (1557-1536) and Thutmosis I (Thutmoses or Thothmes) (1536-1520) campaigned in Palestine and Syria, reaching the Euphrates. The real ruler of Egypt from 1520 until her death in 1480 was Queen Hatshepsut, half-sister and wife first of Thutmosis II, then of her nephew Thutmosis III (1501-1447). Thutmosis III in 19 years (17 campaigns) conquered Palestine, Phoenicia, Syria and reached Carchemish. Amenophis III (1411-1375) preserved this Asiatic Empire by an astute diplomatic policy, as revealed by the *Tell-el-Amarna letters.* His reign was a period of great prosperity and cultural advancement.

Amenophis IV (Akhenaton) (1375-1358), husband of Queen Nefertiti, envisaged one universal god Aton (the sun-disk and its life-giving rays), but his religious reformation did not survive him owing to the opposition of the priests of Amon-Re at Thebes. A gradual loss of the Asiatic cities began in his reign. He built a new capital at Tell-el-Amarna where a new style of painting and architecture can be dis-

1580–1090 cont. cerned. He was succeeded by his two sons-in-law; the second was Tutankhamon (1352-1343) whose richly furnished, unviolated tomb was discovered by Carnarvon and Carter in 1922.

Dynasty XIX. Capital: Thebes (1350-1200): The wars of Seti I (Sethos) (1313-1292) and Ramses II (1292-1225) (under whom Moses probably led the Israelites out of Egypt) were an attempt to regain the Asiatic empire from the Hittites, though only southern Palestine was regained by the peace of 1271. For the final forty-six years of his reign Ramses built prodigiously from the Delta to Abu Simbel in Nubia. Merneptah (1225-1215) repelled the combined attack of the Libyans and the *Peoples of the Sea* (Aegean marauders) in 1221. The movement of these Aegean peoples is connected with the Homeric war against Troy and brought about the end of the Hittite Kingdom.

Dynasty XX. Capital: Thebes (1200-1090): Ramses III (1198-1167) defeated another wave of *Peoples of the Sea*, including the Danaï and Philistines. Under his feeble successors (Ramses IV-XII) the power of of the high priests of Amon-Re increased until Herihor, high priest of Amon and army commander, assumed power.

1090–945 *Dynasty XXI.* The struggle of the line of Herihor and the line of Smendes (a noble of Tanis) for the royal authority.

945–712 *Dynasties XXII-XXIV.* Shoshenk (Shishak of the biblical *Book of Kings*) (945-924) founded a Libyan dynasty with its capital

945–712 cont.

at Bubastis. The high priestly family of Amon at Thebes founded the independent southern Nubian kingdom with its capital at Napata (c. 850). Libyan princes then became high priests of Amon at Thebes. During dynasties XXIII (745-718) and XXIV (718-712) anarchy and civil war prevailed.

712–663

Dynasty XXV. An Ethiopian dynasty founded by Shabaka, King of Napata. After defeating Taharka (688-663), Essarhaddon of Assyria made Egypt (as far as Thebes) an Assyrian province in 671. Ashurbanipal was forced to undertake two more campaigns into Egypt (in 668 and 661) during the second of which Thebes was sacked.

663–525

Dynasty XXVI. Capital: Saïs. Psamtik (Psammetichus), appointed governor of Saïs and Memphis under Ashurbanipal of Assyria, rebelled and by 652 was master of Egypt. Thus began the Saïtic revival—a renaissance deliberately imitating the arts, literature and religion of the Old and Middle Kingdoms. Greek mercenaries and merchants were encouraged to come to Egypt. Necho (609-593), according to Herodotus, failed in his attempt to connect the Nile with the Red Sea by means of a canal, but ordered the successful circumnavigation of Africa by Phoenician sailors. He also reconquered Judea but was completely routed at Carchemish by Nebuchadrezzar of Babylon. His successors were equally unsuccessful in their military campaigns. Amasis (569-525)

663–525 cont. allowed Greek merchants to make of Naukratis a purely Greek city, and the most important commercial centre of the kingdom.

525–404 *Dynasty XXVII.* Egypt came under Persian rule, after Cambyses defeated Psamtik III at Pelusium in 525.

404–332 *Dynasties XXVIII-XXX* were comprised of ephemeral native rulers under whom Egypt was in some degree independent from the Persian kings, despite a further Persian conquest in 354 B.C.

332–323 Alexander the Great conquered Egypt unopposed in 332. When his brief empire faded, Egypt fell to his general Ptolemy, who became king as Ptolemy I in 305 B.C., with his capital at Alexandria.

323–30 B.C. Egypt under the Ptolemies.

30 B.C.–640 A.D. Egypt a province under the Roman Empire, until about 395 A.D. when the Eastern and Western empires split apart, the East developing into the Byzantine Empire. By about 200 A.D. Christianity had spread widely in Egypt, producing the distinctively Egyptian Coptic Church, which arose from the Monophysite heresy. These Christians developed the Coptic language during the third and fourth centuries A.D.

c. 640–1250 The Arab conquest, about 640 A.D., made Egypt an integral part of the Moslem world. In the tenth century Egypt fell

c. 640–1250 cont. to the Fatimid family who founded Cairo as their capital. From 1169 to 1250 Egypt was ruled by the Ayyubid dynasty, founded by Saladin.

1250–1517 Egypt was controlled by the Mameluke Sultans.

1517–1798 Egypt was conquered by the Turks and was incorporated into the Ottoman Empire. By the eighteenth century Ottoman rule from Istambul had become merely nominal.

1798–1801 Napoleon's occupation of Egypt was undertaken ostensibly to restore Turkish rule but actually to sever British trade links with India.

19th century on Mohammed Ali, who rose to power in 1805, was the founder of the royal line which ended in 1952. During World War I the British made Egypt a Protectorate, but granted her independence in 1923 with the accession of Fuad I as Egypt's first constitutional monarch. Farouk I was driven from his throne in August, 1952 by an army coup headed by Naguib but actually engineered by Nasser. A republic was proclaimed in July, 1953.

EGYPT—
FROM ALEXANDER THE GREAT TO AUGUSTUS

In 332 B.C. Alexander the Great took over Egypt to remove it from the threat of Persian domination. When he died in 323 B.C., leaving the empire he had built to the " most worthy ", a struggle for power between his generals ensued in which all the members of the ruling house of Macedon disappeared. Of these generals Antigonus the " One-eyed " came closest to realizing an undivided empire, but he was killed at the Battle of Ipsus in 301 B.C., and thereafter the empire fell apart into separate provinces ruled by different generals, the most important being an enlarged Syria under Seleucus and his descendants, Macedonia under the Antigonidae, and Egypt under the Ptolemies, or Lagidae, descendants of Ptolemy Lagus, Alexander's bodyguard in India.

In Egypt and Syria the Hellenistic " Kings ", as they styled themselves after 307-305 B.C., ruled by right of conquest, relying upon mercenary troops to enforce their power and fostering a well-to-do upper class of Greek settlers to maintain their culture in the midst of alien peoples. Since these rulers were of Macedonian birth and Greek culture, the entire period between Alexander's death and the Roman conquest of the East is usually called " Hellenistic ". In Egypt this was the Ptolemaic period, which ended with the death of Cleopatra.

Among all the states which emerged after the death of Alexander, the Ptolemaic empire seemed for many years the favourite child of history. Although Egypt's position, between the Mediterranean and the Red Seas, was ideal for vigorous commercial and imperial growth, her eastern coast and especially the wide, flat mouth of the Delta were at the mercy of invaders. The Ptolemies therefore built up a powerful fleet to protect the coasts and to maintain the vital freedom of trade, and made of Alexandria on the Delta, Egypt's capital, both a naval base and a fortress. Ptolemy I Soter (Saviour), 323-283 B.C., by surrounding Egypt with territories that strategically and economically complemented the homeland, created an empire that was further enlarged by Ptolemy II Philadelphus and was extended to its widest limits by Ptolemy III Energetes.

Ptolemy I, securing Egypt's western frontier by subduing Cyrenaica, also conquered Southern Syria, a prized but often hotly-disputed area which controlled the trade routes from India through the South Arabian kingdoms, as well as

315

the coastwise trade with Southeast Africa. His conquest of Phoenicia not only secured the trade routes from the heart of Asia but also provided seasoned sailors for his fleets and timber for treeless Egypt. From Cyprus, Syria and Cyrenaica the Ptolemies thrust onward into Greece proper, meeting prolonged resistance from the Antigonids and Seleucids but gaining for Egypt, by force of arms, gold, and clever propaganda, not only a wide-meshed network of naval bases, treaties and friendships but also respect and admiration throughout the Mediterranean world for the name and wealth of the Ptolemies.

Egypt's trade, based as always upon the inexhaustible fertility of her soil, was widespread. All imports were carefully controlled and paid for with coins which for size, beauty and quantity were unsurpassed in the contemporary world. A stringent agricultural policy divided up the land according to its productivity, the most fertile areas being leased by the King and worked by crown peasants. Customs duties further swelled the state income. Thus enriched, Alexandria became the cultural centre of the Greek world, famed for her library, containing over 400-thousand papyrus rolls, her outstanding scholars like Eratosthenes, Aristarchus and Euclid, and her cultivation of medicine, mathematics, physics, geography and astronomy.

In the matter of religion Ptolemy I, while ensuring the loyalty of his Egyptian priests and subjects by worshipping the ancient deities, deliberately created a new god, Serapis (a fusion of the Egyptian Osiris-Apis, god of the underworld and of fertility, with Pluto, the Greek god of the underworld) in order to build a bridge between the different racial groups in his empire. A magnificent temple at Rhakotis near Alexandria was built for Serapis, who for seven centuries was worshipped by the Alexandrians until Christians laid his holy places in ruins. Ptolemy I himself was worshipped after his death as the " Saviour God ", and his son, Ptolemy II Philadelphus inaugurated the cult of the Ptolemaic God-Kings by requiring himself and his sister-consort, Arsinoë, to be worshipped as " The Divine Brother and Sister ". Ptolemy II also instituted the festival known as the Ptolemaia, held in honour of the Greek god Dionysus, who had to a large extent been equated with Alexander and his deeds. As the feast of the Great Dionysia had celebrated Athens and her empire, so did the Ptolemaia glorify the wealth and power of the Ptolemies, especially when held in foreign lands. Ptolemy III Energetes went so far as to declare himself a descendant of Dionysus on his mother's side, thus claiming this Greek god as a Ptolemaic ancestor and protector of the dynasty. Cleopatra's father, Ptolemy XII, styled himself the "New Dionysus", and it was as Dionysus that Antony claimed the lordship of the East.

Under the reigns of Ptolemy IV, V and VI, as political decadence was accompanied by economic decline, the Empire weakened. In 188 B.C. protracted and repeated native uprisings broke out from end to end of the Nile Valley, and for a time the region between the first and second cataracts was ruled by a Pharoah, Harmachis. Inflation and debasement of the currency hit the native population hardest, and abroad loss of possessions cut off supplies of many raw materials. In 168 B.C., during the reign of Ptolemy VI Philometor, the Roman ambassador intervened to save Alexandria from the Seleucid king, Antiochus IV, and from that date Egypt became a client state of Rome. Four years later Ptolemy VI sued to Rome for help against his brother, Ptolemy VIII, who had driven him from Alexandria. Another two years passed and the position was reversed; Ptolemy VIII was seeking Roman aid in return for naming Rome heir to his kingdom. After the death of Ptolemy VI in 145 B.C., Ptolemy VIII Physkon reunited Egypt, but his reign demonstrated as never before the degradation of his dynasty and the corruption of the court. He first married his sister, Cleopatra II, and then married her daughter, Cleopatra III (both niece and stepdaughter to him), whom he also raised to the status of co-regent. Hatred between mother and daughter flourished in an atmosphere of intrigue worthy of an oriental court, encouraged and guided by unscrupulous eunuch officials who were often the true rulers of Egypt.

After the death of Ptolemy IX Soter, son of Cleopatra III, in 80 B.C. Sulla made Ptolemy XI Alexander II king of Egypt, but he was murdered in the same year by the Alexandrian populace for having killed his step-mother, Cleopatra Berenice. As yet the Alexandrians cared little for the wrath of Rome, and entrusted the government to two sons of Ptolemy IX Lathyros, grandfather of Cleopatra.

Yet Egypt was increasingly dependent upon Rome. In 188 B.C. Macedonia had become a Roman province, and the enormous kingdom of the Seleucids was snatched from the hands of its powerless rulers by Pompey in 64 B.C. Ten years earlier Rome had taken over Cyrenaica, bequeathed to it by Ptolemy Apion in 96 B.C. Egypt was isolated; moreover the very complexity of the Ptolemaic succession played into Roman hands. For instance Ptolemy XII Auletes, Cleopatra's father, who assumed power after the murder of Ptolemy XI, was kept in a state of utter docility by the opportune discovery by the Romans of a will of Ptolemy XI making the Roman people his heirs. In 78 B.C. Auletes married his sister, Cleopatra V, who bore two children, Cleopatra VI and Berenice. Cleopatra VII, our Cleopatra, is thought to have been either the third and last daughter of Cleopatra V, or the first child of Auletes' second marriage, which produced her sister, Arsinoë, and her brothers Ptolemy XIII and XIV. At all events, when she was born in 68/69 B.C. the golden century of the Ptolemies was long over and their empire lay in ruins.

After the tumultuous events described in this book, culminating in the death of Cleopatra, Octavian returned to Rome and celebrated his victory with a triple triumph on a magnificent scale. A few years later, in January of the year 27 B.C., he ostentatiously surrendered his power into the hands of the Senate and the People of Rome, and in return was given the status of First Citizen and the surname Augustus. Thus was inaugurated the Roman Empire. The contribution of Egypt, as a source of economic and political power, to this fateful achievement cannot be underestimated.

318

Under Augustus Egypt was placed under an extremely severe form of administration in order to forestall any possibility of revolt. Reserving to himself both the government and the use of its revenues, Octavian—or Augustus as he would become—forbade Roman citizens to settle in Alexandria, made it impossible for an Egyptian to become a Roman senator, and denied Egypt's inhabitants the right of citizenship. In fact a great silence seemed to fall on the country, and although in after years the Roman, and eventually the Arabian occupations restored some of Egypt's former prosperity, Alexandria, giving place to Cairo, declined as a great metropolis and eventually fell into ruins.

Under the settlement of 27 B.C. and in later years not only Egypt, but large parts of the empire from one end to the other, including some of the wealthiest and most populous of provinces, were also assigned to Augustus. The importance of this development, which concentrated three quarters of the empire under the sole and direct control of Caesar and his subordinate officials, cannot be overestimated. In contrast to the " public " or senatorial provinces, where the evils and abuses of the old Republican system remained, it gave the Emperor a free hand in developing a sound administrative system which soon became the envy of the territories not subject to it; and indeed it was finally extended over the whole empire.

Preeminent among Augustus's prefects was the one who now ruled in his name over the wealthy province of Egypt. Indeed Augustus was wise to reserve Egypt for himself, for the man who controlled the enormous resources of Egypt could wield vast political as well as financial power and thus could put pressure on the masses in Rome. In the first place, as Tacitus has told us, Cleopatra's rich treasure enabled Octavian not only to discharge his many financial obligations but also to mount his glittering triumph. Moreover every man in Rome received 400 *sestertii*, the veterans of the capture of Alexandria 1000 *sestertii* each, and in addition 120,000 veterans were rewarded with 1000 *sestertii* each. At a stroke the pressing shortage of capital in Rome was relieved, the rate of interest (an infallible barometer of the circulation of money) fell from 12 to 4 per cent, the price of land doubled, and the minting of countless new silver and gold coins provided an opportunity to celebrate, by means of the designs and legends on the coins, the achievements and plans of the victor of Actium.

All this did Cleopatra's treasure accomplish; but it was soon exhausted. The permanent economic resources of Egypt, however, were inexhaustible, and after the years of war Octavian did all he could to reinvigorate the economy. When Roman soldiers had cleaned out the mud-choked Nile canals, agriculture took on new life and began to supply one third of Rome's requirement in corn each year. Roads were built and trade revived, yielding a considerable revenue in duties. And there was little opposition to the new Roman rule, for whereas Augustus ruled the other provinces as proconsul with the aid of the Senate, in Egypt he was Pharaoh. Events in Egypt were now dated by the regnal years of the emperors as they had previously been by the regnal years of the Ptolemies. Egyptian coins also bore the image of Livia, Octavian's wife, with the double cornucopia of the Ptolemies on the reverse, so that she thus appeared as the successor to Cleopatra.

The Emperor could not continue to wield such autocratic power in Egypt without this having a retroactive effect on his policy in Rome and Italy. There was a temptation, in fact, to turn the Principate into a Hellenistic divine monarchy, and emperors like Nero, and Gaius (who contemplated marriage with his sister, on the Ptolemaic model) more or less succumbed to it. The Roman Empire now had two poles. One centred on Rome and Italy, the stronghold of Roman culture, which Augustus sought to revive through fostering legislation, religion and literature, and the Roman theory of the free state. The other pole was Egypt, with its Hellenistic-Oriental culture and its chosen form of state, the Hellenistic divine monarchy. Between these poles lay the bulk of the provinces, whose cultural and legal structures were intermediate between the two.

In the course of centuries Egyptian influences helped to alter the institutions of the Roman Empire. They could be traced, for example, in the growing centralization of administration, the emergence of the bureaucratic state, the increasing interference of the state in economic affairs, which led to the Roman imperium of the third and later centuries, based on caste and compulsion. Like its Ptolemaic model, it eventually foundered largely on the mood of weariness which such regimentation must induce.

This danger, however—already incipient in the Empire of the East planned by Antony and Cleopatra—was held off for centuries by Octavian's victory. He drove the Hellenistic divine monarchy back into Egypt and tolerated the ruler-cult only there and in those provinces in which he was worshipped along with the goddess Roma. Augustus not only brought to his world a measure of peace, the *pax Augusta*, but also placed at the centre of his new Empire, as its guardian, the reawakened Roman nation, still aware, amid the disorder of the times, of its ancient resources.

ROME: THE REPUBLICAN BACKGROUND

The long history of Rome can be divided into two periods of roughly equal length. After a formative period under the kings, the Republic of Rome was established in 509 B.C. and endured for nearly four hundred years. The Empire, inaugurated by Augustus after many years of worsening civil strife and social disintegration, lasted for approximately the same length of time, finally falling prey in its senility to the fatal incursions of the barbarians. Of this long and remarkable history perhaps the most crucial span of years was that which, at the midway point, saw the dissolution of the Republic and the establishment of the Empire. And it was precisely towards the latter end of this period that Cleopatra flourished and then came to her untimely end.

The story of Cleopatra, so charmingly told by Carlo Maria Franzero, would seem to be merely an episode—albeit a famous one—in the tangled politics that led to the establishment of the Empire. In fact Egypt, the Egypt of Cleopatra, with its fabulous and corrupting wealth, played a rather more important role in these revolutionary years than one might realize. For Rome's penetration of Egypt, the last of the great states of the East to fall under her sway, might be called the final straw that broke the back of the Republic, whose democratic institutions had shown themselves increasingly incapable of coping with the problems engendered by Rome's rapid expansion throughout the known world of the time.

No people who have risen to imperial power have had so long a record of free political development, untrammelled by the oppressions of autocracy, as the Romans. They had long lived together in democratic harmony in a relatively small community, sharing the same traditions, outlook, language and way of life. As they attained to greater power, wealth and glory one might have expected their institutions to adapt themselves readily to the task of maintaining security and a progressive social life for all. But such was not to be the case, for despite the great ability of the Republican leaders and their amazing record of success, the Romans were ultimately unable to create a form of democratic government capable of sustaining the burden and responsibility of world rule. Thus behind the personal tragedy of Caesar and Cleopatra, Mark Antony and Octavius, as told in this book, one can discern the hidden presence of a greater tragedy in which all four played leading roles—the failure of the Roman Republic.

The main outlines of the Roman story stand out clearly enough, although in earliest times it is impossible to disentangle history from legend, or fact from fiction. Rome's beginnings were humble. In time the little city state was dominated by Etruscan kings, and when the last of them was driven out in 509 B.C. the memory of royal rule during the seventh and sixth centuries B.C. was kept alive in legend and story. Indeed such was the hatred of the very name of king that during Republican times the blackest crime of which any Roman could be accused was the ambition to become a king. Nearly five hundred years later, when Julius Caesar had achieved all the power any king could hope for, he still found it impossible to assume the title. And when Augustus began the Empire by setting up his Principate, he paid scrupulous lip service to the institutions of the Republic as did his successors for many years.

Thus Roman political institutions, even under the Empire, were specifically Republican rather than royal, and included the right of Roman citizens to be governed by a settled body of public and private law, as well as the supreme right to appeal to the " people " as a whole for ultimate justice against sentence of death. Power in Rome was *imperium*, from the verb *impero* (" I command "), and when the Romans conferred it upon one of their fellow citizens such as a Consul, their leading official, the Consul was expected to use the full power of the Republic according to his best judgment, and they pledged their obedience to his orders. The Consul appointed Senators, raised armies and taxes, was chief magistrate, and commanded the Roman army. Yet his term was limited to twelve months at a time and a fellow Consul was always appointed with him to act as a check upon his power. In times of dire emergency the Consuls had the right to name an absolute Dictator; but even the Dictator was appointed for only six months, and if the emergency had then been met was expected to return his powers to the Consuls.

Religion played its part in the state through the Pontifex Maximus, elected for a lifetime term, under whom was appointed a "king for sacrifices" to carry on that part of the former royal duties. Interpreting the will of the gods through the reading of omens—a practice inherited from the Etruscans—was carried out by the Augurs, who examined the vital organs of sacrificial animals, observed the flight of birds, the behaviour of the sacred chickens or the nature of lightning flashes in their search for signs. The position of Augur carried much prestige and was greatly coveted among influential Romans.

Even in the early days of the Republic many Romans owned slaves, since slavery was prevalent throughout the ancient world. In Rome, however, emancipated slaves, or freedmen, often became " clients " of their former masters and even gained a vote in the Roman public assemblies.

Gradually they and their descendants grew in numbers to swamp the descendants of free Romans. And since their background and attitude to life was quite different from that of the old Romans, this silent revolution probably did more to alter the tone and quality of Roman civilization than all the overt political revolutions put together.

Nevertheless, as in any expanding society, the Romans had their share of political troubles. The first crack in the Republic of free Roman citizens appeared very early, in 494 B.C., in the guise of a bloodless revolution against the privileges of the ruling class, or patricians, who by virtue of their wealth, their standing in the Senate and army assembly, their social position and bands of faithful clients had increasingly oppressed the lower orders or plebeians. The patricians were subjected to some measure of popular control by the creation of the remarkable institution of the Tribunes of the People, ten powerful officials who could, in the interests of the plebeians, neutralize any acts of the Consuls within the city limits—and the Consuls were of course the supreme officials of the Roman people. Although one Tribune could veto the acts of another, there was no appeal against their decisions except the drastic step of appointing a Dictator.

Another revolution in 449 B.C. was necessary to confirm the power of the Tribunes and enforce respect for the rule of law, and by 367 the plebeians had become legally entitled to provide one of the Consuls from their ranks. Indeed by 300 B.C. the distinction between plebeian and patrician, though not forgotten, had become of less consequence, and in 287 a final popular triumph, carried through without bloodshed or acrimony, provided that the wishes of the plebeians, expressed in their own popular assembly under the leadership of the Tribunes, should be binding upon the community as a whole. With popular representation thus assured, domestic politics were relatively peaceful for nearly two centuries thereafter, which was providential because the state was almost continually at war.

The foreign wars, which by 167 B.C. had made Rome the strongest power in the then known world, conferred greatness upon her, but also sowed the seeds of dissolution which led to the downfall of the Republic. These wars, which may be said to have begun with the sack of wealthy Veii, an Etruscan strongpoint, in 396 B.C. were briefly interrupted when Rome itself was overrun in 390 B.C. by hordes of Celtic or Gallic invaders sweeping down from the North. The story of the conquest of the whole of central Italy by 290 B.C. and thereafter the Greek south by 266 is long and confused, but of great significance for the economic benefits it conferred. Next Rome was locked in the long life-and-death struggle with the Phoenician colony of Carthage across the Mediterranean from Italy, during which, by force of necessity, she learned the arts of shipbuilding and navigation and became a great sea power. In the second Punic War, between 218 and 202 B.C., Rome was all but defeated until P. Cornelius Scipio, a young aristocratic commander of genius, turned disaster into victory. After the Punic Wars Spain fell to Rome, and successful Macedonian campaigns removed fear of attack from the East.

With Rome now the leading power in its world, riches flowed in from conquered and client countries to disrupt the long-held social balance. In 133 B.C. Tiberius Gracchus, in what was in effect the first " share the wealth " campaign, used the office of Tribune to promote economic reforms that would benefit the mass of Roman and Italian citizens and improve the efficiency and honesty of the government. " Tiberius Gracchus ", wrote Appian, " lost his life in consequence of a most excellent design which, however, he pursued in too violent a manner ". He was brutally murdered, and ten years later his brother, taking up the work again, shared Tiberius' fate in a yet more horrible scene of violence along with 3,000 other Romans. Thus was created a new and sinister precedent of violence in public life.

From 123 B.C. onwards Roman political life became steadily less stable, while violence as an instrument of power became more common. Unrest and strife were deliberately provoked by ambitious individuals who used the armies of the Republic for their own ends rather than for the public weal, while the soldiers themselves came increasingly to look to their commanders rather than to the Republic for their well-being. With men of the stripe of Marius, Sulla, Pompey, Crassus, Caesar and even Octavius using their armies as instruments of their own private ambitions, that military tyranny by which, under various disguises, the Romans were to be ruled in the imperial era could not be far off. The days of the Republic were numbered.

Foreign campaigns more and more often became the means in this period whereby able and ambitious Romans could rise to power, using the land and booty from their victories to reward their armies and consolidate their political positions. In 115 B.C. a vigorous ruler, Mithridates VI, seized the kingdom of Pontus in Asia Minor and began a war of conquest, while nearer home successive Roman armies were defeated by hordes of Germanic tribes. Gaius Marius, an efficient and ruthless commander, who modernized and streamlined the Roman army, rose to fame through his defeat of the unscrupulous and semi-savage Jugurtha of North Africa, then later secured the northern frontier against the Germans. An able general, Marius was nevertheless one of the first to set the pattern of using wealth and violence to further his ambitions, and thus inaugurated, with his massacre of Saturninus and his followers in 100 B.C. an era of confused civil war which lasted until the establishment of the Empire.

Saturninus had been a reformer somewhat on the model of the Gracchi. His death, and the murder of M. Livius Drusus in 91 B.C., brought Roman politics to a low ebb and seemed to doom all possibility of reform. In 91 B.C. the restive Italians, their claims for social and political equality with the Romans brushed aside, resorted to arms, and in the bitter " social war " that followed the Romans sustained one defeat after another—in one battle two Consuls were killed and thousands slain with them. Defeated at home and fearful of the attacks of Mithridates abroad, the Romans granted concessions to the Italians, only to find themselves impelled into civil war when the aristocratic Lucius Cornelius Sulla, passed over in favour of Marius as commander of the war in the East, invaded Rome itself in 88 B.C. From this time forward, as Appian wrote, "civil dissensions were decided only by the arbitrament of arms ".

A year later Marius was back in Rome. With Cinna he assumed the title of Consul, but in fact the two were military dictators of a new kind who took a fiendish delight in exterminating their enemies. Fortunately Marius died in 86 B.C. and for a time the strife-torn city experienced some peace. In 82 B.C. however, Sulla's victorious troops once again entered Rome despite the desperate and almost successful resistance of tough Samnite highlanders, who were thereupon exterminated by Sulla in an early example of genocide. Sulla then consolidated his tyranny by proscribing about forty senators and a thousand knights, offering prizes to assassins and rewards to informers, and distributing confiscated land on a huge scale to his returning soldiers. But Sulla was ready to build anew upon the ruin he had created, and his reforms—thorough, intelligent, and competently carried out—made the Senate supreme, limited the terms of the Consuls, and minimized the power of the Tribunes. In 81 B.C. Sulla also appointed three hundred new senators.

Despite the horror of his tyranny, Sulla's reforms might have saved the Republic had not other generals, following his earlier example, refused to give up their commands after successful campaigns. Pompey had overcome resistance to Sulla in Spain, while Crassus had crushed the disastrous slave revolt of 73-71 B.C. led by Spartacus. In 70 B.C. both insisted on being chosen Consuls, and after overthrowing many of Sulla's reforms, Pompey went to the East, cleared the Mediterranean of pirates, concluded the long war against Mithridates, and even captured Jerusalem in 67 B.C. to end a civil war among the Jews. In the meantime Crassus in Rome, jealous of Pompey, whose return was imminent, was seeking to build up a personal party with which to oppose him. Moreover he almost persuaded the Senate to annex Egypt and give him command there, and in an attempt to gain allies hushed up the first Catiline conspiracy—an attempt to gain power by force which failed after it was revealed to the Senate.

Of all the allies seduced by Crassus' wealth Gaius Julius Caesar, then thirty-five years old and hopelessly in debt, proved to be the shrewdest. Implicated as he may have been in the first Catiline conspiracy, and in the plot to annex Egypt, both foiled by Cicero as Consul, he nevertheless outwitted his creditors by winning election both to the position of Pontifex Maximus and to the Praetorship for 62 B.C. Meanwhile the discovery of Catiline's scheme to murder his creditors in a carefully staged revolutionary disturbance obliged the conspirator to flee Rome and gained for Cicero the name of " Father of his country " because of his exemplary conduct in saving Rome from the arms of the discontented Sullan veterans led by Catiline. But in December of 62 B.C. Rome again trembled for its safety: Pompey was returning from the East with thirty-five to forty seasoned troops under his command and laden with unimaginable wealth. Rome was at his mercy. Yet to the amazement of all Pompey laid aside ·his power and returned to private citizenship.

Roman imperial profits, swollen with the riches of provinces newly conquered by Pompey, rose from 200 million to 340 million sesterces a year. This prodigious wealth was further swollen in 60 B.C. by the influx of loot accumulated by Caesar during his pro-Praetorship in Further Spain. His creditors appeased, Caesar claimed the Consulship for 59 B.C. and a province to command as pro-Consul. In order to check his ambition the first Triumvirate was formed—the beginning of the end for the Republic of Rome.

Caesar won over both Pompey and Crassus by implementing his pre-election promises to satisfy their claims, and introduced a comprehensive Land Bill to provide for Pompey's veterans. The opposition of Cato's faction and of Bibulus, the co-Consul manoeuvred into office by the Senate, was so determined that Caesar was obliged to resort to strong-arm methods. A mob of Pompey's land-hungry veterans were let loose in the forum and drove out Caesar's opponents, and the powerless senators, rather than face exile, had to swallow Caesar's law. " Caesar, Pompey and Crassus are at war with everybody ...... for no other motive than their own security and power " wrote Cicero, who shortly afterwards, in spite of Pompey's reassurances, was driven into exile. It was becoming evident that even Pompey was unable to oppose Caesar.

In 53 B.C. Crassus was killed in an abortive war against the Parthians. The Big Three was reduced to Two. After the death of Pompey's wife, Julia, the daughter of Caesar, the relationship between Caesar and Pompey became increasingly strained, but the breakdown was postponed by Caesar's departure for a five-year term of command in Gaul. In Caesar's absence, a young senator took it upon himself to kill Publius Clodius, Caesar's protégé and the leader of Rome's armed thuggery. In hopes of restoring a measure of public safety the exasperated senators appointed Pompey sole Consul. With some of his old energy Pompey mastered the situation, but failed to reckon with the imminent return of Caesar. The end for Pompey was only three years away.

From Ravenna on January 1st, 49, Caesar issued an ultimatum to the Senate: mutual disarmament or war, to which the Senate replied with a motion naming Caesar as public enemy number one. Days after hearing the news Caesar crossed the Rubicon, defying the law which confined him to his province and the custom which forbade him to enter Rome at the head of an army. To some hopeful observers Pompey's position might have seemed strong after nine years rule in Rome, but Cicero was under no such illusion: Pompey was " fatuous and rash ... an inconceivably miserable spectacle ... He has utterly broken down." As for Caesar, Cicero favoured him with the words, " an unprincipled bandit, a disgrace to the Republic ." The Republic's time was running short.

Events moved swiftly to a climax. Realizing that he was no match for Caesar in Italy, Pompey marched south with Caesar at his heels and just managed to escape with a small force to Macedonia where he hoped to build up his army. Seeing that fortune favoured Caesar many waverers flocked to his support and at the Battle of Pharsalia in 48 B.C. Caesar, the public enemy, defeated Pompey, commander of the forces of the Republic. Pompey fled to Egypt and was there murdered. The final act of Caesar's triumph over the Republican forces was played out in North Africa at the Battle of Thapsus in April, 46 B.C.

One man had overthrown the Republic, one man assumed the power formerly held by the senatorial class. Julius Caesar became Dictator in early 44 B.C., and, for the first time in Roman history, he was named Dictator for life. The obsequious Senate heaped fulsome honours upon him and were bound under solemn oath to protect him from harm, with the result that Caesar went unguarded and unarmed through the city. His likeness appeared on coins of the official mint, usually a posthumous honour, and statues of him were erected in temples and in all public places. Caesar had refused the royal title, but this did not prevent Roman citizens naming him " King " in private. To those men deprived of power by Caesar's absolute rule, the situation was intolerable. At least sixty of them began in deadly secrecy to plot his death, and on March 15th, 44 B.C. Caesar was assassinated in the Senate, his body, riddled with twenty-three dagger wounds, falling at the foot of Pompey's statue.

Caesar's assassination, however, only revealed more vividly the bankruptcy and ineffectiveness of the Republican leaders. There ensued a confused, desperate and largely unsuccessful struggle to oppose the men that Caesar had left in power. After a few months of uncertainty, during which Mark Antony claimed Caesar's authority for all kinds of projects which he himself invented, a new alignment of forces began to take shape. The sudden appearance of Octavian, great-nephew and adopted son of Caesar, and only nineteen years old, greatly complicated the situation. Despite the rebuffs dealt him by Antony, who was rapidly frittering away the vast reserves left by Caesar, Octavian's influence was growing.

The appeal to arms did not come until early in 43 B.C. when, after a clash at Mutina in the north in which Antony was worsted, the Senate was rather reluctantly induced to declare him a public enemy. But when a Republican army under Lepidus refused to fight against Antony, Octavian was obliged to seek a compromise. Marching on Rome, he forced the Senate to elect him Consul, although he was only twenty. Then he joined forces with Antony and Lepidus in the Second Triumvirate, formed ostensibly to " reconstitute the Republic. " In actual fact proscription lists were issued against three hundred senators and two thousand knights – a ruthless and bloody reminder of the Sullan terror of forty years before. But the *veterani* at least were quieted by gifts of the lands, homes and possessions of the proscribed.

In the autumn of 42 B.C. the last effective Republican threat was eliminated when Antony and Octavian defeated Brutus and Cassius at the Battle of Philippi, with great loss of life on both sides. Although Sextus Pompeius had kept up a flicker of defiance in Spain and Sicily, by 36 B.C. Octavian had defeated him and at the same time Lepidus had been forced to retire into private life. In the meantime Antony, during the ten years following the Battle of Philippi, had remained largely in the East, allowing Octavian time to consolidate his position at Rome and to slander Antony and Cleopatra in a propaganda campaign of extraordinary virulence. By 32 B.C. Antony's conduct in the East had so outraged the Romans that Octavian saw his chance and declared war—but, astutely, against Cleopatra rather than against a fellow Roman. At the naval engagement of Actium most of Antony's fleet surrendered to Octavian while Antony and Cleopatra fled to Egypt. Antony committed suicide before Octavian arrived in Alexandria, Cleopatra soon afterwards, while Octavian seized the fabulous treasure of the Ptolemies in gold, jewels and ivory. This is what he had come for, and this is what he needed in order to consolidate his power at home.

No independent force now existed in the Roman world that could challenge Octavian, who by his astute diplomacy over the next five years showed that he had profited well from the examples of the careers of Caesar and Pompey

before him. Less than ten years after the battle of Actium
he was commander-in-chief of all the armed forces of the
" Republic, " and thus the personification of the army and,
(by virtue of the *tribunicia potestas*, a new dignity representing
the combined power of the Tribunes) the personification of
the Roman people. The holding of these offices ensured the
success of his autocratic rule, and formed the basis of the
Augustan revolution. In focussing all powers in himself,
Augustus (as he was now called) also inaugurated the Roman
Empire. Although he was never spoken of as a king, for
the rest of his life he reigned over Rome and its Empire as a
king in fact, disguised though his power was by the use of
the old titles. Augustus had finally and completely abolished
the Republican constitution.

GAIUS JULIUS CAESAR (100–44 B.C.)

The statesman and dictator who brought on the civil
wars that eventually led to the downfall of the Roman Republic, was born on July 12, 100 B.C. His name, Caesar, was
the third name (cognomen) of a branch of a patrician family,
the Julii, prominent in Rome from the time of the Punic
Wars. The Julii claimed descent from Venus through Julus,
son of Aeneas. The two branches of the Julii Caesares in
the late Republic were both derived from Sextus Julius
Caesar, Praetor in 208 B.C. Caesar belonged to the less
distinguished branch of the family.

He was brought up in the political entourage of his uncle
Marius, and at the age of sixteen married Cornelia, daughter
of L. C. Cinna. Sulla spared his life with the warning " Caesar
has many Mariuses in him. " In 69-68 B.C. he was governor of Further Spain and in 63 managed to have himself
elected Pontifex Maximus by using heavy bribery. Two
years later he divorced his second wife, Pompeia, who had
been implicated in the trial of P. Clodius for violating the
mysteries of the Bona Dea.

In 60 B.C. Caesar managed by a diplomatic triumph to
reconcile Pompey and Crassus and form the " First Trium-

virate, " under which he secured a large military command. During the next few years he campaigned in summer north of the Alps in Gaul and Britain, retiring each winter to administer Cisalpine Gaul and Illyricum. He subdued the Celtic Helvetii and Nervii, strongest of the Belgic tribes, and in 55 B.C. built his famous bridge over the Rhine. The widespread revolt under Vercingetorix was suppressed in 54-52 B.C. and Gaul finally organized as a Roman province. Immense financial gain to Caesar resulted from the annual tribute exacted.

Civil war broke out over his negotiations for a second consulship, the military opposition to Caesar rallying around Pompey. On January 11, 49 B.C. Caesar took the fatal decision and crossed the River Rubicon—an illegal act since he was deserting the province to which he had been appointed —and invaded Italy with one legion, claiming that his *dignitas* had been insulted. Ahenobarbus, appointed by the Senate to succeed Caesar in Gaul, capitulated at Corfinium, and Pompey was defeated at Ilerda in Spain by Caesar's rapidly moving army. A decisive victory for Caesar followed at Pharsalia in Thessaly.

Pompey fled to Egypt, where he was murdered. Arriving shortly thereafter, Caesar spent the winter at Alexandria fighting Ptolemy XIII, and after confirming Cleopatra as queen and Ptolemy XIV as consort, sailed up the Nile with Cleopatra, then left for Asia Minor and Africa. After the Republican defeat at Thapsus Caesar, back in Rome, celebrated four triumphs for Gaul, Egypt, Asia Minor and Africa— and executed Vercingetorix for good measure. A final victory at Munda was also followed by a triumph—which gave great offense since it celebrated the defeat of Romans. After five months in Rome planning an eastern campaign, Caesar was murdered at the foot of Pompey's statue two days before his intended departure, and shortly after an unsuccessful attempt by Antony, with Cassius and Casca (later his assassins), to place a crown on his head.

The startling brilliance of his military achievements—the conquest of Gaul and the establishment of the Rhine as an imperial boundary—helped to shape the future of Europe. Caesar's administrative and legal reforms were also outstanding in range and imagination, and included his reorganization of the calendar in 46 B.C. which (with small adjustments during the Middle Ages) is still in use today. He showed a penetrating understanding of individual character, although he failed in his later years to appreciate the psychology of politicians in the mass. Nothing in his career is more remarkable than the generosity with which he pardoned his defeated opponents in the civil war—a startling contrast with the blood baths that followed the victories of Marius and Sulla before his time, and of the Triumvirate in 43 B.C.

Undoubtedly Caesar scorned the political conventions, and in his last months was brusque, difficult of access, tactless and discourteous to the Senate. But evidence conflicts as to how far (or whether) he was corrupted by success, how much he welcomed even the most extravagant honours, and whether or not he intended to replace the Republic by an autocratic monarchy of the Hellenistic type. Alternatively, he may never have considered himself to be—nor wished to be —either a king or a god, but may merely have been loth to interrupt, on the eve of his departure for what might prove to be an extremely prolonged eastern campaign, the efficiently-working authoritarian type of government he had set up. If so, it is impossible to say what sort of constitutional settlement he might have made on his return.

Caesar's only certain offspring was Julia, daughter of Cornelia. Brutus, born long after Servilia was Caesar's mistress, despite rumours to the contrary, could not have been his son, and Ptolemy XV Caesar (Caesarion), murdered on Octavian's instructions after Actium, was almost certainly born not in 47 B.C. but after Caesar's death. There is no convincing evidence at all that Caesar was his father, although Cleopatra was certainly the mistress of Caesar in Alexandria in 48-47 B.C. and lived in Rome (with her royal consort Ptolemy XIV) from 46 B.C. till Caesar's death. Gaius Octavius (later Octavian), son of Atia, daughter of Caesar's sister Julia, was adopted by Caesar as his heir in 45 B.C. On

January 1, 42 B.C., by vote of the Senate and people of Rome, Julius Caesar was made a god.

MARK ANTONY (MARCUS ANTONIUS)
(c. 82–30 B.C.)

Mark Antony was the eldest son of Marcus Antonius Creticus of an old plebeian family. Since he was defeated by Octavian in 31 B.C., in the last of the civil wars that destroyed the Roman Republic, much that has maligned him may be discounted as based on the wartime propaganda of Octavian, intemperate abuse by Cicero, and on Octavian's patronage of historical writing after the war.

From 54 B.C. he served on Caesar's staff in Gaul and in 49 B.C. brought troops to Caesar in Illyricum, commanding the left wing at Pharsalia in Caesar's victory over Pompey. In 48-47 B.C. he was *magister equitum* to Caesar, as Dictator, but quarrelled with him in 46 and 44 B.C. While Caesar's assassins were at work, Antony was detained at the door of the Senate House and in the hours and days that followed controlled events with brilliant diplomatic skill. He prevented M. Aemilius Lepidus from bringing in troops to attack the assassins on the Capitoline Hill and engineered the compromise by which on March 17 the Senate granted them an amnesty and confirmed Caesar's " acts. " His famous funeral oration over Caesar's body probably took place on March 20 and, followed closely by the publication of Caesar's will, won him immense popularity with the Roman people.

Antony, Lepidus and Octavian formed the Second Triumvirate at Bologna, beginning their rule with extensive proscription lists which included most of the personal enemies of the triumvirs as well as the assassins of Caesar. The defeat of Brutus and Cassius at Philippi was the result of Antony's superb generalship, and credit for this victory must go entirely to him. Returning to the East the following year, to settle the problems there, he summoned Cleopatra to Tarsus in 41 B.C. and fell under her spell. Together they spent the winter months in Alexandria while the Parthians invaded the

Roman territory which had come under Antony's jurisdiction. At the Treaty of Brundisium he agreed with Octavian to command these eastern provinces while the latter took control of the western, including Italy. This was Antony's first major political error and the beginning of the decline of his power. To seal the treaty of Brundisium he married Octavian's sister, Octavia, and the triumvirate was shortly afterwards renewed until 33 B.C., Antony agreeing to provide Octavian with 130 ships to be used against Sextus Pompey, in exchange for four legions (never sent to him) for the Parthian war.

In late 37 or early 36 B.C. he married Cleopatra at Antioch (as she was not a Roman citizen this marriage, according to Roman law, was invalid) and in the next year severed relations with Octavia. This highhanded behaviour, the disastrous Parthian campaign of 36 B.C., the triumphal celebration at Alexandria for his Armenian victory in 34 B.C. and the reports that reached Rome of Antony's public assumption of the attributes of a Hellenistic divine king, were all avidly seized on by Octavian for skilful propaganda in Italy. Moreover Antony's will in favour of Cleopatra and his children by her, whether genuine or forged, was secured and published by Octavian in Rome. Nevertheless when the final breach between the two former triumvirs came in 32 B.C., Antony's cause was reinforced by both the Roman Consuls and by numerous senators.

Encouraged and financed by Cleopatra, Antony mobilized a fleet, but he was aware that his Roman officers and troops wanted him to break with her. On August 1, 30 B.C. following the naval defeat at Actium, the arrival of Octavian in Egypt and false news of Cleopatra's death, Antony committed suicide in Alexandria.

Personally attractive, Antony was a good soldier and was capable of brilliant political organization, but was out-manoeuvered by the far-sighted scheming of Octavian. His elder son by Fulvia, Marcus Antonius Antyllus, was executed by Octavian in 30 B.C. and his younger, Iullus Antonius, was forced to commit suicide in 2 B.C. The emperors Gaius,

Caligula and Nero were his descendants through his two daughters by Octavia, Antonia *major* and Antonia *minor*, married to L. Domitius Ahenobarbus and Nero Claudius Drusus respectively. By Cleopatra he had two sons and a daughter.

AUGUSTUS CAESAR (63 B.C.–14 A.D.)

The original name of the first Roman Emperor was Gaius Octavius, changed on Caesar's death in 44 B.C. to Gaius Julius Caesar. Augustus was an honorific cognomen given him by the Senate in 27 B.C. He is popularly known, for the period 44-27 B.C., as Octavian, although he never used the name " Octavianus ".

Born in Rome on September 23, 67 B.C., he came of a wealthy and respectable (if obscure) family—his father, Gaius Octavius, was the first in the family to become a senator. The son's career was determined by the fact that Julia, sister of Julius Caesar, was his grandmother, and he was regarded by Caesar as the most promising of his male relations and was appointed heir to three-quarters of his estate.

His adoption by Caesar was his only asset in the days immediately following the murder of Caesar—Octavian was otherwise in an extremely weak position; in particular he was rebuffed by Mark Antony, the generally accepted leader of the Caesarian party, who had taken possession of Caesar's money and papers. On Antony's break with the Senate Octavian illegally raised a force of 3,000 men from Caesar's legions and to this added two of Antony's legions, which he had seduced from him. When the Senate resolved on war with Antony it made Octavian a senator, and after the victory of Mutina (Modena) he found himself in command of the whole victorious army. He was therefore able to enforce his election as Consul in 43 B.C. and to proscribé the assassins of Caesar. Meeting Antony and Lepidus, governor of Gaul, at Bologna he formed an alliance with them known as the " Second Triumvirate, " which was to last for five years.

After the victory over Brutus and Cassius at Philippi in 42 B.C. he crushed a rebellion under Lucius Antonius, brother of Antony, which had been abetted by Antony's wife, Fulvia; but by 40 B.C. it had become necessary to accommodate once more with Antony, who at Brundisium accepted the overlordship of the eastern Roman provinces while Octavian wisely retained the western for himself—apart from Africa which was left for Lepidus. The treaty was sealed by the marriage of Antony and Octavia, Octavian's sister, and at Tarentum in 37 B.C. Octavia was able to negotiate a further agreement whereby the triumvirate was renewed for another five years and was organized against Sextus Pompey, son of Pompey the Great. Although Octavian suffered a personal defeat in a naval engagement against Pompey in 36 B.C., the situation was later saved by Marcus Vipsanius Agrippa who decisively defeated Sextus Pompey. Lepidus, who quarrelled with Octavian after this victory, was deserted by his troops and was deposed.

Octavian was now supreme master of the West, as Antony was of the East. A struggle for supreme power was sooner or later inevitable. Octavian's cause was helped by generous spending on public works and by the conquest of Illyricum (Dalmatia) in 35-33 B.C. Thus he was able to stand as champion of Italy and Rome against Cleopatra and her degenerate paramour. The crisis came in 32 B.C. when the second five year period of the Triumvirate expired and Octavian summoned Antony to lay down his powers. As civil war broke out both Consuls and over 300 senators joined Antony, but Octavian organized a " spontaneous " oath whereby all Italians were forced to swear loyalty to him, and in 31 B.C. he assumed the consulship and command of the war, which was undertaken expressly against Cleopatra rather than Antony. On September 2, 31 B.C., Octavian routed the combined forces of Antony and Cleopatra at the naval battle of Actium, and on August 1, 30 B.C. he entered Alexandria, annexed Egypt, and captured the vast treasure of the Ptolemies. Returning to Rome, he celebrated a triple triumph for the conquest of Illyricum, the victory of Actium, and the capture of Egypt.

As undisputed master of the Roman world, Augustus devoted the rest of his life to the consolidation and expansion of the Empire, the establishment of his own constitutional position as the holder of autocratic power, and the religious, moral and social reform of the Roman people. Moreover, as he is said to have boasted, he " found Rome a city of bricks and left it a city of marble. " With the help of his life-long friend and lieutenant, Gaius Maecenas, he became a patron of the poets Virgil, Horace and Ovid.

The character of Augustus is something of an enigma. Ambition seems to have been his dominant characteristic, and during his climb to power he was often unscrupulous and brutal to any that opposed him. But having achieved power he mellowed and began to display truly statesmanlike qualities. No genius like Julius Caesar, he yet possessed superb tact and skill in gauging and manipulating public opinion, and in the early years of the Principate he managed to reconcile all classes and to rally the republicanism of the more educated section of Roman society in support of his new regime. He died universally respected and beloved, while the system he established endured for three centuries with no essential change.

POMPEY THE GREAT
(GNAEUS POMPEIUS MAGNUS)
AND HIS SONS

Pompey, called *Magnus* because of his supposed resemblance to Alexander the Great, was famed as a general before he entered political life, having defeated Mithridates VI of Pontus, campaigned successfully in Spain, and dispersed the remnants of Spartacus' slave army. Although he was impelled into politics through his long-held rivalry with Caesar, he lacked the ambition to become an autocrat and like his exact contemporary, Cicero, held aloof from the two major parties of the day, the *Populares* and the *Optimates*. Nevertheless the pressures of power politics forced him to join Caesar and Crassus in the First Triumvirate in 60 B.C., an alliance that fell apart after his beloved wife, Julia, daughter of Caesar, died in 54 B.C.

With Caesar continuously away campaigning in Gaul, Pompey for the time being was master in Rome, and when Caesar's protégé, Clodius, was murdered in 52 B.C., Pompey was elected sole Consul. The break with Caesar was now complete, and when the latter marched on Rome in 50 B.C. Pompey was called upon to lead the forces of the Republic against him. Caesar's advance was so rapid however that Pompey was forced to retreat to the east. At Pharsalia in Macedonia in 48 B.C. he was persuaded, against his better judgment, to stand against Caesar and was defeated. Fleeing to Lesbos, and thence to Egypt, he was assassinated by one of his own soldiers as he stepped ashore.

Pompey's two sons carried on the struggle against Caesar. The eldest, Gnaeus, gathering together a formidable army in Spain, forced Caesar in person to take the field against him. Defeated at Munda in 45 B.C., Gnaeus was later captured and executed. After Caesar's death the younger son, Sextus, proscribed by the Second Triumvirate in 43 B.C., gathered a pirate fleet and continued to harass Antony and Octavian from a base in Sicily, thus imperilling Rome's grain supplies from Egypt and Africa. The peace of Misenum, which granted him Sicily, Sardinia and Achaea, soon broke down and his fleet was finally defeated and destroyed by Agrippa, Octavian's general. Pompey escaped to Asia Minor but was captured by Antony's troops and was executed at Miletus.

MARCUS JUNIUS BRUTUS
(85-42 B.C.)

Although Brutus, with Pompey the Great, supported the Republican cause against Caesar, he was pardoned by Caesar after the Battle of Pharsalia and in 46 B.C. was appointed governor of Cisalpine Gaul. In 44 B.C. he was Praetor of Rome and had been promised the governorship of Macedonia, but at the prompting of Cassius became the leader of the conspiracy against Caesar and was himself one of the assassins. After the death of Caesar the Republicans found themselves without a programme, and in August of 44 B.C. Brutus fled east with Cassius, seized Macedonia, and raised forces against Antony. Defeated by Antony and Octavian at Philippi in 42 B.C., Brutus committed suicide.

In 46 B.C. he had divorced his first wife Claudia and had married Porcia, daughter of his uncle, Marcus Porcius Cato Uticensis. A friend of Cicero, Brutus was much admired by the Romans for his respectability and his *gravitas* (seriousness), but he was slow in decision, obstinate, and both extortionate and cruel in financial dealings with provincials. Cicero speaks of his lack of enthusiasm—it seems that the Shakespearian portrait of him is rather too flattering.

MARCUS AEMILIUS LEPIDUS
(d. 13 or 12 B.C.)

As Consul in 46 B.C., Lepidus joined the Caesarian party in the civil wars. In 45 and 44 B.C. he was *magister equitum* to Caesar, and after Caesar's murder rose to importance as commander of the only army near Rome. In the subsequent war he sided with Antony, who after he had been defeated by Octavian at Mutina joined Lepidus in Gaul. At Bologna Lepidus was one of the members of the " Second Triumvirate, " but was soon reduced to an inferior position by Antony and Octavian. Although elected Consul again in 42 B.C., his inclusion in the renewed Triumvirate of 37 was merely formal. In 36 B.C., during the campaign against Sextus Pompey, he attempted to raise Sicily against Octavian but was betrayed by his own soldiers. Octavian then allowed him to remain Pontifex Maximus but forced him to retire from public life, and all political office.

341

MARCUS TULLIUS CICERO (106-43 B.C.)

Cicero was a Roman statesman, barrister, scholar and writer who in vain upheld Republican principles in the civil wars which destroyed the Republic of Rome. As an orator he ranks with Demosthenes and Edmund Burke, and his skill as a barrister was confirmed in 70 B.C. by his famous and unorthodox persecution of Gaius Verres, governor of Sicily, for extortion. His relationship with Pompey the Great seems to have been the focal point of his political career. Elected Consul in 63 B.C. he was instrumental in unmasking the Catiline conspiracy; indeed for this service to the state Catullus hailed him as *pater patriae* (father of his country). In 60 B.C. he declined Caesar's invitation to join the Triumvirate and fled from Rome only just in time to save his life. In 57 B.C. he was recalled and under pressure aligned himself with the triumvirs.

From 49 to 45 B.C. he gave Pompey some indecisive help in the civil war; although he utterly disapproved of Caesar's dictatorship he knew he would be one of the first victims of Caesar's enemies if they triumphed. Cicero was not involved in the conspiracy against Caesar and after the murder retired briefly from politics until the era of his Philippic orations (44-43 B.C.). He pursued the policy of using Octavian as a tool against Antony, but badly underestimating Octavian's intelligence, he died in the proscriptions of the Second Triumvirate.

A gifted but extravagant man, Cicero was noted for the number of his villas and was always in difficulties over money. Moreover he was inclined to exaggerate the weaknesses of his opponents as well as the virtues of his friends. Nevertheless his correspondence—with such men as Caesar, Cato, Pompey, Mark Antony, Marcus Brutus, Atticus and others—forms a priceless commentary on the times and is one of the most important sources for the history of the period. As a philosopher he rejected Epicureanism and was inclined towards Stoicism and agnosticism; his *De Republica* gives his vision of the sublime life of man in the future. His most important contribution was perhaps to give Rome, and th·:; Europe in later times, its philosophical vocabulary.

GNAEUS DOMITIUS AHENOBARBUS
(d. 31 B.C.)

According to Suetonius, Gnaeus Domitius was the best of a family notorious for its pride and cruelty. Like his father Lucius, he was a determined opponent of Julius Caesar and after Caesar's death espoused the cause of Brutus and Cassius. In 42 B.C. he was in command óf their fleet and after Philippi held out alone as a privateer. In 40 B.C., however, he was reconciled to Antony and became one of his chief partisans. Consul in 32, when the final breach occurred between Antony and Octavian, he fled from Italy to the East; nevertheless he could not brook Cleopatra's dominance over Antony and deserted him just before the battle of Actium, only to die soon afterwards, allegedly of remorse.

MARCUS VIPSANIUS AGRIPPA
(63–12 B.C.)

Agrippa, as a Roman statesman, general, organizer and engineer was the right-hand man of Octavian in his rise to power. During the War of Perusia (41-40 B.C.) Agrippa played a leading role, and by destroying the last Republican fleet off northern Sicily was responsible for redeeming Octavian's defeat at the hands of Sextus Pompey. Octavian's decisive victory over Antony and Cleopatra at Actium was largely the work of Agrippa, who commanded the left wing of the three squadrons attacking the Egyptian fleet.

From 27 to 12 B.C. he functioned as deputy to Augustus, alternating between Rome and the provinces. His sons, Gaius and Lucius, were adopted by Augustus, who was anxious to secure the dynastic succession. Tireless and self-effacing in his loyalty to Augustus, he was responsible as an engineer for building the Pantheon in Rome as well as an aqueduct and a sewer. He also prepared a map of the world.

GAIUS MAECENAS (c. 74–64 B.C.–8 B.C.)

Maecenas, a Roman statesman and patron of letters, owed his position and influence to his close association with the Emperor Augustus. Although he may have fought at the battle of Philippi, he first appears in history in 40 B.C. when he was employed by Octavian to arrange his marriage with Scribonia, and was then sent to negotiate peace with Mark Antony at Brundisium. Left in charge at Rome during the Actium campaign, he effectively crushed a conspiracy mounted by the younger Lepidus. An anonymous elegy described him as " Caesar's right hand ". He also encouraged writers like Horace and Vergil and his name has become proverbial as a munificent patron of the arts.

BIBLIOGRAPHY

MAIN SOURCES

APPIANUS. Roman History.

CICERO. Epistulae ad Atticum.

DIO CASSIUS. Historiae.

DIODORUS. Biblioteca Historica.

FLORUS. Epitome Gestis Romanorum.

PETRONIUS ARBITER. De priapismo seu propudiosa libidine
    Cleopatrae Reginae.

PLUTARCH. Vitae.

STRABO. Geography.

SUETONIUS. Vitae XII Caesarum.

MODERN WORKS

AMMIRATA, U. Cleopatra.

BERNATH, D. Cleopatra, her life and reign.

BESTERMAN, T. A bibliography of Cleopatra.

BOTTI. Plan de la Ville d'Alexandrie sous les Ptolémées.

BOUCHE-LECLERCQ. L'Histoire des Lagides.

DAIRVAL. Histoire de Ptolémée Aulète.

DELAYEN, G. Cléopatre.

ELLIS, O. DE C. Cleopatra in the Tide of Time.

ELLIS, O. DE C. The Cleopatra Scandals refuted.

ERMAN, A. Life in Ancient Egypt.

FERRERO, G. Grandezza e Decadenza di Roma.

GARDTHAUSEN. Die Alexandrinische Bibliothek.

GAUDENZIO, P. La Vita di Cleopatra Reina d'Egitto.

GOERLITZ, W. Kleopatra, bildnis einer damonischen Frau.

GRAVIERE, J. DE LA. La Marine des Ptolémées et la Marine des Romains.

IVANOV, M. O. On the antique painting of Cleopatra discovered at Sorrento in 1818.

KIEPERT. Topographie des alten Alexandrien.

LANDI, G. La Vita di Cleopatra.

LARROUY, M. Antoine et Cléopatre; la Bataille d'Actium.

LUMBROSO, G. L'Egitto al tempo dei Greci e dei Romani.

MAFFII, M. Cleopatra contro Roma.

MASPERO. Les Finances de l'Egypte sous les Lagides.

MEYER, P. M. Das Heerwesen der Ptolemaër unter Romer in Agypten.

MOELLER, H. H. Beitrage zur dramatischen Cleopatra Literatur.

NERONTSOS BEY. L'ancienne Alexandrie.

SOGRAFI, S. S. La morte di Cleopatra, a musical tragedy.

STADELMANN. Kleopatra Agyptens letzte Königin.

SUTTON, W. Complete history of the romantic life and tragic death of Cleopatra.

THOMPSON, G. Hymen's Praeludia or Love Masterpiece, based on Cléopatre, by G. de Costes de La Calprenède, Paris 1647-63, London 1652.

WEIGALL, A. Cleopatra.

WERTHEIMER, O. Cleopatra a Royal Voluptuary.

ZOGHEB, A. M. DE. Le Tombeau d'Alexandre le Grand et le Tombeau de Cléopatre.

SOURCES
OF THE ILLUSTRATIONS

INDEX

British Museum bust of Cleopatra, **16**
Bruchion, the, Alexandria, 32, 45, 59, 98, 128, 130, 161, 166, 204, 261
Brutus, Decimus, (*conspirator*), **104**
Brutus, Marcus Junius, 63, **81-2**, **86-7**, **102-3**, 104-5, **106-7**, **128-9**, 250, 269
Bubastes, 36
Buculianus (*conspirator*), 106
Byblos (*Egyptian colony*), 152

C

Caesar, Julius, his "divine descent", 10, 61, 90: his captivation by Cleopatra, 10, **58-60**: accepts bribe from Auletes and gets "Julian Law
Caesar, Julius (*cont.*)
for Egypt" passed, **23-4**: and Pompey, 37, **39-40**, 250: lands at Alexandria, 42: and Cleopatra, **45-115**: sends for Cleopatra, 45, **47-9**: his character, **50-2**: his appearance, 52, 218: dines with Cleopatra, 54: subdues Ptolemy XIV, 57: his son by Cleopatra, 60-1, **68**: his desire to be king, 63-4, **87-91**, 98: travels down the Nile, **64-8**, 192: returns to Rome, 68: his quadruple Triumph, 68, **72-4**, 114, 221: his Spanish campaign, **83-4**, 87: granted title of Imperator, 88: law passed for his marriage with Cleopatra, 96: refuses crown, **101-2**: his will, 102, **109-10**, 127: on the eve of the Ides of March, 102, 103: warned of assassination, **104**: his death, **105-7**: proclaimed a god, 115, 182: *other references,* 108, 126, 127, 130, 133, 135, 145, 163, 172, 177, 178, 227, 232, 235, 269, 280
Caesar, Lucius (*uncle of Antony*), 128
Caesar, Temple of, 114
Caesar Ptolemy (= *Caesarion*), 267
Caesarion (*son of Caesar and Cleopatra*), **68**, 70, 72, 75, 76, 77, 81, **96-7**, 109-10, 115, 124, 125, 127, 131, 133, 145-6, 149, 150,

163-4, 176, **177-82**, 196, 223-4, 225, **235**, 238, 264, 267, **268**, 269, 278, **286-7**
Caesarium, the (*Cleopatra's memorial to Caesar*), **182**, 280
Caesetius (*tribune*), 97
Calendar, reform of the, 18, 31, 79, **98-9**
Callimachus (*writer of elegies*), 31
Calpurnia (*Caesar's last wife*), 58, 63, 71, 72, 76, 88, **103**, 108, 110, 126, 235
Cambyses, 191
Campus Martius, the, 111, 246
Canidius, Publius, **210**, 238, 261, 266, **280**
Canons of Cleopatra, The, 18
Canopus Road, Alexandria, 32, 33, 46, 119, 121, 221, 236, 272, 279
Capito, Fonteius, 188, **193-4**
Cappadocia, 226
Carians, the, 234
Carthage, 27
Casca, Gaius, **104-5**, 6
Casca, Publius Servilius, 106
Cassius Longinus, Gaius, 102-3 **104-5**, 106, **128-9**, 131, 250
Cassius Parmensis, 280
Cato, Marcus Porcius, **24**, 74, 85
Caucasus, the, 91
Caystrus, River, 233
Charmian (*Cleopatra's attendant*), 176, 190, 245, 261, 269, 275, 278, **284**
Charonites, the, 126
Cicero, Marcus Tullius, 76, **79-80**, 85, 89, 93, 98, 99, 127, **128**, 177, 189, 280
Cilicia, 197, 198, 234
Cimber, Tullius, 106
Cinna, Lucius Cornelius, 111
Circei, 99
Cleopatra, no authentic image of her, 9: her birth and parentage, 15, 18: her appearance, 15-6, 77-8: her languages, 17: first meeting with Antony, 26, 92: succeeds Ptolemy XIII, **26-7**: not married to her brother, 37: meets Caesar, **49-50**: falls in love with him, 50, 53: invites him to dine, 54: enceinte by Caesar, 60: birth of Caesarion, **68**: visit to Rome, **68-114**: her statue by Archesilaus, 74: Roman society

This book, designed by
André Mistelli
is a production of
Edito-Service S.A., Geneva

Printed in Switzerland